"A brilliant and necessary analysis of what mothers can do to raise sons who have high regard for women, and so, for themselves. The reconfiguring of the mother/son bond, along the lines Bassoff describes, will do much to make the world a fairer, better, safer, and more humane place."

—Louise DeSalvo, author of
Virginia Woolf: The Impact of Childhood Sexual Abuse on Her Life and Work and *Conceived With Malice*

"A clear and accessible discussion of various mother/son situations, including those involving two-parent families, single mothers, stepmothers, and mothers of gay sons. A book mothers of boys, young and old, will want to read: for insights, for affirmation, and for joy."

—*Library Journal*

EVELYN SILTEN BASSOFF, Ph.D., is the author of *Mothers and Daughters* and *Mothering Ourselves* (both Plume), and is a columnist for *Parents* magazine. She is a practicing psychologist and a member of both the American Psychological Association and the American Association of Counseling and Development. Dr. Bassoff lives in Boulder, Colorado.

"Warm, personal, non-jargoned insight into the complex mother-son relationship. Observations are down to earth and close to home."

—*Kentucky Post*

"Above all, this warm, practical book stresses the fact that, despite unisex clothes and toys and the breaking of gender stereotypes, growing up male is far different from growing up female and requires different handling by nurturing mothers."

—*Anniston Star*

"Makes it clear that it is possible for mothers to raise strong and nurturing men in an age of machismo. Warm and supportive."

—*Childsplay*

Also by the author

Mothers and Daughters:
Loving and Letting Go

Mothering Ourselves:
Help and Healing for Adult Daughters

Evelyn Silten Bassoff, Ph.D.

BETWEEN MOTHERS AND SONS

*The Making of Vital
and Loving Men*

A PLUME BOOK

PLUME
Published by the Penguin Group
Penguin Books USA Inc., 375 Hudson Street, New York, New York 10014, U.S.A.
Penguin Books Ltd, 27 Wrights Lane, London W8 5TZ, England
Penguin Books Australia Ltd, Ringwood, Victoria, Australia
Penguin Books Canada Ltd, 10 Alcorn Avenue, Toronto, Ontario, Canada M4V 3B2
Penguin Books (N.Z.) Ltd, 182–190 Wairau Road, Auckland 10, New Zealand

Penguin Books Ltd, Registered Offices: Harmondsworth, Middlesex, England

Published by Plume, an imprint of Dutton Signet,
a division of Penguin Books USA Inc.
Previously published in a Dutton edition.

First Plume Printing, September, 1995
10 9 8 7 6 5 4 3 2 1

"New Heaven and Earth" by D. H. Lawrence, from *The Complete Poems of D. H. Lawrence* by D. H. Lawrence, edited by V. de Sola Pinto & F. W. Roberts. Copyright © 1964, 1971 by Angelo Ravagli and C. M. Weekley, executors of the Estate of Frieda Lawrence Ravagli. Used by permission of Viking Penguin, a division of Penguin Books USA Inc.

Excerpts from *Mother, Madonna, Whore* by Estela Welldon, copyright © 1990, 1991 by Estela Welldon. Reprinted by permission of Guilford Publications, Inc.

Excerpts from "The Cinderella's Stepmother Syndrome" by Katalin Morrison and Airdrie Thompson-Guppy, copyright © 1985 by Katalin Morrison and Airdrie Thompson-Guppy. Reprinted by permission of Canadian Psychiatric Association.

Excerpt from *Walking to Sleep: New Poems and Translations* by Richard Wilbur, copyright © 1964 and renewed 1992 by Richard Wilbur. Reprinted by permission of Harcourt Brace & Company.

Ⓟ REGISTERED TRADEMARK—MARCA REGISTRADA

The Library of Congress has catalogued the Dutton edition as follows:
Basoff, Evelyn.
Between mothers and sons : the making of vital and loving men /
Evelyn Silten Bassoff.
p.   cm.
ISBN 0-525-93833-8 (hc.)
ISBN 0-452-27462-1 (pbk.)
1. Mothers and sons. I. Title.
HQ755.85.B3639   1992
306.874'3—dc20
94–1868
CIP

Printed in the United States of America
Original hardcover design by Steven N. Stathakis

BOOKS ARE AVAILABLE AT QUANTITY DISCOUNTS WHEN USED TO PROMOTE PRODUCTS OR SERVICES. FOR INFORMATION PLEASE WRITE TO PREMIUM MARKETING DIVISION, PENGUIN BOOKS USA INC., 375 HUDSON STREET, NEW YORK, NY 10014.

In memory of my father,
HANS SILTEN,
a gentle man of principle

Contents

ACKNOWLEDGMENTS

Of the three books that I have written, this one has been the most challenging. I have tried to describe accurately both the mother's experience of raising a son and the son's experience of being raised by a mother. Through personal stories, insights, and wisdom, so generously shared, many people have helped me toward this end. I am indebted to Barbara Adams, Sylvia Ajilla, Terry Andrews, Jonathan Bassoff, Sylvia Bassoff, Dr. Geri Cassens, Sara-Jane Cohen, Hannah Eilbott, Dr. John P. Haws, Caroline Hinkley, Anne Hochmeyer, Jeff Jackson, Dr. Donald Johnson, Art Kaufman, Ellen Kleiner, Judy Kurtz, Dr. Judah Levine, Merete Lupa, Sue Maynard, Allen Overton, Dr. Wayne Phillips, Ginna Newton Rice, Dr. Beth Robertson, Dr. Mary Schlesinger, Dr. Eleanor Mimi Schrader, Dr. Jed Shapiro, Jo Silkensen, Helene Silten, Dr. Howard Snooks, Claudia Stein, Dr. Fred Stein, Dr. Jeffrey Truesdall, Bishop Melvin Wheatley, Rich Wildau, and Donald Williams. Although I cannot honor clients by name, I am keenly aware of their contributions to this book; my hope is that in retelling the stories my clients entrusted to me during psychotherapy I have conveyed the essence of their experiences without compromising their rights of privacy and confidentiality.

A number of friends and colleagues—Ben Eilbott, Dr. Lyn Gullette, Dr. Ivan Miller, Julie Phillips, Dr. Susan Rosewell-Jackson, and Katharine Walker—took time from their busy lives to read my manuscript in its entirety; their commentaries were enormously instructive. I am especially grateful to Katharine Walker, a steady source of support, who attentively followed the development of the manuscript from start to finish.

I owe much thanks to my editor, Alexia Dorszynski, whose encouragement, guidance, and insights have been invaluable, and to my publisher, Elaine Koster, whose confidence in my work has meant so much to me. In addition, I am thankful to Deborah Brody for taking such fine care of the book in its final stages at Dutton; to my long-time friend Alice Levine for her sensitive copyediting; and to my daughter, Leah Bassoff, for her many contributions as research assistant. I also appreciate the secretarial support provided by Bernice Moon at the University of Colorado in Boulder.

Finally, I would like to pay tribute to my husband, Dr. Bruce Bassoff, for his daily acts of love and loyalty, which sustain me.

—EVELYN SILTEN BASSOFF

INTRODUCTION

....

Between Mothers
and Sons

Love alone is useless if it does not also have understanding.
—C. G. JUNG,
"The Philosophical Tree"

My daughter was three when my son was born. From the start, Leah took charge and devoted herself to Jonathan. Although much about my children's early years is now lost to memory, I can easily picture little Leah holding, rocking, carrying, and singing to her infant brother. As they grew older, Leah assigned him roles in her fantasy play: She was Dorothy, he was Toto; she was the nice teacher, he was teacher's pet; and had my husband and I not objected, one Halloween she was to be the Queen and he a *princess*. For the most part, Jonathan, who had always been a handful for me, submitted to his sister's plans without protest; indeed, whenever she was not around, he seemed forlorn.

But one day all that changed. At the time, Jonathan, a

first-grader, always walked home from school with his sister. On this particular afternoon, however, Leah, tears streaming down her cheeks, arrived home alone. Despite her pleas, Jonathan had refused to come with her because he wanted to fool around with some boys from his class.

"When I left him," Leah explained, "he was rolling around on the ground with these guys, throwing things and laughing like a wild man; he wasn't being nice at all." Then, a dark cloud rolling over her face, she proclaimed, "This is a sad and terrible day for all of us—*Jonathan has become a boy*!" Sighing deeply, she added, "Now what do we do?"

Between Mothers and Sons is, in one way, a belated answer to my daughter's question, "Now what do we do?"—a question that, I am sure, most mothers often ask themselves in the course of bringing up sons. It is my attempt to describe what raising boys entails for us women: what we can expect from and how we can best respond to them; how we can deal with the frustrations and hurts that they cause us, as well as with the distances that naturally grow between us; how we can delight in and have fun with them; and, most important, how, in this age of despair and violence, we can help them grow into vital and loving men.

Between Mothers and Sons is, in addition, an answer to a question rarely asked: "Now what *can't* we do?" Mothers tend to "overfunction" in the family.[1] To their own detriment and that of their sons, they often do the lion's share or even all of the parenting. Hence, I write extensively about the boy's necessary relationship to his father (or father surrogate) as primary role model and as caregiver. And I address the ways we mothers—married or single—can bring the fathers back into family life, which is suffering for lack of their physical and psychological presence.

Between Mothers and Sons is also an answer to the question, "And what can our sons do for us?" I am convinced that just as we can help our sons grow into vital and loving men, they can help us grow into vital and loving women. By joining in the excitement of their experiences—playing football or hang-gliding or building a treehouse or a sand castle—we have the opportunity to develop our masculine side, to discover the adventurous boy-spirit in us. As a colleague who is the mother of two grown sons, one of whom suffered a gymnastics injury that has left him partially paralyzed, told me, "From my sons I learned to be tough and courageous." And a client who had recently adopted a six-year-old shared, "My little boy is teaching me to play!"

Between women and men there is presently so much suspicion, contempt, name-calling, and humiliation that the air we all breathe has become poisonous. If we are able to enjoy and empathize with our sons, we may find it easier to enjoy and empathize with males in general instead of seeing them as the enemy, as is so common these days. In my own case, being mother to a son has moved me from a rigidly feminist position toward a more flexible humanistic one. Although I will continue to fight fiercely for my daughter's and all daughters' rights to be respected and valued as women, I will fight every bit as hard to ensure that my son and all sons are esteemed as men.

The major premise of *Between Mothers and Sons* is that if we mothers are to help our sons become vital and loving men, we must learn to respect their unique, separate, male lives. The practice of respect, however, requires an enormous dedication to awareness, tolerance, knowledge, and understanding. For most of us, it is not an instinctive but a conscious effort—a difficult maternal labor.

Webster tells us that to respect means "to feel or show honor or esteem" and "to avoid intruding upon." The word "respect" stems from the Latin "spectare"—to look at, to see—just as do the words "spectator" (an observer), "spectacles" (the eyeglasses that make vision clear), and "spectacle" (a marvel). *The practice of respect requires that we observe and see clearly what is before us so that we may marvel at it.* It is what Sara Ruddick, the author of *Maternal Thinking*, calls "attentive love" and "loving attention"—"a kind of knowing that takes truthfulness as its aim but makes truth serve lovingly the person known."[2] It is what in Yiddish is called *kvelling*—the trembling awe that parents experience when they behold their child in all the child's unique, marvelous complexity. And it is what golden-voiced Aretha Franklin celebrates in Otis Redding's glorious song "Respect."

Paradoxically, the practice of respect also requires that we not insist on seeing too much by probing into matters the other wishes to keep private. Respect implies a certain distance between the subject and the object—an honoring of the boundaries that separate one from the other, a recognition of the other's *otherness*. It is the deliberate act of *not* knowing, when knowing would become intrusive.

An example of the maternal practice of respect comes immediately to mind. A client of mine shared the fact that her nine-year-old son was different in temperament from the other members of the family. Unlike all of them, he was introverted and often sad. Although she was not overly intrusive, my client did not shy away from inquiring about her son's suffering; she listened carefully to his grievances so that she could understand his unhappiness. But she never tried to cheer him out of his gloom, even though his depressed attitude dampened her own moods. Rather, she let him know that he had a right to his feelings, that she was honored that he shared them with her, and that she would never pressure him to act happier than he really felt.

I am also reminded of the single mother of a sixteen-year-old, who told me that her son "is not into talking about his feelings" but reveals himself through his favorite music. "By sharing his treasured tapes of Tom Waits and Eric Clapton with me, my son lets me into his heart and into a world that is not immediately comprehensible to me but which I struggle to understand. I would not miss this opportunity for anything."

For some mothers, the practice of respect is more difficult than for others. Rather than honoring and promoting their sons' individuality, they may project their own fantasies, wishes, and fears onto the boy. Hence, they cannot relate to the child as he really is but, instead, relate to a fantasy child of their own creation. One of my friends, an amiable, bright man in his middle thirties, until recently had a thriving practice as a physician. Quite suddenly, and to the dismay of his patients and his colleagues, he gave up medicine. When I asked him why, he told me that becoming a doctor had been his mother's dream for him—a dream that, out of devotion and love for her, he had made come true—but that he had not been happy in medical school or in his practice. "You may find this hard to believe," he confided, "but I don't really know how it feels to be a fluid, living, breathing person with wishes of my own. I experience myself as a wooden mechanical doll."

In *Between Mothers and Sons*, I include several stories of mothers who *kvell* over and give "attentive love" and "loving attention" to their sons; I also include stories of mothers who fail to respect their sons. My hope is that both kinds of stories can teach us something valuable.

Another premise of *Between Mothers and Sons* is that gender plays an important part in parent-child relationships. Indeed, in the course of bringing up my own children—Leah, who is now twenty-two, and Jonathan, who is nineteen—and counseling many women who are mothers, I have come to believe that bringing up daughters is significantly different from bringing up sons. Between mothers and daughters there is a shared female body and a shared sexual identity, both of which breed deep feelings of familiarity that permeate every aspect of their relationship. Between mothers and sons, however, there is no such sameness; there is, instead, the sense of *otherness.*

Over the past two decades, in our laudable efforts to create an equal, nonsexist society in which girls are given as many opportunities as boys, many of us have downplayed or denied altogether sex-related differences between our daughters and our sons. However, although it is true that gender roles need not be rigid and that there is much overlap between the sexes, it is also true that boys and girls follow different paths in their human development, most notably in their relationship to mother. I believe that Freud's famous— now notorious—dictum that "anatomy is destiny" is an exaggeration. However, I also believe that the bodies into which we are born, whether female or male, color and shape our inner experiences, which, in turn, influence the way we see and move through the world.

If we mothers hope to promote our sons' healthy growth and hope to form loving bonds with them, we must learn to respect their maleness and evolving manliness, which will express themselves in stereotypic but also nonstereotypic ways. For this reason, I write extensively about the boy's struggles to separate from mother so that he can become a man—his own man—and I describe how we mothers can help him toward this end. Because boys growing up in homes where the father is missing necessarily have a harder time becoming independent of mother and feeling secure about their male identities, I include much material on single mothers and sons. Certainly, the maternal tasks facing single mothers of sons are enormously difficult, and single mothers deserve more support and guidance than they have received.

One reason I decided to write *Between Mothers and Sons* was that I wanted to respond to the complex, confused, and often troubled feelings that some of my clients with sons shared with me, feelings that I believe are common among many other mothers. Because so many families are in crisis and because communications between women and men have generally deteriorated, it seems timely to explore in depth the mother-son relationship. I was especially interested in exploring "shared parenting"—the arrangement my husband and I have chosen—because it seems to mitigate power struggles between mothers and sons. I was also moved to learn and write about the special issues that mothers of gay sons face and the complicated roles that mothers of stepsons assume. Although women freely talk with one another about relationships with their daughters and although a huge literature on mother-daughter relationships has developed over the past several years, the mother-son relationship remains shrouded in relative silence, despite the fact that it is the foundation of all female-male relationships.

I also had a personal reason for writing this book: to

explore my relationship with my own son. When *Between Mothers and Sons* was still in the planning stage, Jonathan was about to enter his senior year in high school. Well aware that his time at home was coming to an end, I felt a need to understand and put into words what we had been to each other—and to anticipate what was possible for us in the future. This need took on a special urgency after Jonathan was seriously injured in a baseball accident. During the night my husband and I spent in the emergency room and the benumbed days that followed, I experienced more deeply than ever before how precious my son is to me. Although Jonathan is healthy and whole again, the painful recognition that his life, like all life, is fragile moves me to find new ways to nurture it—to foster whatever in this child of mine is lively, responsive, unique, and growing.

Although *Between Mothers and Sons* is written from the perspective of women, my hope is that it will be of interest to sons as well as to mothers. When I first embarked on this project, I was giving talks around the country on the mother-daughter relationship, the topic of my previous two books. At one of these talks, after I had mentioned that I was beginning a book on mothers and sons, a woman in a back row stood up and called out, "How, in heaven's name, will you ever get material for your book? The last thing men are interested in talking about is their mothers!" The woman's words stopped me short and precipitated a loss of confidence. Fortunately, her dire prediction proved to be wrong. I discovered that sons of all ages were eager to talk about their mothers—to share with me the stories of their childhoods and to explore with me the rage, bewilderment, love, tenderness, and yearning that they often experienced in the relationship with their mothers. I also discovered that just as men needed their mothers to respect their individuality and separateness from them, they also wanted to respect their mothers, to know them as people in their own right.

Between Mothers and Sons draws on the best research and theory in psychology and other social sciences. However, in great part, it is a book of stories—personal stories; stories told to me by clients, friends, acquaintances, and colleagues; fairy tales and folk stories told across cultures and over generations; stories written for children. It also looks at the "stories" that mothers tell their sons: the expectations, hopes, and dreams that they convey about their sons' futures; the affirmations and words of confidence that they express when their sons succeed, falter, or fail. Surely, like the Great Spinners and Fates in myths and fairy tales, mothers enable their sons through their positive faith in them and disable them through negative projections: "By almost every cradle there sits a woman weaving threads of destiny," Jungian analyst and scholar Sibylle Birkhäuser-Oeri writes.[3] My wish is that this book will also generate many new stories for mothers and sons—stories that celebrate their mutual love, understanding, and respect.

Part One

···

THE PLEASURES AND CHALLENGES OF DIFFERENCE

"We"—meaning by "we" a whole made up of body, brain, and spirit, influenced by memory and tradition—must still differ in some respects from "you," whose body, brain, and spirit have been so differently trained and are so differently influenced by memory and tradition. Though we see the same world, we see it through different eyes.

—VIRGINIA WOOLF,
Three Guineas

I

·····················

Bulls and Baseball Bats:
Male Energy

To respect that fury or those giddy high spirits or a body that seems perpetually mobile is respecting nature, much as one respects the strength of a hurricane, the rush of a waterfall.

— SARA RUDDICK,
Maternal Thinking

When I was pregnant with my first child, I experienced her early fetal movements as the quivering of butterfly wings. As she grew bigger and more vigorous, I imagined that the delicate butterfly cocooned in my body had transformed herself into a small bird, for now I felt a flapping within. This imagery was so vivid that shortly before my due date, I shared it with my obstetrician and asked for assurances that I would give birth to a human baby and not a bird baby. He provided those assurances, and Leah was born.

During the early weeks of my second pregnancy, I waited anxiously for the sublime sensation of shimmering butterfly wings. But instead the new life I was carrying announced his presence with a walloping charge. As the months passed, his sudden thrusts and lunges became more frequent, but their forcefulness always took me by surprise. I imagined I was harboring a baby bull rather than a butterfly or bird.

Outside the womb, as well as within it, Jonathan's bullish energy was alien and disconcerting to me. Baby Leah's gentle rhythms had seemed somehow familiar; we were attuned to one another, making lovely music together, dancing in step. With baby Jonathan, however, I felt out of step, engaged less in a dance than in a tug-of-war. When we nursed, he was not content to nuzzle in my arms as my daughter had been; instead, he twisted his head this way and that, more interested in the world around him than in the breast. When he was a toddler, I seemed to be forever chasing after him, pinning him down, tying him in, holding him back. Unlike Leah, who had enjoyed being taken on long walks in her carriage or Snugli, Jonathan hated to be constrained in his umbrella stroller. By stiffening his body and thrusting it forward, he often managed to toddle away from me with the stroller strapped to his back, so that he appeared half-baby–half-turtle. As if this were not enough, after Jonathan mastered unstrapping himself, he discovered the fun of running away with his stroller and ramming it into walls and people. I remember taking little Leah's hand and guiding her to the dioramas of dinosaurs on one excursion to Denver's Museum of Natural History; all the while I pretended that the pint-sized wildman with the stroller who was "terrorizing" the museum's visitors did not belong to me.

Over the years, Jonathan has tamed his bullish energy. Now, at nineteen, he is a gentle and soft-spoken young man, hardly the testosterone-driven terror that he once was. But when he was very young, I was not so sure where his hormones would lead him or me. Indeed, mothering my son when he was little was full of ambivalences. Sometimes I found his wildness and vigor awe-inspiring and funny, but at other times, I doubted my maternal goodness because his relentless physical activity so tired me out that I wished only to get away from it and him. Although this boyish energy tended to overwhelm me, my husband seemed very comfortable with it. When Jonathan was little, the two would roll around the floor together, obviously relishing the movement and struggle. Sometimes, Bruce would crawl about on all fours, rumbling and roaring, while Jonathan, perched on "Daddy lion's" back, would squeal his delight. As Jonathan got older and well into his adolescence, they continued their rough-and-tumble play—wrestling, pushing, prodding, or poking one another, occasionally knocking over a lamp or plant and often making a lot of noise. Their roughhousing made me laugh. But it also made me nervous. "Someone will get hurt," I'd warn, and sometimes someone did.

Surely, my experiences as a new mother are not universal. Some mothers, especially those who grew up with brothers, may feel comfortable with their sons' rough-and-tumble energy from the start; and other mothers may find that their sons do not have this kind of energy at all but are born with docile natures.[1] What is universal, however, is that every son expresses his maleness *somehow* and that every mother responds to it *somehow.* I have two purposes in this chapter. The first is to explore the male nature—that is, to answer the question, "What are little (and not so little) boys made of?" The second is to probe the feelings that our sons' maleness brings out in us mothers—our delight and pride but also our confusion, discomfort, and trepidation; our hopes and dreams but also our negative projections.

In the 1970s, when I gave birth to Jonathan and Leah, it was distinctly unfashionable to acknowledge inborn differences between girls and boys except for the obvious anatomical ones. During that decade of unisex clothes and play-fair toys, liberal and feminist thinkers believed that given equal opportunities, boys and girls would develop gender-free personalities, that they would come to feel, think, perceive, and act pretty much the same. But this evolution did not occur; nor may it ever; nor perhaps would it be a good thing if it did.[2]

Twenty years after the start of the feminist revolution, most will concur that growing up male is still different from growing up female, that mothering a son is still different from mothering a daughter, and that we are wise to respect rather than to deny these differences. To be sure, a male's maleness and a female's femaleness take so many forms that they elude precise and tidy definitions. Perhaps all that can be said with reasonable confidence is that girls and boys, women and men, have a different feel and radiate a different *energy*: they talk differently, they solve problems differently, they play differently, they use their bodies differently, they occupy and move through space differently, they laugh at different things.[3]

In preparation for writing this chapter, I searched in vain for a crisp definition of healthy maleness, or positive "male energy"; what I discovered instead was a bounty of wonderful images. With a mischievous smile, Diane Green, a kindergarten teacher, told me that baby boys come equipped with an "internal vroom, vroom, vroom" that is suddenly set off when they are presented with their first Tonka truck.[4] Julie Phillips, a science writer, evoked the boy-spirit with three words: "Boom, bang, crash." Carol Ryan, a psychiatrist, described boys of all ages as "tough on the outside, tender on the inside." My husband insisted that boys, but not girls, are born with a gene that will make them belly laugh at the antics of the Three Stooges. And long, long ago, someone somewhere mused that little boys are made of "frogs and snails and puppy dogs' tails."

Poet Robert Bly calls primal male energy the "Wild Man"—an image so evocative that I cannot resist borrowing it from time to time. The Wild Man is often undomesticated, "un-nice," and irreverent; he is also vital, sensuous, effervescent, full of feeling but not maudlin, and deeply connected to the earth and the collective history of his male ancestors. "What I'm suggesting," Bly writes in *Iron John*, "is that every modern male has, lying at the bottom of his psyche, a large, primitive being covered with hair down to his feet."[5]

Drawing on ancient Chinese philosophy, John Welwood, the author of *Journey of the Heart*, describes the yang, or masculine energy, as the principle of centrifugal force that separates and pulls away and the yin, or feminine energy, as the principle of centripetal force that draws in and connects. Like thunder and lightning, yang pierces, penetrates, and arouses; like the life-giving earth and its rivers and streams, yin nurtures, accommodates, and flows. To be sure, mature males and mature females have both yin and yang energy, but as Welwood points out, males generally have a larger proportion of yang and are said to "belong to the yang," and females generally have a larger proportion of yin and are said to "belong to the yin"; put another way, *"yang is 'homebase' for men, and yin is 'homebase' for women."*[6] (italics added)

In my search for descriptions of maleness, I came upon an evocative image of the *absence* of maleness; according to the Sambia tribe of New Guinea, a man depleted of his natural male energy is a *wasaatu*: a mushy-soft "sweet potato man," who lacks resolve, self-discipline, and commitment.[7] I also became keenly aware of the distinction between healthy male energy and, for want of a better term, "crazy" male energy—its degenerated form. Healthy male energy has everything to do with being effective and engaged in life; it is focus, determination, and perseverance. The samurai call this vital energy *ki; ki* power causes a man to *leap* into the battle of life rather than to take a passive stance vis-à-vis life's tasks and struggles.[8] Crazy male energy has everything to do with violence and domination. Unfortunately, we do not have to look further than the daily newspaper, with its depressing stories of gun-toting fourth-graders and twelve-year-old rapists, for examples of crazy male energy.

It is critically important for us mothers to distinguish the nonviolent, rough-and-tumble aggression that is pronounced in many healthy boys (which calls for our understanding and acceptance), from the violent, subjugating craziness that festers in sick boys (which calls for professional evaluation and treatment). Unfortunately, some mothers believe that any aggression in their sons—even when it is harmless—is unacceptable. Other mothers err in the opposite direction; they believe that all forms of physical aggression in their sons—even aggressiveness that hurts others or is out-of-control—is acceptable.

In our world, where male violence is on the increase, many women may believe that males are by nature violent, especially if we ourselves have suffered at the hands of brutal men. But this misconception is dangerous. *The boy or man who is violently aggressive is neither a normal nor a typical male.* He may be neurologically or psychologically impaired; or he may have been badly abused, humiliated, exploited, neglected, or exposed to scenes of domestic violence; having learned hurting as a way of life from his parents and other family members, from the popular media, or from the mean streets and schools, he perpetuates the cycle of violence.[9] (Girls, of course, are also victims of abuse and neglect. Abused girls, however, tend to act out against themselves—they are prone to eating disorders, promiscuity, and depression—whereas abused boys tend to act out against others.) The violent outbursts we see in boys are also exacerbated by conditions such as learning disabilities and attention deficit disorder, which are far more common among male than among female populations.[10]

When a boy does not have flesh-and-blood men with whom to identify, as is so often the case in fatherless homes and communities, he may be forced to invent his own concepts of manliness. Some boys turn for inspiration to the pitiful "he-man" images that the popular media promote—the Conans and Rambos and killer cops and life-bashing rock stars. Or they turn to neighborhood gang leaders or criminals whose brutality they mistake for true masculinity.

In fatherless homes and communities, physically active boys do not have male mentors to teach them how to channel and contain their aggressive energy in socially acceptable ways: through sports, martial arts, hunting, sailing, physical labor, and other energetic activities traditionally engaged in by men. Hence, their aggressive energy runs amok and becomes useless or destructive. Then, too, in fatherless homes and communities, young boys are not helped by men to separate from their mothers. An unbroken dependence on and closeness with mother can lead to rage against her and against all women, who are then perceived as dangerously powerful and omnipresent. Men who, during therapy sessions, rail against their "smothering" mothers are often really angrier at their "missing" fathers, who failed to help them break their too-close ties to mother.

Indeed, numerous research studies have shown that boys raised without fathers are less masculine than fathered boys or they exhibit a pseudo, or a "hyper," masculinity that is characterized by excessive aggressiveness.[11] Conversely, as the cross-cultural research of sociologist Scott Coltrane reveals, societies in which there is a high level of paternal involvement tend to be relatively nonviolent.[12]

Just as some sons have distorted or narrow ideas about healthy maleness, so may some mothers, especially those who have not had meaningful relationships with their fathers. They may, for example, expect a son to be rough and tough even if he is by nature gentle; or they may expect him to go out for football or baseball even if his interests lie elsewhere. I once had a neighbor whose bright and animated young son preferred drawing pictures to riding his Big Wheel and who presented his parents with a Christmas wish list that included books but not sports equipment, colored pencils but not electronic toys. As we were having coffee together one morning, my neighbor asked in a worried tone, "Evi, do you think that Tommy's developing normally? Do you think that he could be *gay*?"

In all likelihood, when, past his infancy, a boy breaks free from the symbiotic closeness with mother and begins to identify with a nurturing father figure, he will form a healthy male self. (We will look at this development in detail in later chapters.) And like the clouds in a changing sky, this healthy male self can take various shapes: The boy who stays up all night to tackle a difficult problem in solid geometry expresses healthy male energy just as much as the one who relentlessly tackles his opponent on the football field; the boy who loves books is as vital as the boy who loves baseball; the boy who raises his voice in effective protest against a sadistic teacher is as fierce as the one who challenges the school bully to a fistfight; the boy who will not give in to peer pressure to experiment with drugs, alcohol, or sex demonstrates far more male strength than the boy who is afraid to risk nonconformity by saying no; the boy who protects rain forests against nature's exploiters embodies the spirit of the male warrior just as does the soldier who defends his country; and the man who loves other men can be as manly as the man who loves women.

One of my favorite storybook mothers has always been the cow mother of Ferdinand the Bull.[13] As readers familiar with Ferdinand may remember, he is unlike his friends. While they enjoy running, jumping, snorting, and butting their heads with one another, Ferdinand is an avowed pacifist who prefers smelling the flowers to fighting in Madrid's most prestigious bullfight. And knowing that Ferdinand is not unhappy or weak of will or unmasculine—he is, in fact, the most powerful and strongest of all the bulls in the field—his wise cow mother lets him follow his peaceable nature; she accepts and respects her young bull just as he is.

Another story comes to mind. A celebrated bullfighter disappears during a lavish victory party for him. After searching the grounds, a guest finally locates him in the kitchen. When she comments that it is odd for a famous bullfighter, the pride of all Spain and the symbol of virile manliness, to don a woman's apron and stir the *paella*, he sharply retorts, "Whatever I chose to do is manly."[14] As the bullfighter understands, when a man is sure of his manliness, he need not limit himself to stereotyped masculine behavior but is self-confident enough to engage in traditionally feminine activities. Conversely, the man who is not sure of his masculine identity is more likely to mimic the rigid masculinity of a Rambo or Terminator.

From about ages three to five, when boys are actively

learning to be male and to be like their daddies, they typically behave in gender-stereotyped ways and reject whatever is feminine and associated with their mommies. During the school years, pressures from peers reinforce rigid gender roles. However, as boys mature and become increasingly secure in their masculine identity, they, like the self-confident bullfighter, will become more flexible, more androgynous. I do not think that androgynous development can be forced, that it is a good idea for mothers to impose sewing kits and baby dolls and dancing lessons, for example, on boys; indeed, such impositions are likely to meet with massive resistance.[15] When boys respect and are respected by both the male and female figures in their lives, they have the best chance of becoming masculine men who are comfortable expressing their feminine sides.

Mothers react in a number of ways to their sons' maleness. Historically, women have felt enhanced by the birth of a son: the boy child's chances to become powerful in the world often promised a vicarious power for the mother, whose own possibilities were so limited. My maternal grandmother, who was refused admission to medical school in Victorian Vienna because she was a woman, once shared with me her three doomed personal wishes: to be tall (she was tiny); to have been born a man (she obviously missed out here); and to have had a son who could be all that she could not (she had three daughters). Although opportunities for women are greatly expanding, some women may still harbor the secret belief that the son is their outreach into the exciting world beyond the home. Hence, they may prefer the son to the daughter and take a special delight in his boyish escapades. Of course, when mothers live through their sons in order to feel more powerful, they necessarily burden or exploit them. Oscar Wilde noted that selfishness is not living as one wishes to live but asking another to live as one wishes to live.

However, a son's maleness can also enhance a woman *without* her exploiting him. An animated dental hygienist, while probing my sore gums, told me in great detail and with undisguised happiness about the adventures of her pilot son and about their positive relationship. It was immediately evident to me that this mother, like countless others, was not asking her son to live for both of them but that by sharing in his exciting life she was enlarging her own.

In some ancient myths, the mother's son becomes her consort. Although in modern usage a consort is a companion, partner, or spouse, its older meaning had a spiritual component: a consort energized and awakened another's development in some mystical way. For instance, in some Hindu traditions, yogis would seek out a consort to help them join within themselves the separate and powerful essences of the feminine and the masculine.[16] I have known a few women who were able to release their latent masculine energy as a result of having sons; in these cases, the sons functioned as consorts. I recall a conversation with an old, infirm woman with a beaming face, who told me how she had always gotten a kick out of her fun-loving, irreverent boys: "They were real jokesters—silly fellows. Often they laughed so hard that they would fall to the floor in convulsions, and their laughter made me laugh. I was brought up to be a proper lady, you know, but my sons' wild humor did wonders to lighten me up!"

In a similar vein, my client Lee, the mother of two grown sons, told me this anecdote.

When the boys were little, I wanted to find ways for them to let out their frisky energy. I thought it would be wonderful if they had a sandlot to play in, so I turned our driveway into one. Without a second thought, I ordered *ten tons* of sand from a man who owned a building supply company. And when my husband came home from work and saw these mountains of white sand outside our house, he was in shock. It took him a while to get used to the new look. Anyway, the boys and I had a grand time romping around and digging. Of course, we'd track so much sand and mud into the house that the carpets were soon ruined. But what a small trade-off for all the exuberant fun we shared! I told my husband that I was doing this for our sons, but the truth is that by joining in my boys' play, I was learning to be playful myself. It's as if this wild and care-free *boy-spirit* was being born in me.

To me, Lee's story is doubly wonderful. On the one hand, her boys' boyish energy let loose her own; on the other hand, her delighted responses to her boys' boyish energy undoubtedly helped them love this part of themselves. D. W. Winnicott, an eminent British child psychiatrist, writes that the precursor of the mirror is the mother's face—and Lee's face shone with joy and approval. Interestingly, Lee's older son, who is now in his late twenties and a successful executive at a Fortune 500 corporation, became consort to his mother in another way. Lee had always been a stay-at-home mother, but after her sons were grown she was eager to find work outside the home. However, she did not know how to get her plans off the ground; even the career counselor whom she saw could not get her moving. Seeing that his mother was stuck, her son prodded and pushed her into action. From him she learned how to be more assertive—to become connected to her own masculine energy—in order to land a job in the male-dominated world of business.

Not all women respond positively to their sons' maleness. For some, the son's presence in their lives portends threat and danger. Carol Klein, in her book *Mothers and Sons*, reports that in the dreams of pregnant women she interviewed, there was often a strong subplot of male dominance and violence. "Several remembered dreaming . . . the same dream: each gave birth to a full-grown boy, who stretched her body beyond repair as he forced his way into life. Similar strains of dominance and submission are easily seen in the quite usual dream of a solidly built baby boy pushing his way up, not down, the birth canal, choking off his mother's breath as he insists on taking his own."[17] For some women, the perception of the male baby's maiming them is not limited to their dreams. One woman in Klein's study told her, in the presence of the woman's eight-year-old son, how excruciatingly painful the boy's birth had been for her and how, in comparison to the relatively painless birth of her daughter, he had "ripped her apart." "To this mother," Klein writes, "the son's birth seemed to have elements of violent attack: she, a woman, was already victim to his, a man's, inherent sadism."[18]

As columnist for *Parents* Magazine, I have received letters from young mothers who see in the baby son's male face the despised face of an abusive husband or of the father who abandoned them; their negative projections impair their relationships with their sons and may damage their sons' healthy development. As Marie Bronshvag, who teaches a parenting class in Manhattan, remarked to Myriam Miedzian, author of *Boys Will Be Boys*, "Single teenage mothers abandoned by their boyfriends often take it out on their sons; the sons then take it out on their girlfriends."[19]

And Klein, musing on her interviews with grown men who were unable to form intimate relationships with women, writes,

> Perhaps I was unduly influenced by my memory of the eight-year-old's expression as he listened to his mother's insistence that his life had begun her suffering. But it seemed to me that a number of these men were struggling to make sense of the anger they had suspected, as they grew up, lay behind their mothers' dutiful care. They had glimpsed the connection their mothers unconsciously drew between masculinity and brutality.[20]

I am also reminded of a passage by Christopher Milne, the son of A. A. Milne of *Winnie the Pooh* fame:

> [My mother] was a firm ruler. If there were any obstacles in the way she would ignore them. If any unwelcome facts upset her hopes, she would treat

them as if they didn't exist. I suggested earlier that one of the unwelcome facts that faced her soon after my arrival was that I was clearly a boy, and that for nine years she tried to ignore this by dressing me as a girl. . . . Fortunately, in this particular instance, mind failed to triumph over matter and I remained a boy. But only just; and I was one of her few failures.[21]

In a similar vein, English novelist and playwright W. Somerset Maugham writes, "I was brought up by a very strict mother to believe that men are naturally wicked."[22]

When women see maleness as an inherently destructive energy that is associated with domination and violence, they may, like Mrs. Milne, try to stamp it out in their sons. In a popular book about bringing up sons, the author related how, in an effort to save her son, she separated him from the community of males, picked out clothes for him in the girls' section of a department store, and encouraged him to participate in activities traditionally viewed as nonmasculine. One of my former clients was still more extreme. When she became pregnant, she decided that if an amniocentesis revealed that her baby was male, she would opt for an abortion: "I just cannot see myself tolerating an aggressive little boy in my life," she explained.

To be sure, the great majority of mothers express disapproval of their sons' aggressive energy in more subtle ways, which may nevertheless be harming. "Be nice; behave yourself; mind your manners; don't get into fights; stop acting like a hooligan; be quiet; settle down; and, for heaven's sake, sit still!" thousands of mothers (and female schoolteachers) tell thousands of sons daily in their efforts to socialize them. But sometimes these efforts are overzealous. When a mother not only tames the "Wild Man" but drives him out, she may devitalize her son—rob him of his life essence.

Healthy aggressive energy that is repressed often takes destructive forms, such as hostility, rageful acts, sabotaging, and scapegoating. During the 1960s when I was a schoolteacher in Harlem, I had a colleague who maintained perfect order in her classroom; for most of the school day, her pupils sat at their desks in silence with hands folded in their laps while she lectured. After the three o'clock bell rang, however, my colleague's "well-behaved" little boys routinely knocked over trash cans, broke windows, and got into fistfights. Healthy aggressive energy that is repressed rather than allowed positive outlets may also lead to an inner deadness. Referring to the new-age man, Bly writes, "The male in the past twenty years has become more thoughtful, more gentle. But by this process he has not become more free. He's a nice boy who pleases not only his mother but the young woman he lives with. . . . But many of these boys are not happy. You will quickly notice the lack of energy in them. They are life-preserving but not exactly life-giving."[23]

Oliver, a client, confided that when, as a young child, he expressed his masculine vitality by telling an off-color joke or acting wild, his mother, a woman of great refinement, would accuse him of being boorish—too much like his "vulgar" father, whom she had divorced before my client was born. He also told me that ostensibly for his own good, his mother had discouraged his associations with the neighborhood boys, whom she thought of as "roughnecks" but who, according to Oliver, were merely normal spirited youngsters. To his mother's satisfaction, Oliver did grow up to become a cultured man with impeccable manners who always made a good appearance. More than this, he adopted his mother's disdainful attitude toward the male species and made a concerted effort not to be like them. But as the middle-aged Oliver often told me during the early stages of therapy, he grieved for his own undeveloped masculinity. Having been cut off from the world of boys when he was young, he felt stiff and uncomfortable in the presence of men. Never having been allowed to express his natural male energies, he lacked a joie de vivre.

Although I have implied that mothers enhance their sons by affirming and encouraging their masculine nature I should like to emphasize that a woman's protective instincts may make it difficult for her to do this. In my discussions with mothers of sons, I heard time and again that the mothers were afraid for their boys. As we all know, when boys are boys, they often end up hurting themselves. Girls, who are no less athletic than boys, do not court physical dangers and bodily injury the way boys, especially adolescent boys, seem to. Healthy girls and women will naturally nurture and protect their bodies; healthy boys and men, on the contrary, seem compelled at times to test, challenge, and defy their bodies' limits. Perhaps this is why there are nearly four times as many accidental deaths among adolescent and young adult males than among females in the same age group and why the vast majority of spinal-cord injuries occur in males.[24]

Robert Bly vividly writes about the danger-courting tendencies of young men. At a workshop for several hundred men, the leader handed out two or three thousand strips of red cloth and asked each man to attach a cloth to any part of his body that had been wounded in some way—a cut, a broken bone, a knife wound, a scar. "Many men needed ten or more strips. For some men the entire right side of the body, head to ankle, was brilliant red; on others the red almost covered the head; for some, both arms and legs. When the exercise was over, the room was a sea of red."[25]

As Jonathan's mother, I think my most difficult challenge has been to support his involvement in organized sports in spite of the fact that they came to be associated with physical injury. In the hope that my story will have some resonance for mothers who read this book, I conclude this chapter with it.

Since he was about seven, Jonathan, with his father's enthusiastic participation and encouragement, has channeled his "bullish" male energy into soccer, basketball, and, most important, baseball. In the early years, sports meant having fun—throwing, catching, *and* dropping the ball, running wildly, getting red-cheeked and muddy, making new friends. As Jonathan got older, however, playing ball became serious business. By the time he was in junior high, practicing his skills in baseball had become more important to him than schoolwork, coaches more influential than teachers. Before big games, he frequently complained of stomach pains and tension headaches; if he performed poorly, he would be broken-hearted, often for days. He also suffered a host of minor sports injuries, such as jammed or broken fingers, torn ligaments, and knee problems; instead of being stocked with popsicles and pizzas, our freezer held a variety of ice packs. During the course of bringing up our daughter, my husband or I took her to the emergency room three times: once for eating flowers from our garden, another time for breaking her arm in gymnastics class (which effectively ended her aspirations to become the next Nadia Comaneci), and a third time for a slight concussion after a stray volleyball bounced off her head. By the time Jonathan was twelve, I had stopped counting the trips to the emergency room.

Because of all the upset baseball caused my son (and me), I began to hate it. And when, during his worst slumps, he threatened to quit his team, I hoped that he would, although I knew that his threats were empty ones, that something in Jonathan compelled him to stay with it, to overcome his vulnerabilities, to become *hardened*.

During high school, Jonathan continued to "work" at baseball. When I attended his games, it was obvious to me that the years of disciplined practice, along with his natural abilities, were shaping him into a fine athlete. Just as I had been amazed by his relentless energy when he was a toddler, I was now in awe of his masculine grace and competence. Although he was not a power hitter, he was a superlative outfielder and base runner. Jonathan had cultivated what the philosopher Ortega y Gasset attributes to the skilled hunter: an awareness, an attentiveness, an "alertness" that is full of zest, vivacity, and readiness for the critical moment.[26]

Still, watching him play made me uneasy. The other boys were much huskier than Jonathan, who has a slender physique, and they played *hard*. The pitchers threw fastballs with such force that I gasped each time they came over the plate; when the outfielders madly chased after the long flies hit in their direction, I anticipated that they would collide with the fence or each other. "Someone will get badly hurt," I would mumble to myself . . . and one night my son did.

I was not in the stands when my son was hurt. His team was playing a doubleheader and my husband and I had left for home in the middle of the second game. Jonathan had played exceedingly well up until that point, and certain that he was pleased with his performance, we went to bed feeling very happy for him. Sometime after midnight, an ashen-faced friend of his knocked on our door. Jonathan had been rushed by ambulance to the hospital. Trying to steal second, he had been elbowed and knocked down; after his head hit the base, he lost consciousness.

By the time we got to the emergency room, everything in me had gone numb. It is simply not possible for a parent to take in the possibility that a child who is full of vibrant life, a child who has been nurtured and loved in ten thousand different ways, could suddenly be taken away or be irreparably damaged. Only days later, after I knew that my son would be all right, did I dare to reflect on what had almost happened. Like me, my husband had *appeared* composed at the hospital; he was even able to joke with my son's frightened teammates and coach, who kept vigil with us for part of the night. But two days after the accident, Bruce woke during the night screaming that the room was spinning out of control.

My memories of that awful night in the hospital are blurred, but I recall that after he came into focus, the first question my son asked his father and me was, "Do you know if I was safe at second?" (The umpire had, in fact, called him out.) The second was, "Will I be able to play tomorrow?" (My husband gently told him that it would be a while before he could play.) Of course, I never wanted Jonathan to play baseball again. Perhaps, I fooled myself into thinking, I could interest him in computers.

For a couple of days after he was discharged from the hospital, Jonathan felt so sick that he stayed in bed. But after his headache and nausea subsided, he began to talk about rejoining his team. As a psychologist, I knew that for at least several months after a major concussion, the part of the brain that has been traumatized is particularly vulnerable and that re-injury tends to have very serious effects. Every instinct prompted me to protect my son from putting himself at unnecessary risk. I implored him to sit out the season, but he insisted otherwise. As the days passed, the tension between us grew. He stalked about the house like a caged animal; over my protests, he carried his bat around and took practice swings in the living room.

There are times when the maternal voice has very little influence. I knew this was one of those times. Boys turn to men, not to their mothers, for affirmation of their physical courage. Unfortunately, as we all know, there are men (some of whom become coaches) whose ideas of masculinity are so distorted that they encourage boys to sacrifice their bodies unnecessarily—to hide all feelings of fear or pain and to engage in gratuitous aggression against the competitor in order to prove their manliness. It is from these unbalanced men that boys may learn violence; it is from these unbalanced men that boys need to be protected.

Perhaps the best that mothers can do for their sons when they reject their counsel is to lead them to men who are mature, kind, and nurturing, men who will not take advantage of a boy's vulnerability as he strives to assert his masculine strength but who will rather help him find reasonable ways to express it.

Jonathan, his father, and I finally agreed that Jonathan would abide by the decision of our family doctor—a man whom Jonathan had known since early childhood and whom we all trusted. We also agreed that I would say nothing to Dr. Beasley to influence that decision. To Jonathan's satisfaction, the doctor told him that although there was a small amount of risk, he could return to his team almost immediately.

I accepted Dr. Beasley's decision outwardly, but I was not at peace with it. Intellectually, I understood that I needed to release my protective hold, to trust that Jonathan's coach

—who, fortunately, was a caring and prudent man—would look out for him during practices and games, and to support Jonathan's involvement in sports. But in my heart, I was opposed to Jonathan's playing ball and taking any risk of re-injury. Clearly, in order to resolve my head-heart conflict, I had some inner work to do.

I came to understand my maternal task as twofold. First, I needed to let go the illusion that I could perfectly protect my son from physical harm; as he ventured out into the world, my arms were too short to reach out, wrap round him, and shield him from life's jabs and blows. Second, I needed to accept the fact that as much as I cherished Jonathan and wanted to safeguard him, I would be wrong to *impose* on him my protective maternal love, which might have the effect of holding him back and making him unnecessarily fearful.

Sara Ruddick calls the protective aspect of motherly care "preservative love." "Preserving the lives of children," she writes, "is the central constitutive, invariant aim of maternal practice."[27] Yet, Ruddick goes on to say, a mother's preservative love must be tempered by her "humility," for preservative love becomes degenerate when it is grandiose and unbounded. Only with humility is it possible for a mother to accept the limits of her power and "the independent, uncontrollable, and increasingly separate existences" of her growing children.[28]

An ancient Greek legend about the mother goddess Thetis and her son Achilles also reminded me of my necessary maternal limitations. Thetis tries to make Achilles invulnerable by dipping him, head-first, in the holy river Styx. But the place on his heel where her fingers hold him is not exposed to the magical waters, and he ultimately suffers a lethal arrow through this very spot. Ironically, it is just where Thetis holds on to Achilles in her attempt to make him safe that he becomes most vulnerable. I did not want to repeat Thetis's mistake with my own son.

At Jonathan's invitation, Bruce and I attended the first home game he played after his head injury. As soon as we got to the baseball park, I sized up the players on the opposing team; they looked menacingly big and strong. By the time the game started, it was getting dark, and as my mind flashed back to the night of Jonathan's accident, my heart began to pound. At Jonathan's first at-bat, he took four outside pitches and walked. After the next batter had come up to the plate, I noticed the coach signaling Jonathan to steal. Although a surge of terror shot through me and I wanted to look away, I forced myself to keep my eyes on my son. With the first pitch, Jonathan took off like a charging bull, slid into second—and this time *was* safe. After getting back on his feet and shaking off the dirt from his uniform, he flashed a triumphant smile in our direction.

In that instant, the anxiety that I had stored in my body since Jonathan's accident drained out of me. A great pride in and love for my son took its place. Squeezing my eyes shut, I made a secret vow that from then on, I would no longer dwell on the bad things that could happen to Jonathan when he played sports. Instead, I would join in his excitement and I would respect whatever in him moved his male spirit—or at least I would try to. Joining my husband and a few other people in the stands, I rose to my feet and wildly applauded the dauntless young athlete who had just stolen second.

2

Superman, Bruce Springsteen, and Dad: Male Role Models

Men, after all, must aspire to be men, and although a man may be many different things, being a man, whatever that means, seems always to be of crucial importance.

—GERALD I. FOGEL,
The Psychology of Men

At about age five, my son underwent a strange metamorphosis. From somewhere he scrounged a remnant of red silky fabric, which became his cape. Then, he would pretend to peer through solid masses with x-ray eyes or, with arms arched forward, would dive from chair to couch to coffee table. This bizarre behavior did not abate after a day or two but continued for weeks. At Jonathan's insistence, we all indulged his fantasy: For special treats, his father bought him Superman comic books; I got him a pair of pajamas with a Superman insignia; and his best friend gave him a giant-sized Superman calendar. However, though outwardly I supported Jonathan's infatuation with Superman, secretly I was troubled by it. Was his fascination an unhealthy escape from reality, I wondered? Would he take a flying leap from our rooftop?

One morning, after I dropped off the little red-caped boy at his Montessori class, I decided to pay a visit to its director, Mrs. Gollin, a white-haired woman who, to my mind, knew everything about children. When I asked her what she thought Jonathan's passionate identification was all about, she answered without any hesitation: "It's about acquiring *power*—masculine power." I left the director's office not fully understanding the implications of her explanation but relieved that she did not seem alarmed by my little Superman.

Not long after my talk with Mrs. Gollin Superman disappeared from our family. One morning, to my surprise, Jonathan did not put on his red cape. Instead, he begged for a greasy rag, which looked and smelled like the one the attendant at the gas station used. To his delight, I found a blackened, grimy cloth in the garage. After I presented Jonathan with this "treasure," he carefully pulled it through the loops of his blue jeans, and for many weeks thereafter made it part of the outfit he wore to nursery school each day. Believing that he now resembled the deft and handsome young mechanic who repaired our Dodge Dart, Jonathan seemed contented.

However, just as Superman had abandoned us, so, eventually, did the mechanic. One day, Jonathan, appearing without his rag, flexed his muscles, made grunting sounds, shoved his sister, overturned the furniture in our living room, and announced that he was the Hulk.

In formulating my ideas for this chapter on male role models, I have given much thought to my son's early metamorphoses and have come to appreciate the correctness of Mrs. Gollin's explanation: Jonathan's seemingly strange behaviors had everything to do with acquiring power. Like most little boys, he sought out heroic males and tried to absorb their wondrous strength so that he himself, a small, dependent, vulnerable boy, could feel powerful. I have also come to believe that a boy's quest for masculine power—by which I mean prowess, competence, and effectiveness, *not abusiveness*—through his identifications with vital men is an essential aspect of his healthy development and that we mothers are wise to understand it so that we can find appropriate ways to support it. However, because we have never aspired to become men, such understanding requires an enormous stretch of our sympathetic imaginations.

The young male's struggles to become strong and independent—his compelling identifications with powerful males, particularly with his father—are so tenderly and sensitively described in Felix Salten's classic children's story *Bambi* that I could think of no better way to stretch our sympathetic imaginations than by retelling and interpreting parts of it. (Indeed, I am in agreement with German poet Friedrich von Schiller who mused that more meaning is often found in the make-believe tales told to us in childhood than in the facts we learn through science.)

As those who have read the original version of *Bambi* may remember, the young deer spends his early days with his mother, who faithfully protects, nourishes, and teaches him. But as time goes on, something stirs in Bambi, something begins to pull him away from the world of the feminine and his mother toward the world of the masculine and his father. The young deer is at his mother's side, contentedly nibbling leaves, when he hears a loud rustling in the bushes and observes a herd of elk. As he watches the procession tramp by, he is at once filled with terror and wonder. The elk appear huge to him, like giant apparitions, and the hugest elk of them all, with his wild mane and tree-like antlers, particularly impresses Bambi.

Compared to these kingly creatures, Bambi's mother, whom, until now, he has experienced as all-powerful and all-sustaining, seems suddenly diminished. Next to the elk, Bambi also experiences his own smallness; for the first time, he feels puny. And yet, despite the loss of self-esteem, Bambi is moved by the magnificence of the elks' sheer physical power and, as Salten describes, is "more weirdly affected than ever before in his life."[1] From this time on, the little deer is no longer content to be like his mother or to dwell exclusively in the world of the feminine. Instead, he is increasingly fascinated with the great elk, who represent the primal masculine nature:

> Sometimes he liked to listen to his big cousins the elks. The whole forest would tremble with their kingly voices. Bambi used to listen and be very much frightened, but his heart would beat high with admiration when he heard them calling. He remembered that the kings had antlers branching like tall, strong trees. And it seemed to him that their voices were as powerful as their antlers. Whenever he heard the deep tones of those voices he would stand motionless. Their deep voices rolled towards him like the mighty moaning of noble, maddened blood whose primal power was giving utterance to longing, rage and pride.[2]

In Bambi's trembling admiration of the elk, we sense the young deer's happy anticipation and fear and awe of his own budding masculine power: one day he too will grow antlers and be himself transformed into a mighty stag. It is not difficult to draw a parallel between Bambi's responses toward the powerful physical presence of the elk and the young boy's feelings about the father's male body. Just as Bambi is simultaneously awed and cowed by the sight of the elks' antlers, the young boy is at once impressed and humiliated by the sight of his father's genitals. On the one hand, father's mighty organ suggests to the boy that in time his own small penis will grow and that he will become a virile man; on the other hand, it reminds him that for the time being, he is less than a man—that he is little and weak.

As the story of Bambi progresses, the great stag of the forest, Bambi's father, makes his appearance, and the young deer observes him intently. Gradually a relationship develops, one that is full of effort, passion, and love. Now it is the

father, not the mother, who is the object of Bambi's fascination, and from now on, it will be the father, not the mother,
Bambi emulates.

To be sure, with his father, Bambi is not always at ease.
One day, for example, the young deer, frightened by a recent
shooting in the forest, musters the confidence to ask his father about the hunters who prey on them, but the stern father
does not provide him with comforting reassurances as his
mother surely would. Rather, he tells Bambi, "Listen, smell,
and see for yourself. Find out for yourself." Then the father
"lifted his antlered head still higher" and bade Bambi fare-
well.[3] Bambi's response to this encounter is ambivalent. He
wants to cry because his father is hard, but he is also suffused
with a feeling of growing pride and self-confidence that he
can live up to his father's standards.

Bambi's father does what fathers of sons have traditionally done: He tries to make his child strong; to develop his
capacity for self-defense; to encourage him to explore; to prepare him for the world at large—the world that stretches beyond the mother's sheltering, protective realm. And as long
as it is grounded in affection and respect rather than in
coldness and contempt, the traditional father's demanding,
challenging style of parenting is fodder for the son's psychological growth and masculine development.

Throughout *Bambi*, the differences between fatherly and
motherly care become evident. Bambi's mother, for example,
prepares her young deer for life by telling him about the
forest and the woodland creatures; with great patience, she
answers Bambi's many, many questions and, in this way,
helps him to make sense of his world. The father deer, however, does not talk much with Bambi. But he spurs a different
kind of growth by helping Bambi turn inward to find his own
answers.

"Brooding" is the term that writer J. Lang uses for the
process of sitting close to one's feelings for as long as it takes
for something to "hatch"; "brooding" is what the old stag
teaches Bambi to do. According to Lang, "brooding" is a way
males have traditionally connected with their deepest feel-

ings. "Talking things through," on the other hand, is a way females have traditionally dealt with their emotions.[4] Because we women are usually comfortable speaking the language of feelings and emotions, we may be too quick to condemn our children's fathers if they are not. Perhaps what we need to do instead is remind ourselves that sensitivity can be expressed in various ways and that sometimes it is wordless.

Of course, every son longs for his father's approval. A sweet scene from *Bambi* illustrates that fatherly praise may, in fact, be wordless. Bambi has just told the great stag that he can take care of himself now and that he no longer cries for his mother when she leaves him alone. "The stag looked at Bambi appraisingly and smiled a very slight, hardly noticeable smile. *Bambi noticed it however.*"[5] (italics added)

As his relationship with the great stag deepens, Bambi also deepens his understanding of the world around him. Bambi's early idealization of the father grows into a more genuine appreciation of him. By intently watching the great stag, Bambi learns the deepest secrets of the forest. He also comes to recognize that the great stag's power derives not so much from his physical strength as from his knowledge of the natural world, his compassion, and his commitment to protecting life; and, when Bambi, wounded by a hunter's gunshot, is nursed back to health by the great stag, he comes to know the healing powers of fatherly nurture.

As Bambi matures, he also comes to accept the fact that his father is vulnerable and mortal—that, in fact, he will not always be there for him. The cruel irony for every young male is that as he grows up and becomes increasingly powerful, his father grows old and becomes less powerful. Surpassing the father is problematic for many sons, so problematic that some always hold themselves back from becoming more successful than their fathers. It is also true that being surpassed by the son is so threatening for fathers who are overly competitive and narcissistic that they try to keep the son down.

The story of Bambi exemplifies the natural order: The

old father passes his crown to his son. The story ends as Bambi, now fully grown and magnificent, receives his father's blessing, takes the dying stag's place on the mountaintop, and becomes a father himself. Having modeled himself on his vital and loving father, Bambi has transformed himself into the powerful stag of his childhood dreams. The great antlers that crown Bambi's head represent the cycles of growth and regeneration in which he has participated. But as Felix Salten hints, life will not be easy for the deer. As is true for Bambi's human counterparts, Bambi will have to struggle long and hard to use his masculine power well.

It seems to me that Bambi's struggles to become a great stag reflect every boy's struggles to become a powerful man. As is true for the forest deer, in order to grow into his maleness and adulthood, a boy must grow away from his mother, who is the original source of comfort and a reminder of his babyhood. To ease the considerable pain of loss associated with differentiating and separating himself from the comfort-giving mother, the little boy typically seeks out males with whom he might proudly identify. Moreover, throughout the boy's growing years he will look toward other men to guide and reinforce his own masculine development.

Bambi's admiration—his trembling awe—of the powerful elk is really no different from the feelings that some young boys express for players in the NFL, NBA, or major league baseball. When I was a pupil in elementary school, my male classmates were so enamored of their baseball heroes that they vied with one another (sometimes getting into fistfights) for the closet hooks with the numbers seven and twenty-four—the numbers that their gods, Mickey Mantle and Willie Mays, wore on their uniforms. Now, almost forty years later, I observe my son and his friends watching the Superbowl on TV; they seem at once stirred and transfixed by the masculine beauty, might, and prowess of the players on the field—much like Bambi is as he beholds the parade of the elk. When a player makes an astonishing pass or runs fast as the wind, the boys go wild with joy; reveling in the player's invincibility and godlike power, they must believe, it seems to me, that they are also invincible and godlike.

To be sure, it is not enough for a boy to identify with the sports superstars (or with Superman or the Hulk), for these are fantasy men whose images, carefully designed and manipulated by the media, are unidimensional. A boy also needs to identify with flesh-and-blood men, whose masculinity takes fuller and more realistic forms. Surely, the male who is almost always most important to him and who, through a long, complex process of imitation he internalizes, is his own father; for most boys, the personal father is the great stag of the forest. It is the father who embodies the masculine power that the boy hopes to develop in himself; it is the father the boy longs to see as fundamentally good, strong, honest, and principled. The boy's longing for the father he can admire is beautifully described by novelist and story writer Sherwood Anderson in his autobiography.

> A boy wants something very special from his father. You are always hearing it said that fathers want their sons to be what they feel they cannot themselves be, but I tell you it works the other way. I know that, as a small boy, I wanted my father to be a proud silent dignified one. When I was with other small boys and he passed along the street, I wanted to feel in my breast the flow of pride.[6]

There is a famous story about Sigmund Freud and his father, Jakob, that reveals every boy's great wish to admire his father—*and the disillusionment when he cannot*. During one of their long walks together, Jakob confided to the twelve-year-old Sigmund that one day as he had been walking down the street wearing a new fur cap, someone had knocked it off his head and spat out, "Jew, get off the pavement."[7] When Sigmund asked his father what he had done in response, he expected to hear that Jakob had struck the offender down or at least had words with him. However, his father explained that he had simply retrieved the cap and gone on his way. Because young Sigmund suddenly perceived his father as spiritless and cowardly, the genuine love he had felt for the older man now became tainted with disdain.

This sad anecdote reminds me how devastating it is for all the children of oppressed minorities to observe or hear about their parents being humiliated or beaten down by those in powerful positions. It brings to mind a story that my old friend Avraham, an Iraqi-born Jew, confided to me. As a young child, Avraham had stood helplessly by as an angry mob pushed its way into his house during the dinner hour, dragged his father into the street, taunted him, and viciously beat him. "Many times, on my way to school, I had been attacked by the other children because I was a Jew, but these events did not make as great a mark on me as did witnessing the attack on my father. I have never been able to rid myself of this memory or the rageful feelings that accompany it."

Every boy wants to believe in his father's strength and goodness because this belief allows him to trust in his own potential for strength and goodness. I am convinced that of all the people who can help a boy feel positively about his father, the mother has the greatest influence; it is the mother who "interprets" the world for him, telling him what is good and what is bad; it is the mother whose truthfulness he trusts.

I was moved by a story a former client, Jenna, shared with me years ago. She had noticed that her eleven-year-old son, Brent, was reluctant to engage his father in any meaningful way. Sensing his father's emotional fragility, Brent was afraid that he might say something to hurt his feelings. Although Jenna recognized that her husband suffered from bouts of anxiety and depression as a result of his war experiences in Vietnam, she also had confidence that he would not fall apart or lose control, and she never doubted that he was anything less than a devoted father. Gently, she explained to her son that he need not act as his father's protector or worry about his moods, that nothing terrible would happen to Brent's father if Brent expressed his annoyance with or even anger at him from time to time. She also re-minded Brent that his father had been a war hero—a man of great courage and integrity—of whom he could feel proud and that his father's sad and anxious moods were simply the scars of wartime experience. With his mother's assurances, Brent loosened up around his father. In her wonderful way, Jenna helped her son focus on his father's strengths rather than on his vulnerabilities and fostered the boy's proud iden-tification with him.

Bambi's mother similarly promotes her son's admiration for and identification with his father. Noticing that Bambi is absolutely enthralled by his father's handsome appearance, she tells the young deer, "If you live, my son, if you are cunning and don't run into danger, you'll be as strong and handsome as your father is sometime, and you'll have antlers like his, too"; and hearing these words, "Bambi breathed deeply. His heart swelled with joy and expectancy."[8]

Of course, not all women think well of their sons' fa-thers. However, when they convey their low opinions to their sons, they cannot help but undermine the boys' self-esteem. Indeed, when a mother demeans her son's father, the boy himself will feel demeaned; whenever children are deprived of their wish to idealize their parents, especially the same-sex parent, they lose their own sense of worth, which leads to feelings of shame. This effect is poignantly described in a Jules Feiffer cartoon in which a heavy-hearted boy says, "I grew up to have my father's walk, my father's speech pat-terns, my father's postures, my father's opinions . . . and my mother's contempt for my father."

Sometimes women clients ask me how to handle justi-fiable feelings of anger or disrespect or disappointment to-ward their sons' fathers. Although I cannot give them perfect solutions, I urge them to share their complaints and negative feelings with friends or with me—but not with their boys. I also urge them to let their sons know time and again what *is* admirable or good about their fathers. Joanne, a client, told me that she had to dig deep to find something good to say about her ex-husband, who had been involved in shady business deals and was a pathological liar: "Frankly, I did not think it was possible to say anything nice about my 'ex' to my son since I really loathe the man, but, at your urging, I tried to come up with something. The truth is that he's very intelligent. When I told my son that he has inherited his dad's 'super smart' genes, he gave me a sheepish grin, and it was obvious that he was happy to have this positive link with him."

Nevertheless, when a father physically or emotionally abuses a member of the family, a mother needs to let the boy know that she is outraged. Children who are not told that their mistreatment at the hands of a brutal parent is undeserved come to believe that *they*, not the parent, are badly flawed; and sons who observe their mothers being abused by a spouse are at higher risk for becoming abusive themselves. Moreover, when a father poses a threat to his child's welfare, a mother may need to protect the child by removing him or her from the father altogether. Still, even in extreme situations of paternal abuse that lead to separation between father and child, a mother need not depict the father as an out-and-out monster. While acknowledging his abusive acts and weaknesses of character, she can also make mention of his positive attributes, abilities, and talents so that the son can find something positive in him with which to identify.

In addition to anecdotal material, we have research evidence that suggests that the mother's descriptions of her son's father affect the boy's self-image. In a study comparing sons of deceased fathers with sons of fathers absent for other reasons, the sons of deceased fathers were better adjusted. The most compelling explanation for this finding is that widows, unlike unmarried and divorced mothers, tend to have positive memories of their husbands and to talk warmly about them; the flattering stories that they tell their sons about their fathers help them form the necessary idealizations of and identifications with them.[9]

I learn from my male clients that just as the young boy needs to adore and emulate the father, the grown man also wants to admire him. Recently, Ed, a man in his mid-fifties, revealed that he had just learned that his father, who had died several years before, had twice sexually violated Ed's sister when she was a child. This information devastated my client. Not only did he experience great pathos for his suffering sister, but he was also faced with the sudden loss of "the good father"—the father who had taught him how to fish and to build with his own hands and who had been his first role model.

When I asked Ed how I might help him, he answered that it would be important to preserve some positive feelings for his father. Although Ed did not want to minimize the impact of his father's horrific acts, he also did not want to see him as a monster; rather, he needed to sustain some respect for the man who had guided him toward manhood. In the course of counseling, Ed and I pieced together the happy memories of his boyhood and of a father who, in spite of his exploitation of his daughter, had in many ways helped his son develop into the fine, competent, loving, and loved man that he is.

Ed's situation reminds me of another case. Years ago, I counseled an extremely likable and intelligent college student. David had initiated therapy to make sense out of a tormented relationship with the cold and neglectful father who had abandoned him and his siblings when they were young children. Although David desperately wanted to find something to admire about his father, he could not. Forlorn and increasingly embittered, David resolved to drop his surname as a way of renouncing ties with the despised father: "The truth is that I have nothing in common with this man who *happens* to have fathered me. It's ridiculous that a family name should bind us." Although I could not argue with David's decision, I suggested that he allow himself some time for contemplation before taking such a radical step.

The next week, David came to therapy in an ebullient mood. He announced that he would not drop his family name because he had found a meaningful connection with his father after all. As David explained, it was not their similarities but rather their dissimilarities that bound them. Empathic, sensitive, and capable of relationship, David concluded that he was living out what his incomplete, deficient father could not—that he was actualizing what remained undeveloped in the older man. Now father and son had become a unity of sorts, and although David understood that an in-the-flesh relationship would not be possible with the weak and heartless father, he could maintain a spiritual connection with him. Moreover, by keeping his surname, David was able to sustain ties with all his male forebears, which strengthened his own sense of identity.

In the previous chapter, I briefly described my client Oliver, who, having been cut off from his own father and from males in general, failed to develop a positive masculine identity. Because much of our work in therapy focused on Oliver's rediscovery of the father from whom he had been alienated since birth, it seems fitting to return to Oliver's story.

Oliver's father, a successful building contractor, had agreed to an "amicable" divorce shortly before Oliver's birth. Except for monthly visits, when he delivered the alimony and child-support checks, the father had little to do with his son. Uncultured, lacking social graces, and given to bursts of verbal aggression over his business dealings, he elicited only contempt from his ex-wife and from Oliver. A hefty, clumsy man, he would inevitably break or knock something over when he joined his ex-wife and son for a meal during his monthly visit. Sometimes, in an effort to lighten up the heavy atmosphere at the table, he would make a childish joke or off-color remark, which served only to anger and embarrass the mother and the son. As unwelcome as a bull in a china shop, he must have known that both his ex-wife and his son did their best to push him out of their lives. When this unloved man suddenly died, his son, then eighteen, found no reason to mourn.

In one of our sessions, I asked Oliver whether he could think of *any* good times that he and his father had shared. After a considerable pause, he told me that he did remember one happy occasion. For his tenth birthday, his father, overriding the mother's objections for once, had taken him to a wrestling match, where two long-haired hulks wearing sequined bikini shorts took each other on. Oliver recalled that his father laughed so hard at the wrestlers' posturing—the match had been obviously fixed—that he fell off his seat. Infected by his father's laughter, Oliver also gave himself permission to howl and jeer at the vulgar but good-natured entertainment—something he would not normally do. For Oliver, this memory unleashed other positive ones, which he eagerly shared with me. It seemed that for the first time he could appreciate the attempts his father had made to lighten up the seriousness that hung over the mother's house. Where before Oliver had seen only boorishness in his father, he now saw an appealing playfulness and irreverence.

As Oliver came to value his father's lightheartedness, even the silly jokes and off-color remarks he had made, Oliver began to cultivate his own sense of humor; he even dared to tell a few bawdy jokes to his male colleagues. During one of our sessions, Oliver told me that he felt energized and, with unconcealed joy, blurted out, "I think that my dead father decided to move into that dark, empty hole that was inside me and liven things up."

In recent years, it has become fashionable to minimize or deny differences between mothers and fathers. For example, rather than "mothering" and "fathering," the term "parenting" is often preferred. Moreover, the very real abuses of power associated with patriarchy have caused many sensitive people to see traditional fathering only in a negative light. Families, they contend, would be much nicer institutions if men with children assumed the role of mothers rather than fathers—if they became "male mothers." I disagree with this position.

As a society, we are moving toward greater flexibility in our gender roles and this progress opens up new and wonderful possibilities for men and women and for our children. Today, thankfully, mothers are typically not stigmatized when they choose to pursue careers outside the home, and fathers are typically not mocked when they change their babies' diapers; increasingly, modern fathers do not expect their wives to do all the caretaking, and, increasingly, modern mothers do not expect their husbands to be the sole breadwinners in the family.

Despite the fact that the parental roles mothers and fathers assume overlap and sometimes flip-flop, however, mother love and father love often take different forms. At least in most of the families I know, mothers *tend* to hold their children close and safe while fathers *tend* to push them out into the world; mothers *tend* to affirm and accept while fathers *tend* to challenge and demand. As I see it, as long as these tendencies do not become rigid rules of behavior, they are not necessarily problematic; in fact, the different parenting styles of mothers and fathers promote a child's flexibility.

An example from my own life comes to mind. I recall that after my son had reconciled with his father, who had reprimanded him for writing a shoddy term paper, Jonathan asked if we could talk. Jonathan commented on how different his father and I often are with him. In this instance, Jonathan had also asked me to look over his paper, but I had thought it best to emphasize its strengths rather than its weaknesses. "You accept me as I am, and I need that," Jonathan said; "but Dad pushes me to do better, and I need that too."

As social critic David Blankenhorn writes, "Neither [mother love nor father love] itself is sufficient. But together, they will make a whole and will add up to what a child needs."[10] My close colleague, Dr. Ivan Miller, puts it this way: "Mothers and fathers are dissimilar in the ways that an oil painting is dissimilar from a watercolor. Each is wonderfully various and interesting. Each has a full range of color, but the texture and quality of an oil is certainly not like that of a watercolor."

I agree with David Blankenhorn when he suggests that we should not be so quick to judge mothers' and fathers' different parenting styles in terms of right and wrong. The father who urges his small son to climb to the top of the jungle gym is not wrong, but neither is the mother who warns him to be careful; the mother who softly asks her child, "Where does it hurt?" is not wrong, but neither is the father who firmly says, "You'll be okay, just shake it off."[11]

Maternal nurture and paternal nurture do not always look the same, but each fosters a child's well-being and growth. In going through a portfolio of my children's early drawings, stories, and letters, I came across a note that nine-year-old Jonathan had sent us from camp.

Dear Mom and Dad,
I hate camp. Please drive up here as soon as possible and take me home.
Love from your unhappy son,
Jonathan

Tucked in with Jonathan's note were the separate letters my husband and I had written back to our son, which he had saved and returned to us.

Dear Jonathan,
Because I love you so much, I want you to be strong. I want you to be able to adapt to situations even if you don't like them at first. You are very bright and very good inside. Now you have to learn to make the *best* of things by learning how to be more flexible.
I love you, and I'm confident in you.
Dad

Dear Jonathan,
Dad and I have talked a lot. We both think that you need to give camp a chance. But I really want to know what's getting you down. Please call me when you get this letter—there's a phone you can use in the camp director's office. (I've checked with her, and she said that it will be fine for you to call

home.) When we talk, we can begin to figure out ways to make things better.

I love you and am always here for you.

Mom

In my practice, I have observed that some women who are normally soft and yielding become angry when their children's fathers do not share their style of parenting. "How can my husband be so heartless to insist that our son walk to school on cold winter days when it would take him only fifteen minutes out of his way to drop Brian off by car? If I had a car at my disposal, *I* would certainly drive Brian anywhere," a client laments. Another client, who has a college-age son, confides, "I am furious with my 'ex' for being so hard-nosed with Joel, who is obviously depressed and down on himself. What he needs from his father is some sympathy—the same kind of sympathy that I patiently give Joel day in and day out—instead of this 'pick yourself up by the bootstraps' talk."

A mother may try to "protect" her son from his father's demands without being aware that such "protection" undermines the son's development. I recently observed this tendency in myself. After my husband read Jonathan's carelessly written term paper, he forbade him from partying with his friends that evening and insisted on Jonathan's redoing the paper instead. Jonathan ranted and railed, "How can you do this to me? Don't you know how important it is to be with my friends? I just have to go out tonight." Mumbling insults against "big bad Bruce," he retreated to his room, where he spent the evening writing. For my part, I felt annoyed at Bruce for taking such a hard stand, and when we were alone I urged him to compromise. He would not, and I decided that it would be better for the three of us if I let the matter drop. (Over twenty-seven years of a very good marriage, Bruce and I have learned that not every disagreement between us has to be "processed." In matters of child-rearing, we have learned to take turns not insisting on our own way because we each trust the other's basic goodness as a parent.)

The next morning, Jonathan knocked on the door of his father's study, handed him the paper, and with a warm smile spreading across his face, said, "Dad, I worked really hard on this. You'll see, it's good now." Bruce (who is an English professor) took the paper, read it, and agreed with Jonathan's assessment. I could see that Jonathan was proud of his accomplishment and moved by his father's approval. Had Bruce given in to me by softening his hard stand, I now believe Jonathan would have been less well off. Guy Corneau, French analyst and author of *Absent Fathers, Lost Sons*, writes,

> On the whole, children who have been adequately fathered show more self-confidence, in their studies, in choosing careers, and in personal initiatives.
> A father's love is often expressed in conditional terms, as a way of encouraging the child's achievement: "If you succeed in such a thing, I'll give you what you want." The pressure of this conditional element is crucial in a child's developing sense of responsibility, a willingness to test and go beyond limits, and even a respect for established hierarchies; however, it will be a positive influence only if it is counterbalanced by affection.[12]

Among the many things that I am learning in the course of bringing up my son is that my role in his life is limited. Certainly, there is much that a mother can do to nurture her son and to promote his vitality and his goodness. However, as Robert Bly points out, mothers are not equipped to teach sons what they need to know in order to become men; rather, boys learn how to become men from their personal fathers and from father figures. Between my son and his father there seems to be a special kind of communication, which I do not always understand. When they touch, when they play, when they compete, even when they argue, I know that something life-giving passes between them. What I am learning to do better as time goes on is to step back more and not get in the way of their relationship by acting as a buffer or a mediator.

As I tried to complete this chapter, I was distracted one day by the muffled melody of a Bruce Springsteen song filtering through the vent that connects Jonathan's room to my writing area. Bruce Springsteen and Martin Luther King were my son's most recent role models. He has memorized most of Springsteen's lyrics, which tell of the injustices heaped on the working class, as well as a good part of King's "I Have a Dream" speech. This time around I did not have to ask Mrs. Gollin what Jonathan's passionate identifications were all about. I knew. They were about power. But it was not Hulk or Superman power that Jonathan was seeking; it was the power to speak out against injustice, to be effective, and to make the world a better place. The invincible, supernatural heroes had lost their appeal; men of flesh and blood who take action to help others had captured his imagination instead.

At the dinner table that night, Jonathan, with obvious admiration, told my husband and me that Bruce Springsteen sometimes gives all the proceeds from his concerts to charities.

"It's not to get a tax break," Jonathan assured us. "It's because he's committed to do some good.

"You know," he added, "Bruce really makes *me* feel that I can do some good in the world too; Bruce just gives me that kind of confidence."

"Which Bruce is that?" I could not resist asking. And with a warm smile directed at his father, my son replied, "Both Bruces."

3

....

Growing Pains:
Male Separation

This plant would like to grow
And yet be embryo;
Increase, and yet escape
The doom of taking shape.
      —RICHARD WILBUR,
            "Seed Leaves"

In the last chapter, we explored the boy's (and the man's) necessary identification with other males, particularly with his father. Now, drawing from psychological theory as well as from clinical vignettes and literature, let us backtrack a little and explore in depth the boy's (and the man's) necessary separation from his mother. Stretching our sympathetic imaginations once again, let us try to understand what our sons experience as they struggle to grow apart from us.

From observations and studies of mothers and babies, we know that in the first weeks after birth, the infant has the illusion of being at one with the all-caring mother. There is very little boundary between them, hardly any telling where one begins and the other leaves off; there is only the unity, the sensation of wholeness and harmony. However, as the weeks and months pass, the baby, urged on by some mysterious life force, begins to push away from mother, to break out of their shared orbit, to distinguish its experience from hers, and to lay claim to an increasingly individual and bounded existence. Although this process of separation begins in babyhood, it continues throughout life.

Healthy children of both sexes psychologically separate from mother, but separating has different meanings and follows a different time-line for girls and boys. Because she is female like mother, a little girl, even as she becomes increasingly autonomous, remains identified with mother in an essential way that a boy does not. At some deep level, she seems to know that she is made out of the same cloth as her mother; and so, throughout childhood, she intently observes and stays close to mother, after whom she patterns her reality and her sexual identity. It is usually not until her adolescence that a girl vehemently asserts her differences from her mother, and, even then, the sense of their shared femaleness persists.

To acquire his identity, however, a little boy cannot pattern himself after his mother. In his earliest years, he must begin to turn away from her and toward his father (or a father surrogate); he must begin to make an effort to separate himself imaginatively, or to "dis-identify," from the female with whom he was once joined—the human being who carried him in her body for nine months, who nursed him at her breast, and whom he has undoubtedly regarded as the most wonderful and powerful person in the world—and to "counter-identify" with the male who up until this time has been the "outsider."[1] I am reminded of the words of a five-year-old, which sum up quite nicely the different models of identification for girls and for boys: "Mommies are girls' kinds of humans and Daddies are boys' kinds of humans."

No one knows exactly what combination of factors triggers the separation between mothers and sons. In their book *The Way Men Think*, British researchers Liam Hudson and Bernadine Jacot, who have extensively studied gender development, suggest that boys may be biologically programmed to relinquish the closeness with mother.[2] For example, it is very possible that prenatal development—neurological differences in the structure and functioning of the brain—results in male babies being more restless and intolerant of frustration as well as less attuned to human faces and voices than female babies; hence, boys may be less suited than their sisters for a prolonged symbiotic union with mother. In my own case, nursing my daughter, who would contentedly nuzzle in my arms and gaze into my eyes, was more gratifying than nursing my son, who became impatient at the breast and would vigorously pull away from it to see what was going on around him. For this reason I breast-fed Leah, my "responsive" partner, for nearly two years, and Jonathan, my "rejecting" partner, for less than one year.

Doris Bernstein, the former president of the Institute for Psychoanalytic Training and Research, writes that the boy's anatomy and his bodily experiences help him establish his distance from mother: "The penis is eminently suited for individuation, because it serves as a natural anatomic vehicle for the drive outward." It symbolizes the male's thrusting forward, pushing ahead, going out in the world; it announces, as Bernstein goes on to say, "that men can separate (individuate) and become separate human beings."[3] In contrast, the girl's sexual sensations—diffuse, internal, coming from a mysterious, unseen source deep within—seem to oppose separation; they reflect and reinforce the blurred boundaries between mother and infant.[4]

It is also possible that mothers, in response to their sons' maleness, their "otherness," are from the start more distant with them than with their little girls. Although every mother sees herself in the body of her female child, she does not find herself in the body of her son and, for this reason, she may feel estranged from him. I am reminded of the candid remark made by a seventy-two-year-old woman, who, reminiscing about the birth of her son, remembered that the first thought that came to her when she heard that she had delivered a boy was "What the hell will I do with him?"[5] Indeed, we have evidence that mothers tend to initiate fewer interactions, such as gazing and talking, with their newborn sons than with their newborn daughters.[6]

It may also be that influenced by the cultural stereotypes of the self-sufficient male, the mother sends her infant son messages that he should not act babyish, which may set in motion his attempts at early—perhaps *too* early—independence from her: "Wow, you can hold your bottle all by yourself! . . . Come on now, stop hanging all over Mommy. . . . You're getting to be too heavy to sit on Mommy's lap. . . . Don't be a crybaby. . . . Now, that's my big boy, Mommy loves her big boy!" And partly because the father wants his son to be strong and partly because he feels competitive with the son for the wife/mother's attentions, he also tends to encourage the young boy's early independence from her.[7]

Although we cannot say for sure why a boy grows apart from his mother, we know that he normally does. Indeed, studies of children's behaviors reveal that between ages three and five, a boy will often begin to reject feminine activities associated with mother. He may also repress his wishes to be hugged, kissed, and cuddled by her. And often to the surprise and dismay of his nonsexist parents, he may himself assume sexist attitudes; for example, he is likely to exclude girls from his play, which frequently focuses on stereotypically masculine games of power, strength, and achievement.[8] A little boy may also criticize and mock Mommy or deride females in general; like Aesop's fabled fox who says that the grapes beyond his reach are sour, he may come to devalue the mother whom he is forced to relinquish. As I see it, mothers spare themselves grief if they remember two things: the first is not to take personally their little boy's sexism; the second is to take a firm stand against it when it gets out of hand and become abusive.

During the process of relinquishing maternal intimacy and comforting dependence, the little boy is sure to experience conflict. On the one hand, he is probably terrified of remaining identified with his female parent, of losing himself in mother; on the other hand, he is equally terrified of losing access to her motherliness. An image of my son as a toddler comes to mind. Wherever he went, Jonathan took along two possessions: an orange Tonka truck (which I have come to see as his get-away vehicle—the symbol of his separation from me) and a fuzzy white blanket (his security object—the symbol of his connection to babyhood and to me).

In older boys as well, the inner push toward independence from mother can precipitate a counter pull toward dependence on her. As the mother of a six-year-old observes, "Billy wants me to do things for him that he really could do for himself. He is always coming to me to find the school papers or mittens or cap that he has misplaced. When I refuse, he looks utterly helpless."

If I were to paint a portrait of a young boy, I would, like a Picasso of the cubist period, divide it in two: one half would shine with the bright colors of his fierce independence; the other would be clouded in muted tones of his neediness.

Hudson and Jacot have named the boy's reversal of identity—the cutting away from mother and joining with father—the "male *wound,*" a term that implies injury and possible scarring. Similarly, the great Jungian scholar Erich Neumann describes the young boy's separation from his mother as a traumatic process: a stepping "out of security into danger, out of the unconscious unity with a 'Thou' into loneliness and conscious independence."[9]

Recently, when my husband and I were preparing for a trip to relatively untraveled parts of Greece, I came to understand at a feeling level what it must be like for a little child to leave mother. Although I knew that on my travels I would have my life's companion at my side as well as enough money, a passport, plane tickets, and even room vouchers, I was gripped with angst, and at times, I was not so sure that I wanted to stray from my home-base for a strange land and the adventures that it promised. If a grown person experiences such anxiety at the prospect of leaving the familiar, what great waves of dread must wash over a three-year-old as he cuts himself off from his mother—his mainstay—for the unknown? How vulnerable, how shaky he must feel! Putting myself in baby's place, I could, for the first time, make meaning of the haunting lyrics of the popular lullaby:

Rock-a-bye baby on the tree top,
When the wind blows, the cradle will rock,
When the bough breaks, the cradle will fall,
Down will come baby, cradle and all.

To be sure, the more fortunate little boys will discover that when they disengage from Mommy's holding arms (the tree top of the lullaby), a friendly and nurturing Daddy is there to break their free fall; and they will discover that although Daddy love cannot replace Mommy love, Daddies can also make them feel safe. Thinking back on Jonathan's early years, I remember that when he was about five, he traded my lap for his father's. Although he cringed whenever I tried to hug or kiss him—gestures that made him feel babyish—he had no problem accepting physical affection from his father; indeed, until his legs were long enough to touch the floor, every night after dinner he would hop onto his father's knee.

Less fortunate little boys, however, grow up feeling that they can turn to no one; having relinquished the comfort-giving mother and finding no comfort with father, they may go through life believing that they must bear all their hardships alone. They learn to be stalwart to a fault. Harvard psychologist Samuel Osherson articulates what I suspect many boys and men feel deep down but never put into words:

Early on we experience women as the ones who fill us up, who comfort and take care of us, without having an opportunity in growing up to learn how to fill ourselves and to feel full while truly separate from women. We do not learn to be cared for, to get nurturance and intimacy from men—beginning with the first men in our lives, our fathers, and ending with ourselves. The end result of the boy's separation-individuation struggle is that men carry around a burden of vulnerability, dependency, emptiness within themselves, still grieving, reliving a time when going to mother for help as they wanted to was inappropriate, and they wouldn't or couldn't go to father with the confusion, anger, or sadness they felt.[10]

Hudson and Jacot make an interesting observation. They point out that little boys may react to the loss of the unity with mother, a loss that is necessarily emotionally painful, by defensively forming relationships with things rather than with people. In other words, they may transfer their passions from the realm of the personal (intimate relationships, the mother-child relationship being the first) to the realm of the inanimate (gadgets, machines, abstract thoughts), and from the subjective experience (emotions, feelings, intuitions) to the objective one (logic, numbers, scientific proof). Perhaps it is for this reason that a male tot will become engrossed in the knobs and dials of his parents' CD player but will not show any interest in playing with dolls; and perhaps it is for this reason that a man will devote endless hours figuring out a new software program for his PC but will find excuses not to find an hour to sit and talk quietly with his wife.

The male's turning away from mother and the soft, intimate feelings attached to her toward the world of things and ideas has both positive and negative outcomes. On the one hand, this development may account for the many and marvelous contributions that men have made in the "hard" sciences, mathematics, architecture, engineering, and logic; on the other hand, it may account for the deficiency more commonly observed in men than in women: a limited interest in or ability to form empathic relationships with humans.

When I listen to the stories that my male clients tell me, I find myself making connections between their early separations from mother and their present relationships. For example, from clients' accounts of their early romances, it strikes me that when boys fall in love for the first time they are more vulnerable than girls. In the arms of their sweethearts, young men rediscover the paradise that, as babes, they lost by having to relinquish the unity with their mothers; once again, they are held close, warmed, and adored. But when they lose this paradise for the second time, as early loves inevitably are lost, they are re-traumatized, wounded yet again; as a result, they often shut down emotionally or become jealously possessive and/or clingy in future love relationships. In my experience at least, which contradicts conventional wisdom, girls are generally less traumatized by break-ups with their first romantic partners than are boys; these break-ups do not reawaken for girls an experience of having lost the mother's warmth prematurely as they do for boys.

It seems to me that the early mother-son separation also influences a man's responses to his young children. For example, the new father may discover, to his embarrassment, that he resents his baby or young child who is taking "mother" away from him. Suddenly, he is put back in touch with his early feelings of loss and with childlike yearnings to be "babied" and taken care of himself; shamed by these unexpected feelings, he may defensively disengage from both his wife and his child.

On the other hand, the new father may respond in an opposite manner. My husband has often told me that when he held our infants close to his body, he felt a healing energy surge through him; the tension that he normally carried oozed out of him, and he experienced a deep inner peacefulness. We both have come to believe that by nurturing our babies, he was also nurturing himself—becoming his own lost mother.

The feelings of loneliness, abandonment, and alienation associated with the mother-son separation may also surface in the adult son's relationship with his wife should she withdraw from him. A colleague who specializes in the treatment of men and who is particularly sensitive to the effects of early loss once told me that whenever a married client in a mid-life crisis comes to him, he asks, "Tell me, has your wife recently made changes? Gone back to school? To work? Left you to fend for yourself because she is more involved in her life outside the family?"

Samuel Osherson reminds us of the powerful and lingering influence of the boy's separation from his mother:

> For many men our adult families come to substitute for mother, and we look to our wives for what we had to give up in separating from her. . . . I suspect there is considerable grief and loss associated with letting go of mother as a child and home as a late adolescent, before being ready to leave being cared for and to become an "adult." There are few words in English with as much emotional resonance as "home." When E.T. eagerly says "going home, going home" in his scrappy little voice, he is touching the deepest longings of the adults in the audience as well.[11]

Of course, most men are unlikely to attribute the charged feelings that wash over them when they leave or are left to their early separations from their mothers, which they no longer remember and which are not accessible to their conscious mind.

The boy's separation from his mother shapes not only his development but also his perceptions of her. My husband, Bruce, shared a story from his childhood that illustrates one little boy's conflicting feelings about mother. Bruce remembers coming home from first grade with a soaring fever and his worried mother ministering to him with anxious care while he was sick. During this time, Bruce had two dream fragments, which remain vivid after all these years. In the first, he was desperately clinging to a tree that grew from a rocky precipice while black, tumultuous waters swirled below. In the second, he was transformed into a magnificent steed, but his mother, pulling hard at his mane, prevented him from breaking loose and running free. For young Bruce, the mother on whom he could hang for dear life—the sturdy tree that saved him from falling into the dangerous waters below—was also the mother who, in his imagination, held back his life force, his masculine energy, his "horsepower."

The struggle to liberate himself from the mother whom he perceives as holding and enclosing is also vividly evoked in a dream that analyst and author Loren E. Pedersen describes having had at age seven. In this dream, a house and the roots of a tree symbolize the mother.

I am in my childhood home, a three-story red-brick walk-up flat on the near north side of Chicago. I am walking down the hallway from the second-floor apartment. As I reach the stairway I notice the tree roots are beginning to break through holes in the plaster wall, growing rapidly out from one side of the hall into and seemingly through the other side. As I move downward, more and more of them break out, so that in a short while there are so many that I am completely ensnared. I struggle, climbing downward, trying with greater and greater difficulty to find my way through the roots. They become so thick that finally it seems like it is going to be impossible to get to the outside. I feel increasingly fearful with the certainty that I would not be able to find my way through them. I wake in a panic.[12]

Like the young Loren, when a boy feels trapped by his mother's motherliness, he no longer views her as benevolent but as terrible. Loren's nightmare expresses the son's desperation to break out of the mother's sheltering house, which he suddenly perceives as imprisoning. In the dream, the mother's holding, comforting, embracing arms become strangulating roots that threaten to ensnare him. To "get to the outside," to become liberated from his dependency, Loren must find his way "through the roots" that have grown too thick.

We mothers know that we are not endowed with magical powers of domination and control; we know that we are ordinary human beings who are often confused and sometimes overwhelmed by all that is expected of us as parents. But our young sons do not know this about us. For every little boy, mother—the woman from whose body he came; the woman who feeds, dresses, shelters, and watches over him—is invested with superhuman powers; she is no mere mortal but an omnipresent and omniscient force of nature.

To the very young boy—and in the unconscious of every grown man—mother is alternately experienced as a life-affirming, benevolent force and as a fierce and terrifying one. That she has the power to make and nourish human life out of her own body and the power to annihilate it (or so the son infers) is nothing less than magical to him; and for her "magic," he worships, envies, devalues, and fears her.

Defying and refusing the "all-powerful" mother, which is what a boy does in order to become separate from her, demands a great deal of courage on his part. I suspect that the fantasies of the "terrible mothers" that abound in our fairy tales and myths derive at least in part from the little boy's fears that his separating from mother will cause her to be very, very angry with him: that if he tries to get away from her, she will poison him or devour him or imprison him or claw him or burn him up. In the boy's worst imagination, mother's food becomes toxic; her shelter becomes imprisonment; her holding arms become claws, shackles, or, in young Loren's case, strangulating roots; and her warmth becomes fire. In the boy's fantasy, and the stories that give these fantasies form, he must devise clever ways to "escape" from the "terrible mother"; the "hero son" of our fairy tales and folktales who does brave battle with witches and sorceresses is none other than the little boy who disengages from the all-powerful mother of his infancy.[13]

From experience, I have learned that it is not only the very young boy who imagines that his mother will get very,

very angry with him for leaving her. In my freshman year at college, I dated a young man who was having particular difficulties separating from his doting mother. One lunch hour, as my friend was unwrapping the chopped liver sandwich that his mother had made for him, he noticed that the liver was not the usual brownish color but a strange yellow-green. "What's this?" he asked suspiciously and then, in all seriousness, proclaimed, "I know. My mother's trying to make me sick by poisoning my chopped liver! She's angry that I'm going out with you and wants to punish me." To his embarrassment, my friend later realized that it was the mustard on the chopped liver that had turned it yellow-green.

Despite the struggle, most boys manage to separate from their mothers. However, a small percentage of boys fail in this regard. They may not find the urge to become separate from mother within their biological make-up. In addition, they may be handicapped by a mother who indulges in excessive closeness with them. According to Robert Stoller, who is well respected for his work on gender development, the mother of a son past infancy who is overly intimate with him—fondling, flirting, sleeping, and bathing with him, for example—and who allows no male to disrupt their too-close bond, may cause him to remain identified with her, to internalize her feminine nature, and to fail to grow fully into his male self. On occasion, then, the "terrible mother" who will not let her boy go but who insists that he always remain a part of her is not a boy's fantasy but his reality.

Although the boy begins to separate from his mother when he is very young, the process continues through his life. And just as young boys have a hard time wrenching themselves away from the mother, so do some grown men. I am presently treating a very lovely woman who has fallen into a deep depression because her thirty-year-old son, her firstborn and the "problem child" in whom she had invested almost all of her maternal energy, suddenly, and for no ostensible reason, wants nothing to do with her. Although I have never met the son, I suspect that his estrangement has much to do with his having been less than successful in the past in loosening his ties to mother. Now, out of desperation, he feels compelled to cut their ties altogether. Mother-child separations, I have learned over the years, are often neither kind nor gentle. However, when sons fail to separate from their mothers, their futures are sure to be fraught with psychological problems.

The Jungians call a man's failure to free himself from the all-loving, all-providing mother of childhood the "mother complex." Robert A. Johnson, author of *He*, describes this complex as "pure poison in a man's psychology."

> This is his regressive capacity which would like to return to a dependency on mother and be a child again. This is a man's wish to fail, his defeatist capacity, his subterranean fascination with death or accident, his demand to be taken care of.[14]

Johnson uses the twelfth-century myth of Parsifal and the Fisher King to illustrate the adult man's separation struggle. Parsifal is hampered by the homespun garment that his mother, named Heart's Sorrow, gives him with very loving intentions. As long as Parsifal is encased in his mother's homespun—her protective garment—he cannot realize his natural masculine strength. Consequently, he is unable to cure the wounded Fisher King, who is really an aspect of himself, and to know the splendor of the Grail castle, which is the symbol of his spirituality and his humanity.

The image of a mother's protection as garment also appears in a Yiddish song titled "Oyfn Weg Shteyt A Boym," which is translated as "By the Path, There Stands a Tree." The song tells about a little child who wishes to become a bird so that he can fly to a lonely tree that stands by the path and share a sweet song with it. His mother, wanting to protect the child against the freezing winter winds, wraps him in her warmest coat. But rather than giving him comfort, her garment weighs him down, much as Heart's Sorrow's protective garment encumbers Parsifal, so that when the child tries to lift his "wings," he discovers that he cannot fly. His mother's overprotective love has become the burden that oppresses him.

However, just as enhancing mothers do not prolong the symbiotic intimacy with their sons, they do not harshly drive out or demean all that is needy, tender, and feminine in them. I agree with author Carol Klein who writes, "The delicate balance mothers of sons must achieve is between encouraging a boy's steps toward a separate self and still being available for those pauses which make the rest of the journey less terrifying."[15] Time and again, male clients as well as male friends have told me that their mothers' enduring love and presence have been critical to them. "There is no greater threat in life than that we will be deserted, left alone," child psychiatrist Bruno Bettelheim writes; "and the younger we are, the more excruciating is our anxiety when we feel deserted, for the young child actually perishes when not adequately protected and taken care of."[16]

Carol Klein reports that the vast majority of men she interviewed for her book on mothers and sons remembered a recurring nightmare of coming home from school to find their mothers gone. "With mounting terror, the little boy would run from room to room, looking for his mother or at least some sign that she'd be returning soon. . . . The prevailing mood most of these men described was of deep loneliness, a feeling of being totally helpless."[17]

I am presently treating a young man who suffers from extreme loneliness and who flits from one unhappy love affair to another, much as the men Klein interviewed report dreaming of running from room to room in search of mother. The women my client chooses to be with are always "ice queens"—alluring but cold and ultimately rejecting of him. In a recent session with Jay, we talked about his mother.

"What do you remember about her?" I asked.

"I remember that we never did anything together. Never. She wanted me out of her way."

"And what would you say to her if she were in this room with us?" I inquired.

Jay lowered his eyes, and after a considerable pause, answered in a barely audible voice, "I'd tell her that I miss her . . . and that I'm still trying to find her but that she always evades me." Then Jay buried his head in his hands and quietly wept.

Sadly, it is not uncommon for a little boy to be shamed (by his mother or his father) for revealing his vulnerability and for wanting to turn to his mother for comfort and soothing. According to Robert Stoller, when a boy is shamed for his neediness, he may develop a "frozen, brutal, phallic character"; he may come to abhor any signs of softness, any traces of the feminine in himself and in others.[18]

When a boy is shamed or otherwise discouraged from having a relationship with his mother—when the separation from her has no blurred edges but is too sharply drawn—he is also deprived of the special ways in which she can enrich his life. In order for boys to acquire a masculine identity, they will, in all likelihood, avoid doing womanly things with mom (learning to knit, arranging flowers in a vase, for example), but they will welcome other ways of being with her. It was I who coached my son in geometry; it was my mother-in-law who discussed politics with my husband when he was a teenager; it is my friend who takes hikes in the wilderness with her son and who has inspired his reverence for the natural world; it is countless moms who cheer on their sons at sandlot soccer and baseball games. *For mothers and sons, separating is a normal part of their relationship; severing the bond between them is not.*

Although children consolidate their gender identities—that is, they experience themselves as definitely male or definitely female very early in life—a boy's psychological separation from the mother and identification with the father goes on for many years. The "male *wound*" heals only when a young man becomes fully himself, when he learns to nurture and to be nurtured in intimate relationships but no longer depends on the all-providing mother of infancy and childhood (or her stand-in, the all-providing wife). If he is fortunate, the son is blessed with a mother who helps him pass through his separation from her without undue pain and without permanent impairment.

One way that she does this is by encouraging his relationship to his father or to a father surrogate. Sadly, this is not always easy to do. Some fathers will not assume caregiving roles with their sons, no matter how much their wives encourage them to do so. Other fathers, divorced from their wives, effectively abandon their sons. But a great many fathers want to nurture their sons. I have often observed that when mothers step back a little from caregiving roles, fathers often step into them. A colleague, Dr. Lyn Gullette, shared this sweet anecdote: When her small son tripped and skinned his knee, he came to her for tender loving care. After a short time, however, the boy said, "I think I'll go to Daddy now. I'm finished crying so I don't want to be with you anymore." With an encouraging smile from her, he then skipped away to his father. Like Lyn, the wise mother does not punish or make her son feel guilty when he refuses her nurture and distances himself; although she may be momentarily stung by his "rejection," she nevertheless waves him on with a smile and points him in the direction of his father. If there is no available, loving father, she may pave the way for a relationship between her son and his grandfather or his uncle or some other caring and permanent male figure in his life. What she does not do is keep her son locked up in her woman's care, her mother's heart.

Another way that a mother helps her separating son is by allowing him to return to her from time to time for maternal nurture. As Bruno Bettelheim notes, a boy's short regressions toward the nurturing mother provide the security and strength he needs for the next step in independence and self-assertion. This does not mean that a mother should collude with the boy against his father when he is harder on him than she is, unless, of course, his hardness is brutal. Neither does it mean that she should generally shield the boy from the demands and challenges that are a part of growing up. It means, rather, that when the world weighs too heavily on him, she is there to provide loving support.

When I come home from my office, I usually like to snuggle in my special chair, have a cup of tea, play classical music, and read a good book. Before he went away to college, my son would occasionally come and sit near me. I think he felt restful and safe in my quiet, calm woman's space. When we were together like this, Jonathan sometimes confided his fears and anxieties about growing up. Although I could no longer fix his problems for him, I think that our being together often enhanced him because after a while he usually bounded away from me again, full of new energy. An eloquent acquaintance, Allen Overton, once told me that every boy needs his mother "to feather in and to feather out again."

Still another way that a mother can help her son achieve a healthy separation from her is by affirming his competence and effectiveness. Although the separating boy may appear aggressive or cocky at times, he is, in reality, full of self-doubts. "Can I survive away from mother?" he asks himself. "Is it really all right for me to be different from her?"

As we were washing and drying dishes after a dinner party, a male friend, who is usually reserved, shared some memories of his boyhood with me. Rubin confided that as a small child growing up in a house of powerful matriarchs, he felt almost foolish for being a boy. Both verbally and non-verbally, his mother and grandmothers conveyed to him that although his two sisters always knew "what was what," he could not get things right, just as his father could not get things right, just as all men could not get things right. Probably without realizing that they were doing harm, the matriarchs cast Rubin in the role of *schmegeyge*, a Yiddish word that roughly translates as "bumbler," or "fool." Touching my heart, Rubin explained that, despite the fact that he is an accomplished scientist, he continues to think of himself as ineffective; he is still the little *schmegeyge*, the boy whose efforts at autonomy were met by his mother's and grandmothers' derisive looks and remarks.

I am including Rubin's anecdote because I think that it reflects the experience of many boys and men. In fact, perhaps the most famous story about the boy's struggle to achieve autonomy, "Jack and the Beanstalk," emphasizes Jack's need to be approved of by his mother as he separates from her, and the mother's failure to affirm Jack's new independence and competencies. It also illustrates the boy's defensive tendency to exaggerate his masculine prowess when his mother slights and insults his emerging masculinity.

As most readers will remember, the English folktale begins as young Jack, following his mother's instruction, goes off to sell their faithful cow, Milky-white (who symbolizes the nursing, all-nourishing mother of early childhood) because she has gone dry. On the way to market, Jack meets a man (symbolizing the father) who offers some magic beans in exchange for the cow. Jack accepts the offer, quite pleased with himself for his initiative. Although he expects that his mother will also be pleased, he soon discovers otherwise. Not only does she ridicule and beat him for his foolishness, but adding insult to injury, she tosses the "worthless" beans out the window.

However, after being humiliated by his mother and sent to bed without supper, the little boy is vindicated, as he imagines that his precious beans—which, after all, represent the seeds of his manliness and his budding sexuality—grow into a huge beanstalk. In effect, Jack creates for himself the world's biggest phallus. Because his mother has belittled his first attempt to prove himself a competent, shrewd young man who can manage without her, he defensively exaggerates his masculine prowess. One might say that Jack reinvents himself as the Greek god Priapus, whose male member was so large he had to push it ahead of him in a wheelbarrow.

We all need to be recognized, validated, affirmed, and praised from time to time. This is especially true for young boys, whose struggle to become themselves is both hard and long. Our sons' self-esteem is greatly affected by the way we mothers respond to their humanness, manliness, vigor, virility, sexuality, strength, cleverness, initiative, potency, and independence. Indeed, as Sigmund Freud wrote, the boy who is greatly valued by his mother "keeps for life the feeling of a conqueror, that confidence of success that often induces real success."[19]

The enhancing "mother of separation" (a lovely term coined by child psychologist and author Louise Kaplan) finds ways, through her words and actions, to assure her son that although growing up—becoming increasingly separate and independent from her—is mostly exciting, it is also sometimes sad and sometimes scary. The enhancing "mother of separation" offers support and encouragement all along her son's bumpy journey toward selfhood, but especially at those critical turning points that mark his separation from her and from home: going to preschool, staying overnight at a friend's house, backpacking in the wilderness with dad, spending the summer at camp, learning how to drive, applying to an out-of-state college, getting married. Moreover, the enhancing "mother of separation" gently nudges her son out the door, even when she would like nothing better than for him to stay a while longer.

We should not delude ourselves, however. Even the most loving, the wisest mother of separation cannot heal the son's "wound"; as he relinquishes the near-perfect comfort and protection that she once provided, he will necessarily experience feelings of loss and anxiety that will resonate through his life. But by turning away from the caregiving, all-providing mother, he is forced to develop his own resources so that he may survive and be effective in the world. The positive male principle is all about *agency*, about acting on the world: building, making, fixing, constructing, creating, and loving.

Although a mother cannot heal her son's "wound," she can soothe it and perhaps prevent it from festering or making him sick. As we have seen, she does this by encouraging the boy's movement away from her but also by allowing him to come back to her for warmth, comfort, and assurances. And she does this by encouraging his relationship with his father and with other male role models. Most important, she does this by commending her son's competence and effectiveness as he becomes increasingly independent of her.

For all a mother's great love, however, her son cannot and should not—save for very brief visits—return to the "oneness" and sweet intimacy that they once shared. The boy must leave mother's safe, familiar world behind in order to discover new worlds of his own. And what a heady, exhilarating discovery this can be for him!

> My God, but I can only say
> I touch, I feel the unknown!
> I am the first comer!
> Cortes, Pisarro, Columbus, Cabot,
>   They are nothing, nothing!
> I am the first comer!
> I am the discoverer!
> I have found the other world!
> The unknown, the unknown!
> I am thrown upon the shore.
> I am covering myself with the sand.
> I am filling my mouth with the earth.
> I am burrowing my body into the soil.
> The unknown, the new world![20]

4

....

Love and Sex

"You getting to be," she said, putting her hand beneath his chin and holding his face away from her, "a right big boy. You going to be a mighty fine man, you know that?" . . . And he knew . . . that she was telling him today something that he must remember and understand tomorrow. . . . He watched her face, his heart swollen with love for her. . . .

"Yes, Ma," he said, hoping that she would realize, despite his stammering tongue, the depth of his passion to please her.

—JAMES BALDWIN,
Go Tell It on the Mountain

Like many of his college buddies, Seth, a client, had collected and ogled over *Playboy, Penthouse,* and the "swim suit" editions of *Sports Illustrated.* When a former model who had posed for one of these magazines came to campus to give a talk, he decided to "check her out." To Seth's surprise, the young woman "was nothing like a 'centerfold' but seemed more like a sister" to him. Intelligent and convincing, she described the humiliations of modeling—the dehumanizing effect of being turned into a sex object, whose function is only to titillate. Arguing against "soft porn," she appealed to her audience to recognize women as people rather than as things. After the talk, Seth returned to his dormitory, gathered his collection of erotica, and incinerated it. As he explained to me, "I really *do* respect women. Burning the magazines was one small way of expressing this."

Just as Seth had been moved by the young woman's appeal, I was moved by his high regard for women. It is common knowledge that boys and young men learn from their fathers how to treat women; when fathers honor their wives, their daughters, and women in general, their sons are likely to follow suit. I have also come to believe that young men's regard for women has a great deal to do with the way their mothers (the first women in their lives) have regarded them. Although, in the course of therapy, I never met Seth's mother and did not know firsthand how she related to her son, my strong suspicion is that she had always afforded him—as a person, as a male—basic respect.

Margaret Fuller, essayist and poet, writes, "Man is of woman born and her face bends over him in infancy with an expression he can never quite forget."[1] In this chapter, we will study the many faces of mothers as they respond to their sons' male bodies and sexuality; and we will try to understand how the mother's gaze, along with all the emotion behind it—delight, pride, desire, possessiveness, fear, contempt—shapes the son's self-concept and his ability to be in a love relationship when he reaches manhood.[2]

Until the first quarter of the century, it was customary for a mother to clothe her little boy in frilly dresses and to let his hair grow long. My great-aunt once told me that she had cried bitter tears the day she had cut her son's long, curly ginger-colored locks and saw the boyish face emerge. A part of her—and is this not true for most mothers?—had wanted to keep the child in the world of the feminine forever. But sooner or later, the wise mother lets her son leave this world so that he can embark on the long, hard journey toward manhood.

However, if a woman believes that males are programmed to be sexually violent toward females, affirming her own little boy's sexuality may be highly problematic. For example, in a passage from her book *Every Mother's Son*, Judith Arcana, who describes the male culture as fundamentally "corrupt and oppressive,"[3] reveals her discomfort with her own young son's male anatomy and emerging sexuality.

> Today Daniel gave me something to think about. He showed me his erect penis, and called it Willie. . . . He showed me that erection as if it were an accomplishment—and he said this while we were reading, snuggled up together on big pillows. I feel like I found a stranger in my house, or ants in my bed.[4]

We need to understand that although a mother may be threatened by her son's sexuality, every son wants to take pride in his penis, which is the visible manifestation of his manhood. Indeed, the little boy may sometimes flaunt his penis in what has been elegantly described as "a dance whose aim is to be applauded."[5] Basking in the glow of his mother's acceptance and (unpossessive, unexploitative) love, the child first learns to accept and love his male body. And because every little boy, when comparing his anatomy to his father's, is bound to see himself as puny and inadequate, mother's loving acceptance of his male body is especially important. When mother regards his body and its natural functions, including sexual arousal, as perfectly normal and fine, he will do the same; when, however, she makes fun of them or when she recoils in anger, fear, or disgust, he will not be sure that his body is adequate or that its urges are pure and good.

A friend of mine once confided that the most dehumanizing moment in all his life occurred when he was about twelve; his mother had walked in on him while he was masturbating. Her look of horror so shamed him that he had the distinct impression that he was no longer a young boy but rather a "dirty dog," a feeling that he could never quite shake off. "Could there be any clearer way of making the point that, in anything to do with the erotic, the mother is the child's first teacher, its 'older woman'; and that the child's pleasure is a response to the mother's?" French psychoanalyst Christiane Olivier asks.[6]

I remember the delighted response that a neighbor's baby expressed when he first discovered his "penis power." During one phase of his toilet training, his mother, in an effort to help him make it to the potty without any encumbrances, did not put him in a diaper. One morning, as she and I were chatting over a cup of tea, we looked up to discover bottomless baby George voiding his bladder in the middle of the kitchen, obviously enthralled by the sweep of the grand arc emitting from him. "What are *you* doing?" his mother called out with a note of exasperation. "*I* not doing anything," he beamed back. "*It* do it all by itself!" and the three of us burst out laughing.

I recall as well the story shared by a client who was wonderfully supportive as a mother. When her thirteen-year-old son shyly showed her the single hair that had sprouted under his arm, she smiled and gushed, "Oh, I'm so happy for you!" And another client recently remarked that she got a kick out of her teenage son when he regularly left his jock-strap or a can of deodorant, those unmistakable reminders of his new manliness, on the living room coffee table.

To some mothers, however, there is no delight in the son's penis power, no good-natured laughter in acknowledgment of his newly discovered prowess, no joy in his developing body. "Willie" is potentially exploitative and dangerous: the bludgeon, the ramrod, the missile, the loaded gun. By looking with fearful and contemptuous eyes on her child's male body, a mother increases the likelihood that he will perceive his genitals and sexuality not as wonderful and pleasure-giving but as bad and hurtful. Psychiatrist David M.

Terman, for example, describes one mother who was so disgusted by her son's developing manliness that "as he began to grow body hair, she vocalized her repugnance, and suggested that he shave it off."[7] Not surprisingly, this young man came to feel deeply ashamed of his body as well as of sexual, especially heterosexual, thoughts and feelings. According to Terman, by the time the boy had reached adulthood, he had totally assumed his mother's condemning attitudes toward male sexuality.

Terman's case study brings to mind a client I treated for depression. When I first saw Doug, he was married to a woman who repelled his sexual advances. Rather than recognizing that his wife had a problem, Doug believed that he was at fault for having what was obviously a healthy, normal sex drive. Brought up by a mother who told her children that having sex with her husband was an onerous chore—one of the many services required of a dutiful wife—Doug came to experience his carnal desire as a sign of primitive brutishness. That he married a woman who reinforced these feelings is not surprising, because people commonly seek out love partners who resemble their parents. At the start of therapy, Doug asked me to help him "evolve" toward a spiritual and celibate union with his wife, which he saw as the necessary condition for his marriage to survive. To his surprise, I refused. Instead, after much discussion, we agreed to work toward Doug's loving acceptance of and pride in his sexuality. Doug eventually divorced his wife, who stubbornly refused to deal with her sexual fears, and two years later, he married a warm and sensual woman to whom his manhood was an asset rather than a liability.

We must remember that the great majority of mothers do not set out to devalue their sons' sex or sexuality. It is usually women who have been treated abominably by significant men in their lives who vent pent-up feelings of rage, fear, or contempt against their innocent male offspring. As a columnist for *Parents* Magazine, I sometimes receive letters from new mothers who are concerned that early experiences of male sexual violence or other forms of degradation against them will adversely affect their feelings toward their own sons. Although these letters speak of human pain, they give me reason for optimism. Once a woman brings unconscious feelings to awareness, she is much less likely to act on them; once she knows that past abuse at the hands of a father or a husband puts her at risk for acting vengefully toward her son, she can consciously and conscientiously work against these tendencies. It is the unaware mother who, by transferring unconscious negative feelings about the guilty men in her past to the blameless son, is most likely to do him damage.

One of my clients, Renee, who as a child had been sexually fondled by her father and grandfather, came to believe that all men had exploitative natures; to her, men were the oppressors and women the oppressed. But realizing that this jaundiced view of the world made daily living increasingly uncomfortable—it is, after all, draining to harbor a grudge against half the human race—she set out, with great zest, to challenge her own beliefs. An avid reader and movie-goer, Renee began to search out books and films that allowed her to know what normal, "good" men are all about. Particularly moved by Oliver Stone's *Platoon*, the story of young soldiers in Vietnam, Renee began to understand what had previously evaded her—that tenderness, vulnerability, love, fear, and deep suffering are as much a part of the male experience as of the female one. Not surprisingly, as Renee's sympathy with and understanding of men slowly grew and as the notion of men as the oppressors broke down, she could look upon her own son with more loving eyes and welcome, rather than dread, his development into manhood and his active sexuality.

Until now, I have focused on the effects of the mother's aversion toward the son's sex. However, just as devaluing the son's maleness can impair his self-esteem, overvaluing it, which is a common tendency among mothers, can also pose problems.

Christiane Olivier tells about Thierry, who, from the time

he was about two until he was twelve, would "cup his hand round his precious 'thing' to protect it." Over the years, Thierry became the butt of crude family jokes: "Are you scared it will fly away?" "Maybe you think it hasn't been fixed on right?" Then, one day, an uncle who knew a bit about psychology asked, "Come on, now: if you're all that afraid they're going to take it away from you, who does it belong to? I thought it was yours." To everyone's surprise, including his mother's, Thierry replied: "It's Mummy's."[8]

Although it is certainly conceivable that Mummy had actually fondled her son's genitalia and, in this way, triggered the boy's anxiety, Olivier suggests that her mere longing to be too close to her son is enough to account for his efforts to protect his penis (the obvious and vulnerable manifestation of male selfhood) against her desire. A woman who suffers from pervasive feelings of low self-worth and powerlessness may regard her male child as the promise of her own unattainable dreams and aspirations and thereby attempt to live through him. Sensitive to the mother's needs and desires, as all small children are, and wanting to make mother happy, as all children do, he will try to oblige her—but always at great personal expense and with lingering resentment.

Different self-concepts that females and males tend to have may be, in large part, attributable to the mother's different responses toward them. Although the self-despising mother is likely to reject, in subtle (or not so subtle) ways, her daughter, whom she sees as a clone of her own unvalued self, she is likely to over-cherish her son, whom she perceives as her opposite. A family story illustrates the tendency to devalue the girl child and overvalue the boy child. As I mentioned earlier, my maternal grandmother had desperately wanted a son who would not be held back from achieving in the world as she had been. After my grandmother gave birth to her third daughter, she refused to look at the little girl for several days, and she told me that when she finally did take the baby from the nurse, she felt great disappointment: "I wanted to bring a Peter into the world, a boy who would be strong and powerful, and all I could produce was a little Trudy, who would be a woman like me."

As under-nurtured, under-esteemed, under-loved little girls grow into women, they will most likely suffer from feelings of emptiness: an aching, gnawing sensation of wanting *something*, something vague and elusive; of being always unsated; of feeling flawed and incomplete. The chronic feeling of emptiness is symbolized in many of the behaviors, disorders, and mental illnesses that typically afflict women, such as codependency in relationships, depressions and melancholias, and compulsions to eat and to shop.

Conversely, as over-nurtured, over-esteemed, over-loved little boys grow into men, they may develop unpleasant narcissistic traits, such as feelings of over-entitlement and grandiosity. They are also likely to suffer from feelings of entrapment: a disturbing sensation that their very being—what is most alive, energetic, and potent in them—is not safe from woman's desire and control. Unlike their sisters, who may feel unwanted, they may feel as if women are always wanting something from them, that unless they are on guard, their essence will be stolen from them. "Don't get too close! And never, never try to control me!" men warn their women again and again.

I think that British psychiatrist R. D. Laing captures the unspoken fears and feelings of a good many boys with his terse lines.

> Once upon a time, when Jack was little, he wanted to be with his mummy all the time and was frightened she would go away. Later, when he was a little bigger, he wanted to be away from his mummy and was frightened that she wanted to be with him all the time.[9]

Christiane Olivier foresees that when her young friend Thierry grows up, he will not remember that as a child he had protectively cuppled his hand over his male organ; that his fear of Mummy, now repressed, will turn into aggressive behavior toward women. "You must all know plenty of Thierrys, both young and old," Olivier writes. "Take a look at them. Watch how they shift imperceptibly from self-protection to self-defence. . . . Starting out from fear of the mother, they end up dominating women."[10]

In my work as a psychotherapist, I have found that the adult "Thierry" may also end up running away from women. For example, James, a language professor and a twice-divorced man in his forties, told me that his mother's early dependence on him adversely affects his ability to form a sustaining love relationship. James observed that when a woman expresses her desire for him, he is overcome with anxiety, becomes emotionally cold, and plans to end the relationship. In a recent session, he shared this entry from his journal:

> I see in every woman the specter of Mother, who, disappointed that my father was not more, invested all her love in me and fully expected that I would make her life complete. She had ambitious plans for me; that they were not my own didn't seem to count. I remember that I was always trying to please Mother but never did measure up; in the end, like Father, I was her *failed* hero. Now, when I am with a woman, I can't help feeling that she will want me for her own purposes—to fill her needs—and that, by acceding to her wishes, nothing of me will be left.

In Greek mythology, the monster Medusa turns men to stone with her petrifying gaze. For James, a solicitous look from a woman, reminiscent of his mother's gestures of longing and neediness, seem to turn him to stone. By becoming hard, cold, and silent, he protects himself against her desire.

When a mother over-cherishes her son, when she looks to him to complete her, the healthy parent-child relationship breaks down. Instead of encouraging the boy to separate from her, she draws him ever closer, and distinctions between maternal love and romantic-sexual love may begin to blur. From the biographies of famous men, we can discover many instances of such damaging relationships. Author Carol Klein writes that formidable industrialist Andrew Carnegie promised his mother that he would not marry in her lifetime—a vow he faithfully upheld. And five-star general Douglas MacArthur and his mother were so intensely involved that she followed him to his military posts around the world, a pattern first begun when she moved near West Point to be close to her young cadet: "The two strolled together every afternoon along the school's Flirtation Walk, much to the amusement of the other cadets, who were walking arm in arm with their girlfriends."[11] I suspect that the cadets' amusement masked the disturbing feelings that the sight of this unlikely romantic pair stirred in them.

It is extremely uncomfortable for most of us to witness seductive relationships between mothers and sons; and it is painful to know about overtly sexual ones. Of all the taboos in human history, the one against mother-son incest is the strongest. Anthropologist Margaret Mead notes that every known society has some form of this taboo, and although the taboo often lacks legal sanction, it is invested with the sanction of intense horror. Indeed, in Sophocles' quintessential drama about mother-son incest, when King Oedipus becomes aware that he has unknowingly killed his father and married his mother, he is so horror-stricken that he blinds himself, for to look with wide-open eyes at the acts of patricide and incest is more than even a king can bear.

Deep in our hearts, we all want to believe that the mother-child relationship is somehow sacred and pure, immune to the baser instincts that characterize other relationships, even those between fathers and children; we want to believe that when a mother looks at her son, her eyes shine with love but never, *never* burn with desire. Until recently, even mental health professionals were convinced that sexual violations by mothers against their children were virtually nonexistent; it is only now, as more and more adults are revealing the dark secrets of their early family lives, that some professionals are suggesting that the phenomenon of mother-child incest may have been denied and under-reported by the general population. And, although no one disputes the fact that fathers are far more likely to commit incest with their children than are mothers, it appears that inappropriate sexual relations between mothers and children are not so rare that we can ignore them. Anne Banning, one of the few to have researched this form of abuse, writes:

> Mothers are perceived as nurturing and asexual to their children. There is widespread societal belief that women cannot be sexually abusive to their children and at worst their behavior is labeled as seductive and not harmful. The same behavior in a father is labeled child molestation.[12]

Even Freud, who, during the repressive Victorian era, dared to explore the mother-son sexual bond, would not attribute lust to the mother, only to the son. For Freud, Jocasta is innocent of all carnal longings and is merely a passive participant in the Oedipal drama, while it is Oedipus who realizes the secret, forbidden fantasies of every little boy.[13] Olivier comments that women will quite commonly allude to their little boy's Oedipal stage, but "it never seems to occur to them to think to themselves, even for a moment: 'I'm going through my Jocasta stage.' "[14]

In a modern version of Oedipus and Jocasta, *Murmur of the Heart*, a celebrated comedy by French filmmaker Louis Malle, the incestuous mother is depicted as a generous and life-affirming "older woman" who innocently and selflessly helps her tender fifteen-year-old boy, tormented by the sexual fires of adolescence, become a man. In this film mother and son are at a health resort, away from Papa and other family members, where the boy, Laurent, is taking a cure for scarlet fever. During their time together, he is smitten by the sensuous, flirtatious mother and becomes jealously possessive of her. One night, after a hotel party at which the mother has had too much to drink, Laurent accompanies her to their shared hotel room and puts her to bed. As he nervously takes off his mother's clothes without any resistance from her, they fall into a tender embrace and make love. The morning after, the mother provides Laurent assurances that their act, special as it was, cannot be repeated and is to remain their "beautiful" secret. Father and brothers then appear on the scene, traditional family life resumes, and Laurent, with mother's approval, sets out with a surge of confident energy to conquer young hearts. Mother has indeed helped her son become a man—but *not* a loving one. In the fleeting last scenes of the movie, if we are not taken in by the light-hearted tone of this comedy, we can observe the damaging effects of incest: with his young women, Laurent is sexually aggressive and seemingly devoid of respect or empathy for them. His once tender heart is now hard.

Malle's mostly benign on-screen view of incest is contrary to the real-life experiences of incest victims. It perpetuates the erroneous idea that normal boys want to bed their mothers. Clinical accounts of mother-son incest, however, strongly suggest that unless a son suffers from extreme psychopathology, he will not pursue a sexual or sexualized relationship with a parent. Boys who are seduced by their mothers are necessarily overwhelmed with guilt, shame, disgust, and/or rage, and their future relationships are at risk.

However, although a normal boy does not want to have sex with his mother, he may have fleeting erotic thoughts about her or even become aroused, especially during his adolescence. As one of my male colleagues said,

> When I was a teenager, my sexual urges were so constant and so powerful that I could have been aroused by a telephone pole draped in a skirt. Sometimes when I caught sight of my pretty mother she stirred me. Had she been privy to my prurient thoughts or flaunted her sexuality or indicated any interest, I would have been mortified. But because my mother was always appropriate and acted like

a mother, I was able to let go my erotic impulses rather quickly, before they became disturbing.

Other adolescent boys may respond differently to their sexy mothers; because, at an unconscious level, they are threatened by her sexual powers, they may physically and emotionally withdraw from her or distance themselves by finding reasons to be irritated with her. As Alexia Dorszynski, my editor, puts it, "It's easier to sass your mother than face the implications of her being female."

Although mothers tend to be aware of the teenage boy's heightened sexuality, they may be unaware of the young boy's vulnerability and the fact that their sensual or seductive behaviors may cause him great discomfort, embarrassment, humiliation, or perhaps rage. "Until my husband pointed it out, I simply did not realize that giving my eleven-year-old son full-body massages was inappropriate," a client recently confided. "Because I do not have sexual feelings for my son, I assumed that he would experience my touch as only maternal. My husband helped me understand that if my son got an erection during the massage—which could happen—he would feel absolutely humiliated." Other clients have revealed that they had not given a second thought to crawling into bed in their flimsy nightclothes with their school-aged sons, either in an effort to comfort them or to seek comfort from them. Because they were not sexually aroused by their sons, they mistakenly assumed that their sons would not be sexually aroused by them.

Certainly, perfectly good, responsible, normal mothers sometimes do have sexual feelings for their sons. And it is essential for women to understand that fleeting erotic responses toward their sons when they are babies or young men are not perverse or abnormal. Nevertheless, when a woman is momentarily aroused while nursing or bathing her baby son or by the sight of her son's maturing body, she may be overcome with guilt or shame. Sexual attraction for one's son may also stir feelings of loss. As one woman explains, "I'm so exquisitely aware of my son's youthful beauty and beginnings of manhood. Every single day I marvel that this young man came from my flesh, and yet every day I know I must try harder to let him go toward other love."[15] To be sure, for single women without love partners and for married women with partners who do not satisfy them, the son's unfolding sexuality may be a painful reminder of their own unfulfilled sex lives, and the longings stirred by their sons' maleness may be deeply disturbing.

Robert Bly observes that although our majority culture does not usually address sexual feelings between mothers and sons, other cultures are more sensitive to this possibility and to the dangers of acting on these feelings. Among the Sioux, for example, after a boy reached the age of seven or so, eye contact and direct conversation between mother and son, deemed to be potentially charged with sexual energy, were prohibited. Although such precautions between mother and son may seem absurd or even inhumane to us and although they go against modern concepts of family relationships, we are nevertheless wise to take heed. Bly notes that "the Sioux men, once grown, were famous for their lack of fear when with women, their uninhibited conversations . . . , their ease in sexual talk with their wives."[16]

A mother who goes beyond seduction and actually has sex with her son will not lead the child to manhood but instead will rob him of selfhood. By taking her son back into her body, the incesting mother forces him to fuse with her and thereby to lose the separateness and individuality—the distinct, bounded selfness—that he has struggled since early childhood to achieve; by taking him back, she fills herself up with potent male life but causes the son to regress to a disturbingly diffuse state, one in which he cannot be sure where she leaves off and he begins. As the incesting mother of a little boy candidly explained after a therapist told her about the child's difficulty in knowing appropriate boundaries, "I felt his body was mine."[17]

Because mother-son incest has been under-studied, we know very little about the psychology of women who do sexualize relationships with their children other than that they were probably victims of childhood sexual abuse themselves and that they are usually not retarded or psychotic, as was previously believed. British psychoanalyst Estela Welldon does, however, include in her book *Mother, Madonna, Whore* a rare portrait of an incestuous mother in the form of a letter written by her. In the first part of the letter, the writer describes her childhood: the sudden death of her father and the subsequent invasive, suffocating relationship with her possessive mother. She then goes on to describe her marriage and her relationship with her son.

> I met a nice-looking young man who was kind to me, and I fell for him—or perhaps for a way out. I married him at sixteen and got pregnant. . . . When my son was five my husband was sudenly [sic] killed in an accident. My mother came back to me as if I'd never left her. . . . I soon realized I didn't want my mother with me because I wanted my son for myself, alone without any competition. I created an idyllic relationship with my son to the point that I didn't need any other man in my life.
>
> We went together on holidays. I remember very vividly once at the seaside when miniskirts were fashionable. This was a turning point in my life. My son was then fourteen. I went dancing in the local hotel with some youngsters, and had quite a lot to drink. On my return to our room I saw my son sobbing between the sheets. I was worried and asked him why he was upset. He said that he had watched me dancing and had felt deserted and very jealous of the young men. When he made this statement I experienced an immediate sense of inner peace and great contentment; all previous sufferings and upheavals now seemed futile. I had won; he was all mine. We were together forever, alone. It just seemed natural for me to get into bed with him and console him. But I wanted to show him my love in a more natural way. I was high, elated, and felt

randy. I initiated him in the art of making love. Over a period of time I taught him step by step what to do and how to do it. I created the most wonderful lover and both of us were in ecstasy. This has lasted all these years. . . . Our world was perfect. . . . All my life has been invested in him. . . . I never thought that he could betray me. But after leaving high school he began to show signs of restlessness and self-assertion. First, he wanted to go abroad to further his studies, but I could not let him go. To start with it was easy for me to persuade him to stay, but he is still unmoving in his decision to go away from me. My only other association is with my mother, whom I see every Sunday, and even then I feel so brittle about him taking advantage of my being away and seeing someone else. I take care of myself to make myself look younger; I have always done so. Our days and nights are so very rich.

At fifteen he began to write poetry which showed so much passion and maturity that I felt afraid of his teachers reading it and somehow guessing what was going on. He used to recite it to me, but lately he has refused to show it to me. I've examined his papers and discovered that his poetry is now full of desire for revenge, sarcastic and bitter. He has even hatched a very elaborate plot by which he can get rid of me. I don't care if he does. As I have told him, if he leaves me I'll take my life. Anyway, life seems unnecessary without him.[18]

To me, what is most striking about this mother's confession is her utter disbelief and indignation that the son has a right to be separate from her. Having lost her father and her husband, she now holds the boy in a deathly grip so that he will not get away from her. Merging with him in the act of love, she can feel complete; shackling him to her, she need never feel lonely again. Moreover, because, as a little girl, this woman was invaded by her own mother, who denied her any privacy, she is unable to recognize boundaries between herself and her child. The boy, her creation, is hers, hers alone, to possess and, like a piece of clay, to shape and manipulate. I do not think that this pitiful—and dangerous— mother is exaggerating when she writes that life without her son/lover is "unnecessary"; I suspect that away from the young man, she feels like "nothing"—hardly there at all.

Although this mother's behavior is extreme, the tendency to use one's child as an object of self-aggrandizement is common. The terrible irony is that women who are weak and powerless in the world—those who are deprived of opportunities to be effective, to realize their dreams, ambitions, and talents—are the ones most likely to become tyrants toward their children by treating them as possessions or extensions rather than individuals in their own right. And sad to say, the grown sons who have been tyrannized by their mothers often retaliate by disempowering their own wives and other women, thereby ensuring the exploitation of the children in the next generation.

Although empty mothers look at their sons with hungry, devouring eyes, women who are, by and large, fulfilled can look upon them without want or desire. We hear much about the woman who is broken-hearted and feels betrayed when a son becomes sexually interested in a girl and diverts his sweet attentions from mother to the younger woman. We even hear about the woman who anticipates with dread her son's future love life. For example, in their book *In-laws/ Outlaws*, Penny Bilofsky and Fredda Sacharow tell the sadly funny story of a mother in the maternity ward who, showing off her newborn son, remarked with passion, "See my wonderful son? Just think, somewhere out there—maybe she's not even born yet—there's a little girl who is going to take him away from me. I hate her already."[19] Less known are the stories of women who delight in their sons' sexual development and romances, but these stories deserve to be recounted and celebrated. Following are five such stories that women have shared with me.

"Mike was a late bloomer," Sally told me. "Frankly, I

used to be a little concerned that, unlike his friends, he didn't date when he was in high school. But in his first year of college Mike fell in love with a wonderful young woman. I watch them together, and he is so tender with her that I am sometimes moved to tears. Perhaps I'm being obnoxiously self-congratulating when I say this, but I do believe that his capacity to love a woman is in part a tribute to me, a sign that having been loved well, he is able to love another so naturally. Knowing this, I feel very proud."

In a similar vein, Harriet, who has had three unhappy marriages that have ended in divorce, pointed out that knowing that her middle-aged son and his wife have created a good and enduring marriage brings her peace of mind. "What a relief it is to me that Aaron has not followed in my footsteps but has been able to make a successful marriage—and, of course, I give my daughter-in-law a lot of credit for this too."

Gwen confided, "You know, ever since Rod has been dating Chloe, he seems more relaxed, more at peace with himself and the world. During his middle adolescence, he had been so argumentative that living with him was sometimes quite an ordeal for me. Chloe's gentle care has softened him, and I am so grateful that she has touched both our lives."

Angela shared these sentiments: "Sometimes the world seems full of anger and cynicism. I look at young people— my son and my daughter especially—and despair for them because they have so little to believe in. The political leaders, the people in authority have all betrayed their trust. And yet, despite all this, they fall in love. So it occurs to me that things are not so hopeless after all; as long as young people can fall in love, there is still cheer in the world."

And my own mother-in-law, Sylvia Bassoff, reminiscing about my marriage twenty-seven years ago to her only son, recently told me, "Now, Evi, when you and Bruce got married, how could I have been anything but delighted when it was so obvious to me that you were making my son so happy?" Then, with a twinkle in her eye, she added, "And how could I have been anything but thankful to the girl who would put up with all my son's *meshugass*?" (the Yiddish word for "crazy antics" and "neuroses").

May 22, 1992: It is a sweet-smelling spring evening in Boulder. Jonathan sits down beside me on the front steps of our house to go over his plans for the senior prom. "We need to make sure that the evening will be very, very special for Katie," he tells me, and I assure him that, more than this, he will make it magical. We go through his list: "Order corsage, rent tuxedo, make dinner reservations at the Greenbriar."

"Should I also buy red roses for Katie?" he asks.

"That would be lovely," I respond.

"And the car, Mom?"

"Yes, of course, you can drive the new Acura for the evening," I assure him.

"I'll get it washed and vacuumed," he adds.

I look at my son and am flooded with loving feelings for him. Would I have imagined a few years ago that the dirty-faced little boy whom I chased around the house with a washcloth would be having a discussion about cummerbunds and red roses with me? Could I have fathomed the joy I would feel in anticipating Jonathan's prom night? Or the deep gratitude toward him for allowing me to share in the preparations for this event and in his excitement? I think not.

My son and I continue to talk. I agree that having a special candlelight dessert after the dance is a fine idea. The plans all set, he starts to take off. "One thing more," I call out after him, "those girlie posters that you have hanging up in your room . . . well, you know, Katie might be offended by them. Don't you think you should take them down?"

Jonathan smiles sheepishly and says, "Haven't you noticed? I already did."

Part Two

FAMILY
PORTRAITS

*Other things may change, but we all begin
and end with the family.*
—ANTHONY BRANDT

5

....

Between Husbands and Wives: Toward Shared Parenting

The Father and the Mother, since they are . . . never hidden or separated from each other, are called Companions. . . . And they find satisfaction in permanent union.

—The Kabbala,
Zohar III

A month ago, a young married couple who were in the process of adopting a baby boy began therapy with me. Although both came from families in which the mother was the dominant parent and the father was mostly disengaged from family life, this young couple envisioned bringing up their child together, as co-equals. Could I help them? they asked. Could I teach them to be different from their own parents? Without hesitation, I agreed to try.

Inspired by the hopes of this young couple, I describe in this chapter—in part by sharing my own story—how married people grow and flourish as individuals, as companions, and as parents when they bring up their children together. For mothers of sons, a strong parenting partnership seems especially desirable. With the husband/father's active participation in child rearing, the relationship between mother and son has a better chance of thriving. Having been a boy himself, the husband/father can help his wife better understand their growing boy's reactions and needs so that she can respond to them appropriately.

However, before I describe "shared parenting," it will be helpful to explore why men, even those with the most noble intentions, often find it difficult to become involved fathers, and why women, even those who profess to be eager for their husband's participation as fathers, may undermine their efforts.

Statistics regarding men's participation in family life are discouraging. They indicate that American men tend to spend astonishingly little time with their young children. For example, it is estimated that more than three-quarters of fathers do not regularly take *any* responsibility for their children's daily care.[1] Not surprisingly, a significant proportion of the letters that I answer for my monthly column on marital problems in *Parents* Magazine have to do with fathers who underfunction and mothers who overfunction.

"My husband spends very little time with our three-month-old son; he rarely plays, holds, or cuddles him. . . . Right now, we just get into fights when I complain about his lack of involvement, and I feel so discouraged," a young mother confides.[2] "It seems that my days are filled with nothing but cleaning and caregiving. My husband refuses to help out. . . . What can I do?" a worn-out homemaker and mother of a seventeen-month-old baby asks.[3] "[My husband] spends most of his time playing with and walking the dog, while I am juggling part-time work and the care of our two children. . . . I am concerned that my husband seems to be paying more attention to the dog than to his children," still another frustrated mother complains.[4] Other women write that their husbands go out drinking and carousing while they are left at home with the children; and I recently received a letter from a wife who explains that her husband has abandoned the family not for another woman but for his personal computer, to which he is exclusively and passionately devoted.

A new term—"father hunger"—has entered the American language. Father hunger describes the deep craving for physical and emotional interaction with the father; it is also the loss and emptiness felt as a result of being deprived of such interaction. In recent years, much has been written about the deprivations of sons raised by single mothers. But we also need to remember that sons who grow up in two-parent homes often have very little relationship with their fathers; for many boys in intact families, father is a vague and disconnected presence.

Although, when first coined, the term father hunger referred to the son's experience, it can easily be extended to the daughter and also to the wife/mother. Today, all too many married mothers, like their sons and daughters, are hungry for the husband/father's involvement in family life. For to be held primarily responsible for the child's happiness and daily care—especially when they may also hold jobs outside the home—has left many women feeling burdened, irritated, resentful, and *oh-so-tired*.

It is, of course, tempting to attribute some terrible character flaw to the father who is not interested in his children. After all, how could a normal person with feelings not want to nurture and be involved with his sons and daughters, especially when they are very young and eager for his affections? As a result of interviews with several fathers, I have come to believe that feelings of incompetence, uselessness, or insecurity—rather than personality defects—usually account for a man's disengagement from his children.

"I am being asked by my wife and by society as a whole to take a larger role as a parent, which is only just and right—and something that I also want for myself," Sam, a self-assured and successful attorney told me; "but when I'm taking care of the baby I'm on very shaky ground. To be honest with you, I really don't know what the hell I'm doing!"

"When I watch my wife breastfeed our newborn, when I see that she is so wonderfully equipped to soothe him, I feel superfluous as a parent. The most that I can hope for right now is to become the helper-parent—and a bumbling one at that—and this role feels demeaning to me," another young father confided.

And looking despondent, a middle-aged father told me, "I just assumed that my wife always understood the children better than I could, and I turned them over to her. Now that they're adults, we're like strangers. I hardly know them. I wouldn't know where to begin with them."

For some men, being nurturant threatens their masculine image. For example, if men have had no models of nurturing males, they may see themselves as being motherly, rather than fatherly, when they change a diaper or wipe a runny nose or rock a feverish child in their arms. I am currently counseling a young man who confided that for fear of being ridiculed, he dared not tell his boss that he had taken the day off from work in order to stay home to nurse his son who had the flu; rather, he had lied and said that his car had broken down.

There is a vast difference between the ways females and males are prepared for parenthood, and males are clearly at a disadvantage in this respect. From the first years of life, most girls get ready for motherhood. They identify with and imitate their own mothers; they practice their versions of motherliness by nurturing doll babies and, perhaps, by taking care of younger siblings or by babysitting for the neighbors' children; they are encouraged to be soft, gentle, sensitive, tender, and yielding—qualities suited to caring for babies. And starting with the first menstrual period, they are given monthly reminders of their life-creating potential, which stimulate fantasies of having babies someday. Hence, long before females become mothers, they have undergone basic training for this role.

Most fathers, we must realize, did not undergo comparable training for parenthood. As little boys, they did not identify with and mimic their mother's motherliness and incorporate the soft, feminine qualities associated with caregiving; aspiring toward manliness meant imaginatively separating from her and her womanly ways and identifying with father instead. But in all likelihood, father was so busy "doing" in the world and "bringing home the bacon" that he did not have the opportunity to become an intimately involved parent. Observing father, most boys grew up with the understanding that a man's responsibility is to make money for the family, not to nurture and be close to the children.

We should also recognize that pregnancy is a very different experience for the expectant mother and the expectant father. Moment to moment, day after day, month after month, the mother-to-be comes to know the baby growing within her body; when she gives birth, it is not to a tiny stranger but to one with whom she is already deeply bonded, intimate, and in harmony. By contrast, the father-to-be does not usually develop a significant connection with the womb-baby. Putting his hand on his wife's belly to feel the movements of the fetus cannot compare to the maternal experience of growing a baby in one's body for nine months. Unlike the biological mother and child, the biological father and child encounter one another for the first time in the delivery room or the maternity ward; nine months after the relationship between mother and baby began, father and child start theirs. Is it any wonder that fathers are usually more awkward than mothers with a newborn?

In addition to feeling incompetent, useless, insecure, and estranged, a father may also harbor a secret resentment toward the new member of the family. Before baby came along, he was his wife's one-and-only. Now he must share her sweet love, her warm body, her tender ministrations. Or he may discover that his wife is totally wrapped up with baby care and not interested in having any physical or sexual intimacy with him. When the "interloper" is a boy, the new father may—to his chagrin—experience surges of jealousy. Suddenly there is another "man" in his wife's life who is clearly her number one. Thus, feeling displaced, feeling second best, the new father may defensively withdraw from his wife and his child. To avoid the perceived rejection, he does the rejecting; he goes off—to the office or the golf course or the neighborhood bar—and leaves them behind.

We married mothers have a choice in the way we react to our husbands when they are distant, unavailable, or uncomfortable as fathers. We can revile or rebuke or ridicule them; or we can try to understand their insecurities, and if they are willing, work with them in a spirit of kindness to overcome the obstacles that stand in the way of their being committed family men. Surely, the latter course is the better one.

In *Broodmales*, a book by anthropologist Nor Hall, I discovered a delightful story that illustrates the mother/wife's positive influence in the development of the nurturing husband/father. According to a Basque myth, during the time of the Great Flood, Aitor, the god of creation, and his wife sought refuge on a mountaintop where, in a cave shielded from the lightning and thunder, she gave birth. When the mother was ready to leave the cave and search for food, she asked Aitor to lie on a bed of skins and protectively hold their newborn child in his great arms, and he readily complied with her request.[5]

Nor Hall explains that among the Basque the human father patterned himself after the nurturing father/god, Aitor. As soon as a man's wife was strong enough to leave the childbed, he lay in it with their newborn babe, sheltering the young one against his chest, *inspiring* the young one with his manly father's breath.

Contemporary mothers can learn from the Basque practice. We too need to turn the newborn (as well as the child and the adolescent) over to the father so that the two can inspire each other and begin to participate fully in each other's lives—and so that we are no longer burdened by the full responsibility of childcare.

Earlier in the chapter, I referred to Sam, a new father who described himself as being on very shaky ground when it came to caring for his newborn. Three months after our first interview, I met with Sam again and found him to be much more at ease in his paternal role. In fact, he seemed head over heels in love with his baby son. When I asked Sam to account for the positive change in him, he told me that his wife, Nicole, had insisted that he spend some time alone with their baby every day.

> Nicole didn't tell me what to do with the baby. She didn't add to my feelings of ineptness by patronizing me. She just assumed that I would figure it out, and I did. Except for feeding and changing, I discovered that my son didn't need me to "fix" him—to do for him. I learned that it was okay to sit with him and to stare at him, and to become part of his growth process. Well, it was really much more than okay; it was almost surreal, so spectacular, to watch this marvelous, precious life—how each moment had a palpable meaning for him. You know, I feel so sorry for all the fathers who turn over their babies to their wives, who never get the chance of experiencing their babies' magic.

Researchers Martin Greenberg and Norman Morris, who have studied the father's potential for involvement with his newborn, use the term "engrossment" to describe the "feelings of preoccupation, absorption, and interest" that release paternal impulses. When a father is engrossed in his child, the child becomes dear to and cherished by him, and the father, in turn, "feels an increased sense of self-esteem and worth."[6] But in order for this gentle form of relatedness to emerge and feelings of paternal confidence to develop, fathers need to have time alone with their babies. And if the relationship with their children is to flourish, fathers also need continued one-on-one time with them as they grow older.

In Robert Benton's film *Kramer vs. Kramer*, we observe the powerful effects that *simply being with one another* has on a father and his young son. This is a story of a man—so removed from his son that when we first meet him in the film, he does not know which grade the youngster is in—who is suddenly forced to take full responsibility as a parent. During the moment-to-moment intimacies of everyday life—the child watching in bemused disbelief as the father botches the French toast that is to be their breakfast; the father watching in horror as the child slips from a jungle gym—the two grow to love each other fiercely. The day-in, day-out acts of caring transform a self-centered, emotionally absent father into an empathic, nurturing, and present one.

In the movie, Mrs. Kramer has to walk out on her family in order for her husband to begin paying attention to his son. In real life, however, less drastic solutions are usually in order. When new (and also experienced) married mothers write to me or tell me during therapy that they are at a loss to get their husbands to become more involved as fathers, I almost always give them three pieces of advice. The first is: Make sure that your husband and your child have opportunities to be together without you. And make sure that you *don't* leave your husband with a list of childcare instructions; let your husband discover his own style of relating to your child, which will be different, but no less "right," than your own.

The second piece of advice is: Don't imply to your husband that nurturing a baby is a feminine activity. Instead, assure him that in your eyes, being a close, caring, and committed father is a mark of manliness. Let him know that in order to thrive children need both mothering and fathering, and that while you're equipped to mother, only he can father.

The third piece of advice is: Make sure that you and your husband have opportunities to be together without your child. Do what you can to keep your marriage vital. Although the physical and emotional demands of baby and early childcare may dampen your interest in sex, remember to tell your husband every day that you love him very much and that in time you will want to make love with him again. If your husband knows that he is as important (and as attractive) to you now as he was before you became parents, he will not come to see his child—especially his male child—as his replacement, his competitor.

Recently I reread Homer's *Odyssey* and was struck again by the beauty of the reunion scene between the father and the son. After more than a decade of wandering, Odysseus, the mythical king of ancient Ithaca, returns to his faithful and strong wife, Penelope, and to their only child, Telemachus. Beholding the princely adolescent boy, the stranger-father, Odysseus, now grown old and compassionate, speaks the longed-for words to Telemachus: "I am that father whom your boyhood lacked and suffered pain for lack of. I am he . . ." and,

> Throwing his arms around this marvel of a father,
> Telemachus began to weep. Salt tears rose from the
> wells of longing in both men, and cries burst from
> both as keen and fluttering as those of the great
> taloned hawk, whose nestlings farmers take before
> they fly. So helplessly they cried pouring out tears,
> and might have gone on weeping till sundown.[7]

Reunited with his wife and with his teenage son, Odysseus belatedly assumes his responsibilities as a family man. He guides Telemachus into a confident and powerful manhood. Together they battle Queen Penelope's scheming suitors who were trying to usurp the kingdom, and together they triumph over them. As resplendent as Odysseus's homecoming is, however, I cannot help but believe that, unlike Odysseus, the most heroic fathers do not *return* to their sons and their wives. Rather, if at all possible, they choose not to leave them in the first place. They choose *to be committed to them*. And I also cannot help but believe that loving wives can often encourage their husbands to make this choice.

We should not discount the fact that just as many husband/fathers have great difficulty breaking away from the traditional forms of family, in which father was the designated provider and mother the designated caregiver, wife/mothers may also resist the changes that shared parenting calls for. For example, Cheryl, a client whose depression brought her to therapy, said:

> Because my husband has chosen to spend lots of time with our two sons—to be there for them in a very real way—he has lost his competitive edge in the law firm where he works. In the evenings and on weekends he's with the boys and me, not at the office preparing briefs. Because he's not as competitive as the other attorneys, I know that he won't be promoted to partner, that he won't ever make much money, the way my father did, and this bothers me. My father, because he was a very successful businessman, provided my mother a comfortable and secure life, and I would like such a life for myself. I am ashamed to say this, but I've lost respect for my husband. Even though he is a wonderful father and a loving husband, I see him as, well, not powerful in the world.

For Cheryl the prospect of becoming a successful career woman, which I have encouraged her to do, is not attractive; in her heart she believes that providing for the family's material needs is the man's job, not the woman's, and she thoroughly rejects the option of becoming the higher wage earner. Cheryl reminds us of something that we may occasionally forget: our own parents remain extraordinarily strong influences throughout our lives. Many, many women expect their husbands to be like their traditional fathers and are deeply resentful of them when they are not. (And, of course, the reverse is also true.)

Some women, like Cheryl, are reluctant to give up the protection of the powerful provider/father; other women are reluctant to relinquish the power of being the primary parent. Even women who say that they are eager to share parenting with their husbands, to become equal partners in the home, may unwittingly act in ways that undermine collaboration. Several vignettes from my practice come to mind.

A young father complained to me that whenever his wife left him with their two pre-schoolers for a few hours, she taped to the refrigerator door a detailed list of instructions— what and when to feed them, which games to play, and so on—so that he felt like "mother's little helper" with his own kids. As a result, he made excuses to "get out of *babysitting*." How very sad it is that in this man's eyes, the act of fathering was comparable to the duties performed by a hired sitter.

A woman who brought a six-month-old to a therapy session shook her head disapprovingly each time her husband tried to distract the restless child with finger food or a toy; obviously feeling increasingly useless, the young father gradually withdrew his attention from the baby.

A husband and wife who were in marriage counseling were concerned about the delinquent behavior of their teenage son; the wife corrected her tearful husband whenever he tried to explain to me what he thought was going on for the boy: "No, no, you're getting it all wrong, Joe, that's not what's behind his acting out," she would say impatiently. Lacking confidence in his own perceptions as a father and deferring to his wife's interpretations, Joe became increasingly quiet as the therapy hour progressed.

One of the reasons that some women are not eager to turn over their children to their fathers is that they are convinced that by nature or training men are incapable of sensitivity, empathy, and keen perceptions. Put more bluntly, a good number of women believe that men are "jerks." This firmly held belief can, of course, become a self-fulfilling prophecy. Many husbands, fully trusting their wives' perceptions of them as unfeeling or unattuned (as "jerks") come to believe that they cannot handle the emotional aspects of relationships and, for this reason, avoid heart-to-heart connections with their children. When an adult child telephones his parents in the hopes of having a "real" conversation with *both* of them, how many millions of fathers take a minute for small talk and then nervously say, "Gotta go now. I'll put Mom on the phone"?

Another reason that women assume a superior position in family matters—a "[Mother] Knows Best" persona—is that parenting is perhaps the only realm in which women are allowed to be expert and powerful. "God couldn't be every-where, and so invented mothers," the well-known proverb tells us. Although giving up the role of the all-knowing, all-nurturing, ever-present parent may in one way be a relief, it can in another way feel like a profound loss because for many women there is no other powerful *and* safe role to take its place. Sad to say, two decades after the women's liberation movement began, successful women are still being ridiculed and criticized. The general suspicion of and verbal attacks against Hillary Rodham Clinton during the 1992 pres-idential race compared to the trust and warm approval of grandmotherly Barbara Bush are vivid examples of this tendency.

Although a woman may consciously want her husband to take an equal part in parenting their children, at an un-conscious level she may be threatened by his participation and see it as an impingement on her territory. This experi-ence is movingly described in Linda Rennie Forcey's auto-biographical passage from her book *Mothers of Sons: Toward an Understanding of Responsibility*.

Although I believe I have a wholesome relationship with our youngest son who was born shortly before I returned to graduate school and is truly a product of "shared parenting," I have lapses concerning my redefined mothering identity from time to time. One such lapse was the time he at age 12 had an emer-gency appendectomy. On this particular day I had called from work to "check on things," only to dis-cover my husband had taken our son to the hospital in time to see him being wheeled off to surgery, his hand tightly clutching his father's. After the opera-tion (successful) my husband, who is prone to insomnia and late night hours anyway, said he wanted to stay in our son's room for the night in case he awoke frightened or in pain. This certainly seemed like a sensible decision and I scampered home to bed.

But I could not sleep. Something was wrong. I felt extremely anxious. Surely our son would be expecting me, his mother, to be by his bedside when he awoke, I thought to myself. Not stopping for breakfast I dashed back to the hospital at the crack of dawn, theoretically to relieve my husband but in reality to be "the essential one" for our son.

When I arrived three big tears rolled down our son's cheeks and he said, "Daddy, don't go. I felt so safe with you all night by my side." My body stiffened. For a moment I felt almost an uncontrollable rage toward the child. I wanted to shake his poor sore little form and scream: "I am your mother and you feel safe with only me alone." The irony of it all! Here before my very eyes had been the most beautiful proof that the mothering of sons can be shared and when I am shown not to be the essential one I almost go berserk![8]

Similarly, my neighbor, Merete, a writer who shares the care of two young sons with her husband, Mark, recently confided that upon returning from a weekend professional trip, she could not help but feel terribly hurt when her older son advised her that from now on he wanted only his daddy to take him to the pool because he had more fun swimming with him. But Merete's feelings of wounded pride quickly passed. "After my crying jag, I thought to myself, how wonderful it is that my son can take what he needs to grow from each of us. How fortunate he is to have two parents with different strengths. And what a relief it is that I don't have to be everything to him!"

Looking back at my own early years as a parent, I see how easy it is for a mother to insist on being the essential one to her child—and how, if she succeeds, everyone loses. During my daughter's early years I had the luxury of being a stay-at-home mother. Partly as a result of the amount of intimate time we spent with one another and partly as a result of our shared femaleness, Leah and I developed a wonderfully close, exclusive relationship; like Cinderella's tiny foot and the glass slipper, we fit together perfectly. During our new period of parenthood, my husband was busy establishing his academic career as an English professor and, necessarily, could not be with our little daughter as much as I was. One New Year's eve, little Leah, who was almost two, and I were playing together, totally wrapped up in one another, as we often were. When Bruce tried to join us, we both acted mildly annoyed and let it be known that he was intruding on us. I know that I did not mean to hurt my husband's feelings, and when he stormed out of the house and stayed away for several hours, I was appalled at his "overreaction."

The next morning, the first day of 1973, the two of us talked for a very long time. Bruce explained how rejected he felt when we had cast him from our cozy nest. Because he spoke from his heart, the icy anger that I felt toward him for having walked out on me New Year's eve quickly melted. But more important, having been made aware of his considerable emotional pain, I resolved never again to relegate him to the role of outsider or lesser parent. Twenty years later, we are both thankful for this decision. Still, I remember, with a little shudder, how "natural" it had been for me as a young mother to assume the role of primary parent and that had my husband not strongly objected, I might very well have pushed him to the periphery of our family permanently.

It is not easy for husbands and wives to become equal partners as parents. As we have seen, cultural and psychological factors get in the way of their bringing up the children together. Indeed, the traditional division of family responsibilities, in which fathers provide financially and mothers provide emotionally, is a tidier arrangement than the alternative form of sharing family responsibilities. Sharing authority, especially in an area as emotionally charged as parenting, necessarily stirs conflicts and competition, which can make life "messy" at times. However, for more and more couples, the traditional division of family obligations is becoming unworkable. In most of today's households, both wives and husbands are wage earners, both have interests and curiosities that draw them away from the home, and both have yearnings and responsibilities to be close to their children during their growing-up years. To my mind, shared parenting offers a practical solution for contemporary couples; it also encourages stronger bonds between parent and child, wife and husband—and, for these reasons, is worth struggling toward.

In recent decades, we have witnessed the breakdown of marriage, which brings untold suffering to the children of divorce and also to the broken couples. When husband and wife commit to the shared care of their children over the many years of the children's dependency, they are also committing to each other. In the course of protecting, nurturing, worrying about, disciplining, and rejoicing in their children *together*, mother and father—husband and wife—are drawn into a daily intimacy from which a strong, deep, enduring, unbreachable marital love can grow. Jungian scholar and writer Robert A. Johnson calls the down-to-earth, everyday relatedness between husband and wife "stirring-the-oatmeal."[9] To stir the oatmeal together means to find value, meaning, and love in sharing the million and one humble, ordinary, tedious, troublesome, and tender tasks that parenting entails. To stir the oatmeal together is not particularly romantic but wonderfully nourishing and sustaining.

When sons and daughters grow up with parents who love each other they too thrive. Children who know that their fathers and mothers are bound by their marriage vows grow up trusting that love lasts, that promises are kept, that commitments are real. Children who observe their mothers and fathers working out problems in an atmosphere of mutual respect grow up believing that conflicts do not destroy relationships but can be resolved. And children who are nurtured by fathers and mothers grow up understanding that males can be as tender and as caregiving as females. Indeed, the surest way to ensure that a little boy will one day become a nurturing father is for him to grow up with a nurturing father.[10] A lovely example comes to mind. When my neighbor Merete was away, I caught sight of Mark mowing the lawn and, simultaneously, carrying and comforting Jakob, their one-year-old. Then I noticed four-year-old Mattias. There he was, shadowing his father, pushing a toy mower while holding a small stuffed animal close against his chest.

Because shared parenting is a new practice (one that, for the most part, our parents and our grandparents did not know), married couples are not familiar with how it works. In the hope that my own story can be helpful to parents who want to participate equally in their children's upbringing, I would like to conclude this chapter with it.

One great advantage of shared parenting for me was that I did not have to give up motherhood to pursue a meaningful and demanding career or give up a career to ensure that my children would be well cared for. I was able "to have it all." Of course, having it all meant lots of hard work and juggling and patience. While Bruce was first making his way in the academic world, I took responsibility for the everyday functioning of the household and was the one who mostly cared for the children—although Bruce was still very much involved in family life. When I began to work on a Ph.D., Bruce became responsible for the family—although I remained involved. (Those were busy years; Bruce used to joke with his friends: "Evi and I schedule in times we can go to the bathroom.") After both of us had established our careers, we divided our household tasks more evenly, but neither one of us became the primary parent; we both continued to enjoy strong, nurturing, and loving relationships with our children, albeit very different ones; equality as parents, we discovered, did not mean sameness.

Just as a woman's body is softer than a man's, I am softer with the children, the one to whom they tend to turn for comfort and unconditional acceptance. In contrast, Bruce is more likely to set and enforce limits with them. Our children never seemed to find these distinctions problematic. Similarly, Bruce has not minded taking the role of the "heavy" more of the time as long as he could count on my not undermining his efforts at discipline.

Bruce and I also brought different energies to our family life: Bruce is a "wild man" who loved to engage the children in vigorous play, and I am quiet by nature and spent hours with Leah and Jonathan drawing or painting or collecting leaves and pine cones. Interestingly, just as Bruce assumes a stereotypic male role and I a stereotypic female one in some areas, we also deviate from the traditional gender roles. For example, Bruce is, by far, the better cook; I am the higher wage-earner. He is the one who thinks to leave music on for our parakeet when we are at work "so that the little fellow won't feel too lonely"; I am the one who does the taxes. Indeed, for me, one of the more difficult aspects of shared parenting was sometimes feeling guilty that I was not the one doing all the nurturing. When, for example, my husband attended Jonathan's Little League games while I stayed home to write or when he caringly prepared a delicious meal for all of us on his days to cook and I settled for take-out on mine, I could not help but think that I was not only remiss as a mother but somehow lacking as a woman.

When, at times, I felt especially unsure of myself, Bruce would boost my confidence by assuring me that I was a very good mother and a womanly woman as well; and he would point out what my guilty feelings had temporarily prevented me from seeing: that Jonathan and Leah were not suffering from undermothering but, on the contrary, were thriving under our shared care.

There have also been times when Bruce needed my assurances. Because he spent so much time with our children during their growing-up years, he was not as competitive in the "publish or perish" world of academia as he might otherwise have been, which translated to fewer and lower salary raises and to the improbability that he would ever become a "star" on campus. When Bruce was downcast, I could be the loving friend who provided assurances—the one who pointed out how valuable and priceless his contributions to our family were and that in his role of good father and husband, he had become more of a man to me than he would have if he had achieved the most dazzling career successes.

The insecurity of being undervalued as a parent has alternately plagued Bruce and me. Just as Bruce felt excluded during our daughter's infancy, I felt excluded during periods of Jonathan's life. Without intending to demean, Bruce—so passionately involved with our son—nevertheless would sometimes take care of all his needs, set all the rules for him, and leave me with hardly a parenting role at all. On several tearful occasions, I shared with Bruce how being left out in these ways diminished me, and he, sensitive to my grievance, made efforts to let me in. I also began to share with him my perception that too much father-son closeness was not healthy for either Jonathan or him.

One of the husband/father's traditional roles is to act as a buffer between the mother and child, so that they do not remain permanently fixed in a symbiotic relationship; by helping the two to separate from one another, the growth-promoting father ensures that each will develop an autonomous, independent life. Similarly, aware that Bruce and Jonathan's attachment had become skin-tight, I saw that one of my roles as a growth-promoting wife/mother was to help *father and son* separate. Especially as Jonathan entered his teen years, I encouraged Bruce to be less with him and more with me—and this new arrangement worked well for all of us. Jonathan gradually transferred his attentions from his dad to his peers; Bruce and I turned more of our attention toward one another.

My colleague Dr. Ivan Miller, who has a gift for turning abstract ideas into lovely images, compares the development of the married couple to a garden of flowers, vines, shrubs, and trees that is tended by a devoted gardener. To flourish, flowers must be regularly watered and fertilized—in the same way that a husband and wife must feed each other with kind words. So that they will not collapse under pressure, vines may need wire supports; similarly, a husband or wife who is in danger of breaking under life's pressures requires the other's reliable support. In addition, in order to develop a pleasing form and not grow in the wrong direction, shrubs and trees must be regularly pruned. Married partners also tame and shape (but are careful not to "cut down") one another's parenting behaviors when they get out of control.

What is especially accurate about Ivan's image is that it reflects the continuous interaction between the husband and wife who parent together. I know that the collaboration between Bruce and myself as parents has deepened our love and friendship for one another. Over twenty years, we have shared immense joys as well as worries and fears about the children. When either of our children was unhappy, the two of us would talk and try to figure out how to be of help. When one of us was handling things inappropriately, the other would tactfully offer criticism. Because we have an ongoing dialogue, I am aware of the personal struggles that Bruce confronts in his effort to be a good parent and, similarly, he is aware of mine. And knowing the fatigue and pressures that being both caregiver and provider, parent and professional, necessarily entail, we have learned to be especially sympathetic when one or the other feels like there is just too much to do.

Although I almost always knew that our arrangement was strengthening our married love and enabling each of us to be fuller human beings, I was, until very recently, not absolutely convinced that my nontraditional mothering had benefited our son. Leah had often told me that she was glad and proud that I was both a mom and a career woman—that my dual roles gave her confidence that she too could combine the pleasures of work and family love. But Jonathan had not provided me with such verbal assurances.

I am, however, just beginning to understand that my *not* having been all-available to Jonathan (once he had passed babyhood and had been weaned) accounts, in great part, for the mutually loving, engaged, and respectful relationship we now have. Because I was not *the* essential one but one of two essential ones, because I was not the one on whom he depended absolutely or the one who always controlled him, Jonathan did not and does not feel in awe of or overpowered by me; to him, I am certainly not a goddess, but neither am I a witch. For the most part, Jonathan and I are easy around one another; indeed, we can talk for hours. Jonathan's warm and open relationships with girlfriends indicate to me that females generally do not threaten him; that, unlike many, many males, he does not have to fend them off or evade them or assert his superiority over them.

Years ago, feminist theorist Dorothy Dinnerstein wrote that there will be real hope for the human condition only when the primary parents are both mother and father; only then will mothers (and women in general) no longer be perceived as all-powerful and responsible for the ills that beset humankind. Looking at my own son's development, I believe Dinnerstein may be right. In order to grow up into loving and kind husbands and fathers, our sons need *less* mothering and *more* fathering.

In late summer, 1992, Bruce and I drove our freshman son across three state lines to his new college. The trip to Iowa was a rite of passage for each of us three: for Jonathan, the beginning of independence away from home; for Bruce and me, the end of active parenting. When we arrived at the university, we helped Jonathan carry his things to his dorm, and we made small talk with his roommate. After leaving him in his new room, we two—feeling ancient and utterly out of place among the throng of college students—retreated to a motel for the night.

The next morning, as planned, we met Jonathan to have breakfast and to say our goodbyes. When the time for leave-taking came, our son, looking shockingly manly, took our hands and quietly said, "Thanks, Mom and Dad . . . Dad and Mom. Thank you both for everything." And for the first time in many years, he did not flinch when I moved toward him for a kiss.

Arm in arm, choking back our tears, Bruce and I walked back to our compact car, which, no longer packed with Jonathan's duffel bags and cartons of books, Bruce Springsteen tapes, baseball bat and glove and rolled-up Ricky Henderson poster, basketball and weights, seemed uncomfortably spacious.

On our first day's drive back home, Bruce and I talked mostly about Jonathan and a lot about Leah. But on our second and last day of driving, we talked more about ourselves. Passing through the cornfields of Iowa and Nebraska, we planned a dream trip to the prehistoric caves of southern France; we brought each other up to date on our writing projects; we talked about building a grape arbor in our back yard like the ones that we had admired on our trips to Greece. And instead of playing Jonathan's Bruce Springsteen tapes, as we had done on our trip to Iowa, we played our favorite songs and we sang along with them.

Our house is quieter these days—and much more tidy. Bruce and I eat out frequently. Except for the times that Jonathan and Leah are home on school breaks or vacations, we have no reason to close our bedroom door at night. After all those years of being four, then three, we are most often two again—but much, much changed (we think for the better) from the young couple we once were.

The Father and the Mother . . .
are called Companions. . . . And they find
satisfaction in permanent union.[11]

6

······················

Single Mothers

Sifting through the paper one Sunday morning, I came across an article on single mothers by *New York Times* reporter Tamar Lewin, which begins with the following vignette.

ATLANTA—As Janice Edwards drives home after work to the small, neatly kept house she bought last year, she tells the proud story of how she kept her family going since her husband left her five years ago, just before their second child was born.

"I thought we'd fall apart with no man there," she said.

"There was a time I had no money for formula, no gas, no water, no electricity and I didn't know what in the world we would do."

What Edwards, 27, has done is work—an office job during the day, and another job after hours, at Kmart, or, at one point, delivering newspapers from 2 to 5 a.m.

"I'm going to work 17 jobs if I have to, but I'm going to take care of these children," she said.

"I'm not going to listen to people who tell me single mothers are bad. I'm not single by choice; I'm single by force, and I'm not going to listen to those negative things."[1]

Lewin notes that in her dozens of interviews with single mothers, "the feeling that was expressed most often and most strongly was a great pride in finding that, against all expectations—theirs and society's—they are managing reasonably well."

In my personal life and in my role as psychotherapist, I too have gotten to know mothers who, like Janice Edwards, do what they have to in order to care for their children—and, quite frankly, I am in awe of their fortitude. From time to time, I have asked myself whether I would have had the necessary grit to do a good enough job if, as a young woman, I had been forced by circumstances to raise my daughter and my son alone. Or would financial pressures and the children's relentless needs and demands have worn me down to despair or ineffectuality? I just don't know.

Although I have not been put to the test of single parenting, in this chapter I would nevertheless like to share with my readers what I have learned from the research in this area—the bulk of which focuses on the effects of divorce—and from personal stories about single mothers and their sons. My hope is that this fund of knowledge and record of experience can deepen the understanding of the divorced, never-married, or widowed mothers who are, in fact, put to the test.

Although the break-up of a family is traumatic for children, research findings indicate that the majority—50 to 70 percent—of youngsters do not appear to have significant long-lasting problems as a result of divorce; certainly, this is testimony of the resiliency of the human spirit. Of course, the grimmer interpretation of this research, which we should not try to whitewash, is that, even years after the divorce, 30 to 50 percent of children suffer from its effects. These children are prone to angry, aggressive behaviors or to sadness, depression, and feelings of low self-esteem; they tend to have trouble in school and in establishing intimate relationships as they grow up.[2]

New research on the effects of divorce also suggests that the gender of the custodial parent plays a part in the child's adjustment. Although there is hardly any information on the best custody arrangements for infants and toddlers, we have some research evidence that on the average, boys past the age of six do better when they live with their fathers whereas girls do better when they live with their mothers. At least in relation to independence, maturity, self-esteem, sociability, as well as anxiety, aggression, delinquency, and depression, youngsters who live with the same-sex parent appear to have an advantage.[3] Of course, we need to recognize that other conditions, such as the presence of siblings in the home, economic security, and, most important, the stability of the primary parent, will positively affect a child's adjustment. Thus, although the gender of the parent should be considered when custody arrangements are made, it should not be the only consideration.

The most obvious explanation for the poorer adjustment of older boys who are raised exclusively by their mothers is the absence of a viable connection to their fathers. Mothers can nurture, teach, discipline, and provide financially for their sons, but they cannot, of course, model male behavior. Robert Bly tells the story of a young man named Keith Thompson who, after his parents' divorce when he was twelve, lived with his mother. Throughout high school and college, Keith remained closer to women, whose company he enjoyed and whom he genuinely admired, than to other men. After graduation, he worked mostly with women and was further sensitized to their concerns. At about this time, he had a disturbing but revealing dream, which Bly describes.

> He and a clan of she-wolves were running in the forest. Wolves suggested to him primarily independence and vigor. The clan of wolves moved fast through the forest, in formation, and eventually they all arrived at a riverbank. Each she-wolf looked into the water and saw her own face there. But when Keith looked in the water, he saw no face at all.[4]

Interpreting Keith's dream, especially the final image, Bly suggests, "When women, even women with the best intentions, bring up a boy alone, he may in some way have no male face, or he may have no face at all."[5] It is through his connection with his father—and all his male ancestry—that a boy feels himself to be *real*, to have a firm identity, a well-defined "face."

Boys who are brought up exclusively by their mothers respond to this arrangement in a number of ways. Although Keith embraced the world of women and seemingly became too identified with it, other boys and young men may do the opposite. My client Rose, a pleasant, soft-spoken woman who is the divorced mother of two adolescent daughters and a young adult son, explains that however hard she tried to please Albert, he acted irritated and impatient with her and his sisters. Last November, in her relentless efforts to create a warm family feeling, Rose decided to celebrate the four-day Thanksgiving holiday with her three children in a mountain cabin nestled at the foot of the Rockies. During the preparation of the traditional dinner, however, Albert became increasingly gloomy, putting a damper on the others' high spirits. As the day went on, the young man's mood got only worse, and the holiday was miserable for everyone. Rose was, understandably, terribly disappointed, but out of the shambles of this family experience, she gained an important insight.

> I always was afraid that, because of the divorce and the fact that I'm a working mother, my son would have *too little* of me—not enough family closeness and not enough mothering, which is why I have always made it a point of planning lots of activities for the four of us. But I understand now that my son is no longer a little boy that the opposite may be true. Living with me and his two sisters, he has been overwhelmed by *too much* female presence. During our miserable Thanksgiving celebration in the cabin in the mountains, he must have felt positively claustrophobic. There was no getting away from the three of us women. And there was no other man with whom Albert could hang out and relax into himself.

As I have discussed in previous chapters, most boys, in their efforts to become men, struggle hard to differentiate themselves from mother and all that is feminine. As Rose discerned, her son probably felt overwhelmed in the midst of his matriarchal clan; the thick female presence all around him threatened to snuff him out.

Beyond the anxiety of being subsumed by his mother's and his sisters' female energy—losing his male face, as Bly might say—Albert may also have been threatened by their sexuality; it cannot be easy for a young man, who, much of the time, battles to contain his erotic urges, to live in intimate quarters with three attractive women.

Freud has taught us that the father, by virtue of his dominating size and generally powerful presence, makes it clear to the son that he will not tolerate the child's sexual claim to mother; through his implicit threat of punishment (castration) for sexual transgressions, he helps the little boy give up dan-

gerous fantasies about mother. The strong father, by disapproving of the "mama's boy," also discourages the adolescent
boy from getting too cozy with mother. What Freud did not
say, and what I think may be equally as important, is that the
father's presence also assures the son that mother will not
have to turn to the boy for the sexual and emotional fulfillment that she finds with her husband; in other words, the
son is let off the hook because his father is "taking care of
business." Without the paterfamilias, the threat of an eroti-
cized relationship between mother (or other females in the
household) and son becomes greater; in the absence of the
strong husband/father who gratifies his wife's sexual appetite, the boy may imagine, sometimes with good cause, that
his mother hungers after him.

Because the taboo against incest is so strong, we shy
away from talking about the erotic overtones in the parent-
child relationship. And yet, they undoubtedly contribute
heavily to the tensions in the single-parent home and may
explain, in part, why children of divorce seem to do better
when they live with the same-sex, rather than the opposite-
sex, parent. It is likely that without being conscious of his
fears of intimacy, the boy fends mother off by acting dis-
agreeably or even abusively toward her.

But although boys may oppose mother in certain ways,
they may try to meet her needs in other ways. Through my
conversations with sons of single mothers, I have learned
how common it is for them to feel responsible for mother's
well-being—to take it upon themselves to replace the missing husband/father by becoming her loving, strong, sensitive,
care-taking companion and confidant. And although this devotion may flatter the mother and empower the boy, who
takes pride in being mother's protector, it also exacts an emotional toll from him. Neil Kalter of the University of Michigan,
who has studied the effects of divorce on 500 families, writes
that when youngsters are called upon to help with single-
parent stresses, they "become distracted from the normal developmental tasks of gaining greater independence from their
family and investing emotionally in relationships with friends

and important adults outside the family. As they are pressed into this service, they are drawn back into the maternal orbit, partially sacrificing their efforts to establish a life of their own outside their family."[6]

Many stories about the plights of the "little man of the house" come to my mind, but the one that touches me most is a story that a childhood friend, whom I will call Joyce, shared. Joyce's background is unusual. As a baby, she lived with her widowed mother, Louisa, and her older brother, Eric, behind barbed wires in an internment camp set up in Oswego, New York, for Jews who had been liberated from the Nazi concentration camps.[7] After the family's release from the Oswego camp in 1945, the three moved to an apartment in upper Manhattan, where Louisa got a full-time job as a seamstress. Like many other children born into hardship, both Joyce and Eric were very responsible children, and they gave their hard-working mother little reason for complaint. Joyce, who was blessed with a fun-loving nature, was a happy little girl, despite her harsh beginnings; but Eric, old beyond his years, enjoyed few childish pleasures. Recently, when Joyce was visiting me in Colorado, she told me this sad story about her brother's bar mitzvah.

Eric was under five feet tall when he turned thirteen. As if it were yesterday, I can picture him standing in front of the rabbi and looking up at the great man with a shy, sweet smile as he awaited the benediction. The rabbi gently laid his hand on Eric's shoulder, and then in a full, deep, very serious voice told him that, from this time on, Eric was responsible for looking after our mother and me; he told him that he knew he had always been a good boy, but that now he had to be even more helpful; now he was the man of the house.

I noticed that everyone in the congregation, including my mother, was beaming and obviously agreed that the rabbi's words were wise and just. But I also noticed that my brother was sinking under the weight of the rabbi's words, so that he looked even smaller than he really was.

I loved Eric and felt so sorry for him. In fact, I had a great impulse to run up to the pulpit and scream at the rabbi, "Don't do this to my brother. Don't take his young life away like this. He shouldn't have to take care of Mom and me! He's just a kid, and he should be allowed to have fun now." But, of course, I stayed seated on the wooden bench in the synagogue and didn't say a thing.

Eric, in fact, heeded the rabbi's words—although at great emotional expense to himself. Long after it was appropriate to do so, he remained bound to his mother, always wanting to please her but never quite measuring up to her impossible expectations of him. In fact, it was only after Louisa died that Eric, then in his middle forties, psychologically released himself from her hold and proposed marriage to the woman he loved. Eric's story brings to mind the achingly sad words of French novelist and diplomat Romain Gary, who also believed that he owed his life to his mother and, for this reason, could not savor loving and being loved by other women. "I am not saying that mothers should be prevented from loving their young," Gary writes; "I am only saying that they should have someone else to love as well. . . . If my mother had had a husband or lover, I would not have spent my days dying of thirst beside so many fountains."[8]

Certainly, when a woman diverts some of her attention from her son to another, she frees the boy to leave her—to find his own relationships—without feeling that he has betrayed her. Allen, a man I have interviewed several times during the writing of this book, helped me understand, however, that the mother who *indiscriminately* takes sexual partners may cause her young or adolescent son considerable emotional pain.

Allen cannot remember his birth father, who deserted the family when Allen was still a baby. He does, however, vividly remember the many men from his childhood, whom he sneeringly calls "sharks," who visited his beautiful mother. When he closes his eyes, he says he can still hear the scary sexual noises that came from his mother's bedroom; he imagined these sounds were her screams of pain.

> I hated these men; I wanted to hurt them so badly. But, of course, I was no match for them. I was just a skinny little kid, less than half their size. Still, more than anything in the world, I wanted to be able to protect my mother from them. Failing over and over again, I began to feel useless. I am fifty-one now, but I still am incapacitated by these feelings of utter ineffectuality. Part of my sense of helplessness comes from growing up black in a racist society, but another part comes from growing up with a mother who could not resonate with a little boy's sensitivities. If she has been more discreet, I would not have suffered so.

Of his mother's many lovers, there was one, however, whom Allen came to trust, revere, and even love. For unlike the others, who saw him as nothing but a nuisance, the man who became his stepfather took a genuine and gentle interest in him. When Allen's mother eventually left this marriage, Allen was devastated.

Of course, the emotional repercussions for sons when their mothers date or remarry are vastly complicated. We will address them in much fuller detail in the next chapter.

Though sons living with single mothers face many psychological difficulties, a boy growing up under his mother's care is not doomed to be maladjusted or unhappy. We have only to look at our president, Bill Clinton, for an example of a fatherless boy who, in addition to having become a powerful leader, is obviously at home in the world and emotionally connected to other people. Certainly, even the most resourceful mother cannot *undo* the harm of father loss; there is, as Bill Clinton described, always a "hole" where father should be. But a single mother can often *mitigate* her son's loss and thereby help him grow in beautiful ways.

If she is separated or divorced, the clearest way for a custodial single mother to help heal her son's wound and lead him toward manhood is by encouraging a vital relationship between him and his father. After all, the need for his father is a basic, indisputable need of every boy. To be sure, visiting with father cannot undo the boy's disappointment and anger that they no longer live together all the time, but at least it can soothe the hurt feelings. However, for mother, these visits may be painful events. We saw in the previous chapter that married women are often critical of their husbands as fathers and may subtly undermine their efforts to be close to the children; surely, we can expect divorced women to be far more mistrustful of their ex-spouses. Moreover, when a woman does not like her husband well enough to stay married to him, turning her beloved child over to him may go against her protective instincts. Yet this is what the good and wise mother is often called upon to do.

I am currently counseling a lovely, sensitive Dutch woman, who earns a small income by giving violin lessons. While still living in Holland, Tanne fell in love with an American businessman, who won her over with his clean-cut good looks and midwestern friendliness. "Living in a rainy country, I imagined Pat as a ray of sunshine sent by God to beam down on me," she reminisced, "and I gladly followed him to the United States to become his bride and to start our family." A couple of years after Tanne had their first and only child, Pat fell under the influence of a fundamentalist Christian sect, whose dogma, especially its anti-gay and pro-life activism, offended the liberal-minded Tanne. As Pat became more and more zealous, the two drew further and further apart, and ultimately they split up. When they negotiated their divorce, Pat did not argue against Tanne's wishes for child custody, but he did insist on generous visitation rights with their seven-year-old son.

With a sinking feeling Tanne packs the child's duffel bag

for his weekly overnights with his father and listens to the boy's enthusiastic accounts of his growing attachments to his father's evangelical friends. Nevertheless, believing that her son should love and honor his father, whom she acknowledges is a good father, she does nothing to undermine their relationship or to demean her ex-husband's religious values in front of the child, although she does let him know her principles differ from his father's.

"I have learned to bite my tongue a lot," Tanne explains. "Still, on my bad days, I worry that Pat will turn our son into a religious zealot; luckily, on my good days, I have faith that the child will take from me and from his father what he needs in order to grow and that he will eventually reject the rest." In supporting the father-son relationship, Tanne does the right thing, even though doing so sometimes tears her heart in two.

Sometimes, even more than encouraging an active involvement between her son and her ex-spouse, a mother, acting in the best interests of the child, turns the boy over from her custody to his father's. This maternal act of care is beautifully rendered in John Singleton's film *Boyz 'n the Hood*, in which a mother relinquishes her cherished and only son to his father's care not because she is weak or lazy—on the contrary, she is fierce and capable—but because she understands that from this time on, the ten-year-old boy, who is acting out in school and pushing too hard against her, needs father love and father limits if he is to survive the brutal world of the ghetto. It is out of mother love, not in spite of it, that this woman steps back from the son who would cling to her for comfort and leaves him in the tough hands of his father—the hands that will mold him into manhood and that will also learn to nurture him.

Its focus elsewhere, Singleton's movie does not attempt to explore the feelings of self-doubt that normally beset the noncustodial mother. In our society, and in most others, the mother is expected to be her child's primary caretaker. If she gives up or is denied custody she risks being characterized as a "bad mother," an "unnatural woman," a "selfish person."

More painful still, she may worry that her son will interpret her decision to turn him over to his father not as an act of love but as an act of abandonment and rejection. Certainly, noncustodial fathers often suffer deeply as a result of the lost contact with their child, but noncustodial mothers, in addition to suffering the wrenching pain of loss, may also begin to question their self-worth.

For all too many single mothers, sharing parenting responsibilities with their son's father is not an option. Whether by choice or by circumstance, father has left the family circle for good. Or his behavior is so destructive that he poses a psychological or physical danger to his son, who must therefore be kept away from him. Or in the case of the never-married mother, the son's father may not be known.

No one can, of course, replace the missing parent in a child's life. But in the absence of a biological father, a mother can lead her son to other male models of strength and integrity. For example, a boy's grandfather(s), his older brother(s), his uncle(s), his therapist, his clergyman, or his stepfather— men who are invested in and consistently there for him— can fill a good portion of the empty, aching hole left by the lost father.

A woman who remembers her childhood father as distant and cold or as harsh and authoritarian may feel awkward promoting a relationship between her son and his grandfather. And yet, very often, the inadequate father evolves into a more-than-adequate grandfather and wonderful role model. Relieved from the pressures and stresses that accompanied his fatherhood, he is able to enjoy his grandchildren much more than he enjoyed his own children. My own husband, who, as a little boy, lived for a year in his maternal grandparents' home, loves to describe the lavish feast of smoked sturgeon, lox, freshly baked pumpernickel bread, and homegrown pickled tomatoes that his Russian-Jewish grandfather set out for him each Sunday morning. To this day, Bruce has a craving for pickled tomatoes—grandpa's love food—and whenever he eats them experiences a deep sense of wellness. It is interesting that the nurturing grandfather Bruce remembers contrasts sharply with the unkind, inaccessible childhood father my mother-in-law remembers.

As I listen to men tell their life stories, I am struck by their frequent references to the good grandfather and the impact he had on their personalities. During his presidential campaign, for example, Bill Clinton credited his widowed mother for passing on to him her "fighting spirit," and his "golden-hearted" grandfather, with whom he had lived during his mother's absence, for imbuing him with the principles of humaneness. President Clinton remarked that as a child growing up in the segregated South, he had not failed to notice that his grandfather, who ran a grocery store, had quietly defied the conventions of bigotry by always treating his African-American and Anglo customers with equal respect, kindness, and generosity.

An interesting piece of research by psychology professor Martin Hoffman links the development of conscience in a sample of seventh-grade boys to the presence of the father. Dr. Hoffman found that boys who came from fatherless homes received lower scores than boys with fathers on measures of moral development such as guilt following transgressions, acceptance of blame for wrongdoing, compliance with rules, and internalized moral standards.[9] I think that we can justly say that grandfathers too can help boys develop strong consciences and standards of right and wrong; indeed, traditionally, the elders of a tribe or of a community have been the rule-makers and the rule-enforcers. In addition, grandfathers can bestow on their grandsons a "male face": a life-affirming sense of identity and connection to their ancestry. It has been said, quite correctly, I believe, that a child develops a feeling of belonging by finding his place within the history of his family and that no one explains this history better than a grandparent.[10]

Other men who are temporary rather than permanent presences in a boy's life, such as his coaches, the fathers of his friends, his mother's male friends or "significant other," and his teachers, can positively affect his healthy development. "It is too early for me to be thinking about 'letting go,'" the widowed mother of a seven-year-old told me, "but I think a lot about 'letting in'—welcoming those people into Todd's world who can give him different experiences than I can. For instance, my son loves to tag along with his best buddy's family, which is a two-parent family, and I'm so pleased that they are glad to include him and that he gets to see what a family with a mother *and* a father is all about." This enhancing mother says that she has come up with some unconventional ways to expose her son to the world of men: "When we go to the library, I intentionally pull out books from the shelves that are written for little boys *by men*. I have discovered that these male-authored books about sports heroes and sensitive woodsmen and brave Indians and just ordinary, everyday things speak to Todd in a special way. They are like the stories his own daddy—were he still alive— might have told him."

Although it is true that relationships with vital and loving men are important for a boy, it is also true that the relationship with his own vital and loving mother has great significance for him, especially when she is the person on whom he primarily depends. How a woman feels about her life necessarily affects how her son lives his own. When she finds fulfillment in her work, her creative activities, and her relationships with friends and family, she releases her child from the onerous task of making her happy and of becoming her devoted "little man"; and, similarly, she has no reason to turn to her child to fill her up. According to the most credible research on divorce, for children of all ages, the psychologically distressed parent, especially the custodial parent, is a key source of emotional pain for them and an obstacle to their healthy development.[11] The following story—whose source I have, unfortunately, forgotten—illustrates that the opposite is also true: the joyful mother is a healing salve for her child and promotes his growth.

A renowned psychiatrist was treating a sensitive, upperclass young man for chronic melancholia. Of course, the doctor inquired about his patient's childhood. The young man then told him that he remembered with great clarity one particular incident. On a dismal, wintry night—the very night his parents were to attend a masquerade ball—he came down with a fever and was to be left in the care of a housekeeper. His mother, a pretty, cheerful young woman, swooped into his sick room to kiss him goodbye; costumed as Marie Antoinette, she was stunning in her powdered wig and shimmering scarlet gown, and during her brief visit, she filled the boy's room with her radiance. All during the night, while he was wrestling with a rising fever and aching muscles, he could not help thinking about her.

The doctor thought that his patient's story was a metaphor for a neglected childhood. "How sad and all alone you must have felt when your mother, rather than staying by your sickbed to give you comfort, traipsed off to her ball!" he told the young man. But his patient felt misunderstood. "No, that was not my experience at all," he offered. "The image of my mother, who was so beautiful and joyful, made me feel better that night. In fact, although so many years have passed, it is the memories of this lively, happy woman that can sometimes pull me out of my doldrums."

In presenting this story, I do not mean to suggest that mothers abandon their caregiving responsibilities, which often require them to put their children's needs before their own (children who have lost one parent may be especially needy), or that they transform themselves into self-indulgent pleasure-seekers. However, I am suggesting that they try to bring joy into their own lives. My advice may strike some single mothers as burdensome rather than as freeing. "In addition to everything else that I have to do to bring up my kids, is being happy also part of my job description?" a tired single mother may ask herself with a heavy heart. My answer is "Yes—with qualifications."

Surely, every thinking, feeling person, in reaction to life's travails and the world's sorrows, feels depressed from time to time. And, equally surely, a single mother, who is typically burdened by more than her fair share of stress and hardship, experiences periods of great frustration and unhappiness. Especially during the months following the death of her husband or the break-up of the family as a result of divorce, a woman naturally suffers deeply and gravely. Were she alone in the world, she would have every right to allow herself an unbounded and prolonged bereavement. In those circumstances, she might take years to do nothing but mourn and rage against the fates for her terrible losses—the loss of a partner-in-life, the loss of financial security, the loss of the family home, the loss of relationships with in-laws and perhaps old friends, the loss of all that might have been. But because the single custodial mother is not alone, and because a child's well-being depends in large part on her emotional stability and psychological availability, she is called upon to contain her grief and to limit the mourning period; to do so, she may require the help of a psychotherapist and perhaps anti-depressant medications.

The antidote to depression is not assuming a false cheerfulness, however. It is, rather, *engaging* with life: developing one's interests, nurturing one's talents, taking social actions, envisioning and acting on what is possible. These are the essences of joyful living. And a single mother, who is choosing for her children as well as for herself, cannot afford not to choose a positive life.

In choosing a positive life, a woman who is raising her children alone requires support from other caring people. No single mother should allow timidity or pride to stand in the way of asking for this support; there is too much potential harm for both the mother and child who live in isolation from others. "I know that a twenty-five-year-old woman is supposed to be liberated from her parents," a woman I counseled explained; "but maybe the rules need to be changed for twenty-five-year-olds with babies. If I had not temporarily moved back to my parents' home after my husband walked out, I don't know how I would have made it. My parents are enormously helpful. And when I feel guilty that my son and I are imposing on them, they smile and say, 'That's what families are all about—to be there for one another in rough times.' "

Another single client, who does not enjoy close relationships with her family and would not think of asking them for support, has often told me how invaluable long-term therapy has been for her. "Wives can turn to their husbands when they feel down or confused. Well, I can't do that, but I can turn to you. And what a comfort that is!"

In my role as psychotherapist, I have listened to the stories of many single mothers who struggle in their maternal role. Although each story is unique, a common thread runs through many of them: the shameful (and undeserved) feeling of inferiority that necessarily feeds depression. All too often, my single clients who are divorced or who have never been married describe themselves as "flawed," as "misfits," as "not measuring up," or as having or being "less than" their married women friends. The following clinical vignette illustrates how devastating these feelings of shame can be.

Today, Jeanette manages very well in her dual roles as single mother and as paralegal. But five years ago, after her divorce was finalized, Jeanette sank into a self-hating depression. Because she could not bring herself to talk during our early therapy sessions, I asked her to make drawings for me. A very pretty woman with lively blue eyes and an abundance of curly auburn hair, Jeanette portrayed herself as an ugly hag with greenish black blood spurting from an undersized heart. The putrid blood, she told me, symbolized the "badness" inside her, and the tiny heart was her inability "to be a good wife." Sometimes, Jeanette drew a house—really a windowless, cinderblock prison—for her hag. "She is so bad that I want to shut her away," Jeanette would say. And in her real life, Jeanette did shut herself away; she stopped visiting her friends and would not even pick up the phone when it rang.

For Jeanette, her new status as a divorced woman and the single parent of a five-year-old had generated intense feelings of shame. Although her marriage to a corporate executive had been miserable, as a corporate wife she never-theless felt she had a rightful place in society: she "belonged"; she was "acceptable"; she had money. But as a consequence of her divorce, Jeanette's sense of personal se-curity and identity had crumbled: "I feel like a terrible failure because I couldn't make my marriage work and because I'm not able to give my son, Scott, a 'real' family life. I don't know if I'll ever shake the feeling of being a complete loser."

One of the ways Jeanette eventually tried to repair her wounded self-esteem was by setting out to prove to the world—but really to herself—that as a single parent she could provide for her son everything (and more) that a mother *and* father ordinarily give their children. When Jeanette was not busy attending or studying for her law class-es, she was doing committee work at Scott's school or baking chocolate chip cookies or fund-raising for the junior soccer league or throwing pitches to Scott in the backyard. As one would expect, in time Jeanette's efforts to become superpar-ent wore her down; and exhausted by the frenetic schedule she had imposed on herself, she came down with a number of stress-induced medical problems. For the first two years after her divorce, Jeanette swung back and forth between feeling like a wretched failure and defending against this painful feeling by trying to prove that, as a single mother, she could do it all.

Dr. Susan Rosewell-Jackson, a close friend who is a sin-gle parent and who also specializes in counseling single women, points out that for single mothers the message "You're not okay" comes not only from within but is contin-uously reinforced from without.

It comes from insensitive teachers who make you feel inadequate because you don't have the time to oversee your child's homework every night or go to school meetings in the middle of the day; it comes from the loan officer at the bank who turns you down because you're an unmarried woman and then, with a condescending smile, suggests that you get your mother to co-sign; it comes from the married women you meet at social gatherings who ask you, "And what does your husband do for a living?"; and, most painfully, it comes from your own children who tell you how much they miss having a "normal" family and who blame you for this deprivation.

If she is to overcome depression and lay claim to a vital life, the single mother must learn to challenge the destructive inner and outer messages that undermine her and find ways to affirm her own goodness and rightness. Perhaps, like Janice Edwards, whose story introduced this chapter, she can say, "I'm not going to listen to people who tell me single mothers are bad. . . . I'm not going to listen to these negative things." And perhaps she can surround herself with people who value and pay tribute to her. Jeanette, who is now cured of her severe depression and managing quite well in her single life, no longer needs weekly therapy sessions; but she still visits me about once a month because, as she says, "I just find it reassuring and affirming to hear from you again and again what I really know in my heart: that I'm doing fine, that my son is doing fine, and that there's nothing wrong with me for wanting to remain unmarried."

Certainly, it is important for single mothers to be aware of the difficulties that a son growing up without his father faces so that they can try to ameliorate them. But it is also important for them to recognize what is good and right about their families. Judith Wallerstein and Joan Berlin Kelly, whose longitudinal research on the effects of divorce is much respected, observe, for example, that "young boys separated by the divorce from a psychologically ill father and placed in the care of a well mother were sometimes able to make extraordinary progress."[12] What I have observed in counseling Jeanette over the years—and I am sure is true of many other divorced mothers—is that as a single woman she is a much better parent than she was as a married woman. No longer in an impossible marriage that drained her energies and dampened her goodwill, she is able to delight in the relationship with ten-year-old Scott. And he, in turn, is flourishing. Jeanette, who finds fulfillment in her paralegal work and through her friendships, does not depend on Scott to make her whole; but as she says, "I just get such a kick out of him; he is a terrific little guy." Without a doubt, Jeanette and Scott are a *real* and happy family.

I would like to end this chapter with a tribute to Baya, a single mother whom I know only slightly, but whose son, Sebastien, is a dear friend of my own son and, like Jonathan, attends an out-of-state college. During the winter break from their respective schools, Sebastien and Jonathan were back in Boulder and hanging out with each other a lot. One evening when I came home from work I found a note from Jonathan saying that he and Sebastien had gone to Mc-Nichol's Arena, which is about an hour's drive away on the interstate, to see a Denver Nuggets game. When I came upon the note, it had already begun to snow. Concerned for the boys' safety, I called the weather station and heard that we were in for a heavy snowfall. Although I have trained myself not to fret about my children nearly as much as I used to, I knew that I was in for a long night of worry and that I would find no peace of mind until Jonathan was home again, safe and sound. Indeed, I spent the evening trying (unsuccessfully) to do some reading and nervously checking in with the highway patrol for reports of the latest accidents. When, close to midnight, the boys had still not arrived, I decided to call Sebastien's house in the hope that they were there. Baya answered the phone somewhat groggily and told me that they had not come back. Picking up on my anxiety, she assured me that there was no reason to worry.

"But the roads are probably treacherous," I protested.

"No, they're snowpacked but not slick, and the visibility on the highway is okay too," she said confidently. "It will take the boys longer than usual to drive home from Denver, but they shouldn't run into major problems."

"How do you know all of this?" I asked incredulously.

And Baya explained that, just a little while before, rather than sit home worrying and feeling helpless, she had taken her car out and assessed the road conditions herself. I understood then that Baya, over years of parenting two active sons single-handedly, had become an expert at staying calm, cool, and collected in the face of small and big crises. I also understood better than ever before why Jonathan's friend, Sebastien, had turned out to be such a competent young man.

7

....

Single Mothers and Their Significant Others

I wonder why love is so often equated with joy when it is everything else as well.

—FLORIDA SCOTT-MAXWELL,
The Measure of My Days

Among the many seminars that I attended as a doctoral candidate in the 1970s, I remember with surprising clarity one on postdivorce adjustment. I recall that the presenter, an impressively cheerful graduate student, showed us a handmade chart that depicted the divorced person's stages of grief— denial, fear, anger, loneliness, letting go—as steppingstones climbing a steep mountain trail. After describing each of these stages, he displayed another chart, which was labeled "Destination: Freedom and Happiness." On it, in rainbow colors, he had illustrated the end of the trail: a mountaintop surrounded by an expansive, cloudless sky. With new-age optimism, the seminar leader insisted that having successfully mastered the stages of mourning for the lost marriage, the divorced person was free to create a new and better life and to search for new and better loves—to enter what, in the jargon of the 1970s, were called "experimental," "transitional," or "healing" relationships.

Moreover, he assured us that these sexual liaisons would not pose a problem for the children of the single parent as long as the parent was willing to talk openly about them. Accordingly, free-flowing communication between parent and child always led to good family adjustment; honesty was the all-purpose medicine that healed or, better still, prevented emotional pain. Implicit in his discussion was another message: Children are tougher, more resilient, and more adaptable than we think; we don't have to go out of our way to protect them from real life.

My counseling experiences over the past twenty years contradict the optimistic prophecies of the speaker. I have observed that the single mother's temporary love partnerships often create problems for her sons (and daughters). The wise single mother understands these difficulties and protects her children from them. In this chapter I present three mother-son stories that explore these problems and their possible solutions. I also present a fourth story that illustrates the positive relationship between a young boy, his mother, and the special man who becomes part of their lives.

I first saw Alicia four years ago when she was contemplating leaving her husband, a man who drank too much, could not hold down a steady job, and showed little interest in their eight-year-old son. At our first meeting, Alicia appeared old and worn beyond her thirty years. Her pretty features were hidden by a mask of anxiety, and her vitality was shrouded by her dull, depressed manner. During our year of therapy, Alicia gained the confidence to leave her ne'er-do-well spouse. She filed for divorce, and after the papers were signed, her former spouse all but disappeared from her life, visiting their son only occasionally. Alicia had been a working mother during her marriage; after the divorce, she took a second job to make ends meet. When Alicia terminated therapy, she and her little boy were "doing okay," although financial stress and unremitting hard work weighed her down.

When, three months ago, Alicia returned for a second round of therapy, I was surprised by her appearance. She looked years younger and vibrant. Never having had the inclination to adorn herself, Alicia now sported large, dangling turquoise earrings, which brought out the green-blue light of her eyes; and instead of the baggy sweat suits that she used to wear, she had on a black sweater that revealed her shapely figure.

I was not surprised when, with a flush of pride, Alicia told me that she was dating. At her second job as a waitress in a restaurant that catered to the business community, she had met several attractive men, more than one of whom had asked her out. For Alicia, who had seldom felt desirable, her romances were a great ego booster. Moreover, the new men in her life brought bouquets of fresh flowers and lightheartedness into what had come to be an all-work, no-play existence. With a hint of embarrassment, Alicia also confided that her ex-husband had never fulfilled her sexually; the men she was dating were practiced lovers and "turned her on," so that for the first time in her life, having sex was compelling.

What brought Alicia back to therapy was not her own depression, which had long since passed, but the serious problems that she was having with her twelve-year-old son. According to Alicia, Marc, who as a younger child had been tender and caring, was now mostly angry and demanding. Whenever Alicia brought one of her male friends to their home, Marc would be especially disagreeable. In fact, he was usually quite rude to his mother's dates, making a point not to return their greetings or deliberately cutting them off in conversation.

Alicia was well aware that Marc missed his father, whom he loved and idealized despite the man's character flaws. She also knew that she could not bring the missing father back into her son's life; at best, she could remind Marc of the happy moments that they had shared, and when the irresponsible father did make one of his infrequent contacts with the boy, she could cooperate with their plans. Although Alicia was often furious with Marc for his unpleasant manner—and, quite rightly, insisted that he act with civility—she also ached for him and recognized his great father loss. She urged the boy to see a counselor, but like many boys his age, he would have nothing to do with a "shrink." Moreover, when she tried to talk to him about his problems, he typically shut down.

Alicia asked me if, despite the boy's silence and his certain unwillingness to come to therapy sessions with her, I could nevertheless help her to understand him better and to make changes in their lives that would help him. I thought I could. For the next three months, we two women talked a great deal about the ways that Alicia's love affairs might be affecting Marc.

Alicia pointed out that the men she brought home usually made efforts to engage Marc. For example, she noted, "A fellow I'm dating now genuinely likes children. He tries to talk football to Marc; he offers to go to the playground with him and toss a ball around; he hints at fishing trips—all the things that I don't do with Marc. But Marc rejects these offers outright." Alicia also commented that this man is much more responsive to Marc than his own father, who never wanted to teach or play with him, and that she is surprised that Marc rejects the attentions of her male friend.

Listening to Alicia's description, I remembered and shared with her a story about my own son. As a youngster, Jonathan had a pet turtle, Dribble, that did little more than peek out of his shell from time to time and surreptitiously eat the shreds of lettuce that were placed in his bowl. As far as I could see, Dribble did not know Jonathan from Adam; and yet, Jonathan loved him dearly and tended to him with utmost devotion. One sad day, Dribble did not peek his head out of his shell to nibble his lettuce, and after poking and prodding him, we concluded that he was dead. Jonathan was devastated. A few weeks after we laid Dribble to rest in our backyard, I asked Jonathan if he wanted another pet turtle, and he said no. Having given his heart to Dribble, my little boy was determined not to give his affection to any other turtle in the world; he would remain true to Dribble.

Similarly, it seemed to me that Marc, out of loyalty to his father, would let no other man take his father's place—or even come close. Although, to Alicia and me, Marc's father appeared to care little about his son and did not deserve his devotion, Marc, nevertheless, remained bound to him.

There was another, even more compelling, explanation for Marc's rejection of Alicia's men friends: Having suffered partial abandonment by his father, Marc probably dared not form an attachment to other men, who could also leave him behind and break his heart again. Congenial as they seemed, the men Alicia brought into their lives gave no assurances that they would stay or would be committed to Marc. Quite rightly, young Marc may have been protecting himself against the trauma of repeated loss by refusing to become attached to them. In Jodie Foster's film *Little Man Tate*, we watch the wounding of a fatherless boy who forms an attachment to a friendly and charming young man, only to discover that this attachment, which means the world to the boy, is of little consequence to the young man; it is the boy's suddenly jaded expression and his slumped posture that tell us that the wounding is not superficial but deep and piercing.

Alicia noted that although Marc mostly seemed indifferent to her dates, at other times he was fiercely competitive with them. When, for example, one snowy Sunday morning, Alicia's male friend cheerfully offered to clean the walk but then could not get the snowplow started, Marc smirked and remarked to her, "Just look at him. He's a real jerk. *I* can always get the plow to start." If Marc had been able to put into words all that was in his heart, he might have said: Mommy, I want you to believe that I'm better and stronger and smarter than all the men who court you. I want you to love me most of all because this is my best assurance that you will never leave me for one of them. And, Mommy, I want you to remember that the only men who have a right to you are my father and me; one day, the three of us will be back together again, you'll see.

My friend and colleague Katharine Walker, a Jungian analyst and specialist in divorce counseling, maintains that the rivalry between the son and his mother's lovers may be a basic and primitive feeling common to all sons. She points out that it is powerfully recounted in Homer's *Odyssey.* "How arrogant you are—beyond all measure—you who would win my mother," Telemachus, the adolescent son of Penelope and the absent father, Odysseus, sharply tells the suitors who clamor after his mother. "Feast with pleasure for now. . . . But I shall then implore the gods, who live forever, asking Zeus to grant me my requital: all of you would then die unavenged within these halls."[1]

And when the wandering Odysseus does at last return home to his wife and his son, father and son set out together to slay every one of Penelope's suitors.

> Telemachus, dear son of bright Odysseus, strapped
> on his sharp sword, clasped his spear, and stood
> beside his father, armed with gleaming bronze.[2]
> . . . And terror took the suitors; through the hall
> they fled like cattle when the gadfly darts to sting
> the herd, in spring, when days grow long.[3]

In myth, Telemachus acts out what, in reality, the mortal son of a single mother may fantasize—at least some of the time: with his father as his ally, he annihilates his mother's suitors, whom he considers competitors and interlopers.

Just as the son may feel naturally rivalrous with the mother's lovers, the lovers may also feel rivalrous with the son. Carline, a therapist and single mother I interviewed for this chapter, remarked: "The competition for my attention between the men in my life and my son was always a problem for me and produced much tension. One would try to draw me away from the other, and I often felt torn between their clashing demands. It was as if each was insisting, 'Put me first.'"

The fact that there is competition between a boy and his mother's lovers does not mean that a positive relationship can never develop between them; it sometimes does. Carline noted that by putting her son first and thereby assuring him of his importance to her, she could sometimes lower the intensity of his competitive feelings for her lover and thus foster friendlier relations between the two. However, to assume that friendships between a mother's sons and her lovers are natural or easy to bring about would be naive.

Alicia claims that despite all his bluster, Marc is an insecure child. In the presence of her men friends, he acts superior; with her, he is often cocky and bossy; but when he thinks no one is looking, Marc sucks his thumb. Children thrive when their environments are stable and predictable and when their bonds are meaningful and enduring, but they are made insecure by too much change and transience. It is likely that Alicia's having multiple partners is one reason for Marc's insecurity.

In *Sex and the Single Parent*, psychotherapist Mary Mattis presents a telling anecdote. A man she was interviewing for her book discussed the series of "uncles" he had known when he was a child. He explained that he used to fantasize that he, like they, would vanish some morning and that he had worried about where he would go when he disappeared from his own home. Underlying this fantasy is the notion that if mother is casual about the men who share her bed, she may be casual about all other intimate relationships—even the sacred mother-child relationship—and that love bonds, rather than being permanent and precious, are transient and replaceable.

In addition to Marc's insecurity regarding her transient relationships, it is likely that Alicia's open sexuality is also very troublesome for him. Indeed, he has angrily accused her of keeping him awake "because you and the guys you sleep with make so much noise at night."

Typically, children and adolescents are *not* curious about their parents' sex lives. They shield themselves from the awareness that mothers and fathers are sensual and sexual creatures because this awareness stimulates forbidden fantasies; it threatens to sexualize their own feelings toward their parents, and such sexualized feelings always generate guilt and anxiety. Not surprisingly, although they may be sophisticated enough to know better, children and teenagers from intact families nevertheless half-believe that the number of times mom and dad had sex with each other correlates with the number of children in the family; and they are comforted that their parents do not act amorously in front of them. Although they may be delighted to see mom and dad give each other an affectionate hug every once in a while or go out on a romantic date occasionally, they would rather not see them in a passionate embrace. But because new love partners are often turned on when they are together, children of single parents who date are forced to recognize their parents' sexuality in a way that children of married parents, whose sexuality is usually contained and tamed, are not.

In the previous chapter, I included a lengthy quote from Allen, a fifty-one-year-old man, who, drawing from his own boyhood experience as the son of a single parent, was able to describe the rage he had felt toward his mother's many lovers and his sense of personal powerlessness from being unable to protect her against their advances. Allen also told me how painful it was for him to live in a home that seemed to be always sexually charged. With his bedroom separated from his mother's by paper-thin walls, he was exposed to the sounds of his mother's sex acts night after night; and even when his mother was not engaged in sexual activity, his mind would spin out of control with sexual images of her. Continually stimulated sexually, he would brace himself against the forbidden sensations of arousal.

The consensus among child psychologists and family therapists is that children are distressed when their parents flit from partner to partner and are indiscreet about their sexual activities; open talks about love and sex are not enough to soothe this distress; good communication is not the salve that quells all emotional pain.

Perhaps as a reaction to our country's Puritan ethic, Americans tend to become especially incensed when we are asked to limit our sexual expression, which we may see as one of our inalienable rights; yet the need to contain sexual impulses is not new or unique to our society. Every culture sets limits around sexual expression in order to assure the well-being of children and of the community as a whole.

"I am usually not comfortable telling the parents of my young clients to curb their sexual activities. When I do this, I rather feel like the Pope or the censorial parent," Katharine Walker explains. "And so, instead of lecturing at them, I sometimes make my point indirectly by telling them the following Native American story, which I heard as a girl growing up on an Indian reservation in New Mexico."

In this story, Trickster, a spirit with mostly human feelings, has a great deal of trouble controlling its genitals. The genitals run around the earth impregnating maidens and causing mayhem and furor. In order for it to keep its genitals under control, Trickster devises a strong leather pouch, puts its genitals inside, and ties the pouch to its waist. In spite of this effort, from time to time, the genitals do slither out of the pouch and run around the countryside impregnating maidens and causing mayhem and furor.

When this happens, poor Trickster, in shame and embarrassment, must chase after them and tuck them safely inside the pouch again where they will do no harm.

After having heard this story from Katharine, I, in turn, retold it to Alicia, who did not flinch at its meaning. Alicia feels that having an active social and sex life is important for her now. She is not ready to settle in with one man and believes that her multiple love relationships have enhanced her self-esteem and have helped her become a happier person and a more relaxed mother. However, Alicia has come to understand that in the best interests of her twelve-year-old son, she must find a better balance between serving her needs and his. Because she realizes that Marc's exposure to her sexual relationships is disturbing him, she has decided not to bring lovers to her home any longer but to go to their place instead. And although she is not willing to give up dating, she is ready to limit it somewhat so that Marc does not feel deserted by her. She also has come to believe that pushing Marc into relationships with her men friends is a bad idea—that she can help him find more appropriate role models among his uncles and his grandfather, men who will always be part of his family.

One might say that at this time Alicia is devising her own leather pouch—a pouch that is not too restraining but that is nevertheless sturdy enough to protect her young son from mayhem and furor.

Dr. Susan Rosewell-Jackson decided, after her divorce, not to date actively while her three children were minors and in her custody; this choice, which sharply contrasted with Alicia's, presented its own difficulties. Recently, I had a two-hour lunch with Susan and her thirty-year-old son, Jeff, so that we might talk about their postdivorce experiences and put them into perspective.

Jeff was fourteen when his father moved out; according to him, the loss left him feeling "empty" and the emptiness made him "surly and impatient with everyone and everything for years." Reflecting on the past, Jeff does not believe that he could have tolerated the presence of his mother's love interests then.

After the divorce, we had to make one adjustment after another. We moved to a new neighborhood. We had to get used to a lower standard of living. My mom went back to work and to graduate school, which meant another loss for my sisters and me. Also, I took part-time jobs after school to help out, which resulted in my being cut off from my school friends. I was reeling from all these changes. I just think that if, in addition, I had been asked to make relationships with my mom's boyfriends, I would have completely lost it.

Jeff also pointed out that the parents' divorce can be a source of shame for a child. Just as a divorced woman often feels flawed as a result of failing to stay married, a child of divorce may imagine that he or she is inferior to peers who come from intact families. The high incidence of divorce these days does not necessarily change the child's perception that it is a stigma. For Jeff the shame he felt coming from a divorced family was worst during his adolescence, when he was especially sensitive to the judgments of his peers.

> It was bad enough to explain to my friends and their parents that I came from a divorced family—which to me meant an abnormal family—and that my father lived in another state. I don't think I could have also handled explaining to them that the guy hanging around my mother was her new boyfriend. I probably would have tried to hide this from them rather than risk their snide remarks or raised eyebrows.

Susan was keenly aware of Jeff's distress as a result of the family's break-up and, like him, believed that bringing a serious relationship into their lives would be a mistake. In the years just after the divorce, her main objective was to stabilize her family and to create a home for her children that felt safe, comfortable, and inviolate. Susan's readiness to sacrifice her own adult pleasures for the welfare of her children brings to mind the wise words of Mother Teresa: "A living love hurts. . . . If you really love another properly, there must be sacrifice."

Nevertheless, sacrificing one's personal pleasures poses dangers of its own. The mother who forfeits the joys and passions of adult love and sex may look to her son for compensatory companionship; she may expect him to meet her emotional needs and fill up her deep well of loneliness. When he does not, as is inevitable, she may resent him and become hostile.

Moreover, as was discussed in earlier chapters, the burden for the boy who becomes too central in his mother's life is heavy indeed. When a son perceives his mother as lonely and needy, he may feel a responsibility to take care of her. Necessary separation from her may then feel like a terrible abandonment or betrayal of her. A fifty-year-old bachelor once told me, "I suppose I could never make the necessary break away from my mother because I felt so sorry for her. I was convinced that my calling was to protect her forever." When the son is mother's "little man," he may assume too much power; he may see himself as her equal partner, not as her child, and become somewhat of a household tyrant, thinking nothing of ordering her about.

Fortunately, Susan was well aware of the destructive potential of maternal self-sacrifice, and this awareness enabled her to avoid the pitfalls that other women in her situation often fall into. During lunch she told me and Jeff,

> Along with my conscious decision not to bring new men into our family, I also consciously decided to build a full and rich life for myself that went beyond my commitment to the children. My work and graduate studies engaged me; I found deep pleasure in my solitude; and I cultivated a loving friendship with you, Evi. I also believed that at some future time, when the children were grown and out on their own, I would have the chance to develop a meaningful relationship with a special man, and this proved to be true. I never sacrificed my life; I just sacrificed the immediate gratifications that I thought might create additional problems for my children.

Jeff listened intently to his mother as she spoke and then softly said, "Thank you, Mom." He also went on to say that during the years immediately after his parents' divorce he had been self-absorbed, aware only of his own problems, as young people tend to be. Only now, as a grown man, could he appreciate his mother's earlier struggles and efforts.

We have been exploring the problems that can arise when single mothers bring male lovers into their sons' lives. Let us now examine some of the dynamics between the lesbian mother and her son. Jeff described how embarrassing it would have been for him to explain to his friends that the man hanging out with his mother was her new boyfriend. It is not hard for us to imagine the conflict for the boy who is called on to explain to his friends that the woman hanging out with his mother is her new girlfriend. After all, ours is not a society that looks upon its homosexual members with kind and accepting eyes. As John Balzar, who writes for the *Los Angeles Times*, asks, "How many generations of contemporary Americans, particularly American boys, entered grade school and learned homophobia casually along with their ABCs, long before discovering anything of the fluttering of the birds and the bees?" And he reports that although a majority of Americans have come to believe that homosexual acts should be legal, about 80 percent of Americans nevertheless believe that homosexuality is wrong.[4]

"My fifteen-year-old son, Jason, has never brought a friend home," Bernadette shared during an interview. "He is ashamed that he is the child of a lesbian mother. Even though Jason is attracted to girls, he believes that *he* will be taunted—called a queer or a faggot or, most insulting of all, a dyke—if his classmates find this out about *me*. Just as I was once forced into the closet because I am a lesbian, my son now hides in the closet because he is identified with me."

I asked Bernadette if Jason might not also be afraid that by bringing his friends to his home, where they would likely meet her love partner or, in some other way, figure out that she was a lesbian, he would expose her to their derisions. Lowering her eyes, Bernadette whispered, "Yes, I am sure Jason tries to protect me by keeping my sexual orientation a secret. He doesn't want people to laugh at me or see me as a degenerate. It hurts to know that he carries this burden."

Just as Jason tries to protect his mother by guarding the secret of her homosexuality, Bernadette used to try to protect him by keeping her homosexual identity from him.

> I did not want him to suffer humiliations because of me—to be told by his peers or their parents that he comes from an unacceptable home. I was also horribly afraid that the court would deem me an unfit mother and remove my little boy from my custody, which I was sure would do him irreparable harm. And so, for several years after my divorce, I kept my sexual orientation a secret. I had a few clandestine affairs with women, whom I met at bars, but I presented myself to the world as a conventional, hardworking single mother. Yet, I knew that leading a false life was also hurting my son, that my secretiveness was burdening his life with anxiety and confusion, that he had a right to know who his mother really was.

Just before Jason entered public school, Bernadette did tell him that she was a lesbian—and, to her great relief, he was not upset by her disclosure. No doubt, never having been taught that homosexuality was "wrong" or "unnatural" —that teaching was, however, to come later—he had no reason not to accept his mother as she was. Soon after her disclosure, Bernadette introduced Jason to Diana, the woman with whom she was forming a serious relationship. Perhaps because he did not see his mother's female friend as someone who could replace his father and perhaps because Diana was warm and caring, Jason became attached to her. The two would draw pictures and play ball; and when Jason did not feel free to share his innermost thoughts with his mother, he would talk to Diana. Away from society's disapproving eyes, in their protected and hidden nest, Jason was relaxed with the two women who cared for and loved him.

Then, quite suddenly, Diana left Bernadette . . . and Jason. Despite her lover's abrupt leave-taking, Bernadette was not particularly bitter; the full relationship with Diana had enriched her, and she was thankful for the time that they had together. Moreover, Bernadette had not really expected that the relationship with Diana would go on forever. As she told me, "The prejudices against homosexual people and society's lack of recognition for our love relationships make it hard for us to stay together." For Jason, however, letting Diana into his life, only to have her disappear from it, left him forlorn; unlike his mother, the little boy could not look at this loss philosophically.

Bernadette has been with her present partner for two years. Like Diana, Helen is warm and caring. She would like to engage Jason, but he keeps his distance from her. Doubtless, Jason's earlier losses—the loss of his father after his parents divorced, the loss of Diana—have taught him to be wary of people who try to get close to him.

Of course, there are several other plausible explanations for his coolness: Jason is a teenager now and, in all likelihood, wants to separate from his mother's world rather than become a part of it. Coming into his own sexuality, Jason may also feel uncomfortable being close with Helen, who is an attractive woman. And having been around female caregivers for most of his early years, Jason may now be trying to get away from them; indeed, Bernadette notices that he chooses to spend more time in his father's home than he used to. In addition, Jason the teenager has seemingly learned what Jason the child had not: the popular idea that there is something wrong with women who love other women.

Bernadette encounters some of the same difficulties heterosexual single mothers face in new relationships. For example, she often feels torn between her partner's and her son's wishes for her loyalty; and she is saddened by the fact that her partner and her son are not closer. However, as a lesbian, Bernadette also confronts particular difficulties. Because she knows that her son may be a target of hostility if his friends find out about her homosexuality, Bernadette wavers between helping Jason hide her identity and trying to be open about and proud of it. She also worries that Jason may not feel positive about being a male. "I am concerned that Jason will come to experience his sex as less than wonderful because I, his mother, do not find men sexually attractive—because I did not find his own father, the man Jason takes after, attractive," she told me.

In addition to her specific, legitimate concerns, Bernadette also reveals an irrational lack of confidence in her goodness as a mother. She confided, "I am tormented by an inner voice that screams, 'There's no way that *you* can be a good mother; *you're* not a normal woman.' " Every mother looks for affirmations from others that she is doing an adequate job as a parent. I suspect, however, that Bernadette gets far less affirmation than she deserves. Opinion polls show that Americans tend to be especially intolerant of homosexual parents, whom they see as warping their children's moral and sexual development. The voice that screams at Bernadette and tears her down is the collective voice of neighbors, family members, acquaintances, and strangers whose angry judgments she anticipates.

After my interview with Bernadette, I turned to academic books and journals and found that Jason's experiences were typical for sons of lesbian mothers. Jason's unhesitant acceptance of Diana reflected the positive feelings that boys tend to have for their mothers' female lovers; and his distress after Diana's departure was not different from the anxiety that clinicians frequently observed in young children who had lost the care of the mother's female partner. (It is interesting that daughters tend not to have as positive relationships with their mothers' female lovers as do sons.)[5] As Jason grew older, his fears of being harassed and ostracized by his peers should they discover the truth about his mother and his consequent secretiveness about her sexual arrangement matched the reactions common among older children and adolescents with lesbian mothers.[6]

As I reviewed the research literature, I experienced a certain sadness. It occurred to me that in every community, every neighborhood, every school, young people like Jason are fearfully guarding the secret of their parents' homosexuality from their peers. Isolated by their silence, they cannot know that they are not alone but that many other children share their experiences; afraid of breaking their silences, they cannot join with these children to explore their complicated feelings and to come to accept themselves and their parents.

For many single mothers, the hoped-for outcome of dating is marriage, or in the case of lesbian mothers, an enduring and committed relationship. Researchers and clinicians tend to agree that when the single mother brings a loving, mature, here-to-stay partner into her life, both she and her son can reap enormous psychological benefits.

In an impressive longitudinal study and six-year follow-up of 180 divorced families, researcher E. Mavis Hetherington reported positive outcomes for stepfather-stepson relationships. Although stepfathers initially tend to describe stepsons as having behavior problems, over time they see them as becoming less difficult. Stepfathers are generally warmer and more involved with stepsons than with stepdaughters, and in enduring remarriages, stepsons frequently report being close to their stepfathers, enjoying their company, and seeking their advice and support.[7] (As we will see in Chapter 8, stepmothers unfortunately do not normally experience the kind of companionable relationships with stepsons that stepfathers do.) In my practice, I have observed and heard accounts of several positive stepfather-stepson relationships. However, the story that is most vivid for me and with which I will conclude this chapter comes from my personal experience.

During graduate school, I had a special friend, Nicholas, with whom I spent endless hours studying and discussing. Nicholas was a frequent visitor to our home and enjoyed our family life; although he had never married and was childless, he was perfectly at ease with our two young children and they with him. About two years into our friendship, Nicholas met a young woman who interested him in ways that his previous girlfriends had not, but because Elaine had a young son, Nicholas was hesitant about pursuing her. Entering into a relationship with Elaine, he was well aware, also meant entering into a relationship with her four-year-old boy.

Despite his initial uneasiness, Nicholas began seeing Elaine, and as his attachment to her deepened so did the one to her son, who had never known his biological father. Nicholas, a skilled woodsman, taught little Greg how to use a compass, how to tie knots, how to pitch a tent, and how to imitate the calls of wild animals. Not surprisingly, Greg, who owed no allegiances to a biological father and who seemingly had no difficulty sharing his mother's love with Nicholas, came to adore Nicholas. But Nicholas was not only Greg's good-time companion; he also set limits for the little boy, who could get out of control. Rather than shield her son from Nicholas's acts of discipline, Elaine supported them. It is not always a simple matter for a single mother who has been used to being fully in charge of her child to allow someone else to step in as disciplinarian, but Elaine seemed glad to let Nicholas share in Greg's upbringing. And because Greg was very young, he accepted Nicholas's authority without question; an older boy probably would have vehemently resisted it.

It was not long before the three looked very much like a traditional family. Far from resenting the fact that his love partner had a son who required their time and attentions, Nicholas seemed to thrive in his role as paterfamilias; and he took in stride the hassles and annoyances that are part and parcel of family living. Not surprisingly, Nicholas and Elaine decided to get married, and when they did, Greg was their proud ring bearer.

Over the years, Nicholas and I drifted apart. However, because we live in the same town, I run into Nicholas, Elaine, and Greg (who is now a high school senior) from time to time. And when I do, I am struck by the fact that Greg, who is blond and lanky, has somehow come to resemble Nicholas, who is dark and burly. The boy and the man who has cared for him all these years obviously belong together.

....

I began this chapter with my recollections of a 1970s seminar on postdivorce adjustment. If I could turn back the clock and encounter the cheerful man who led that seminar, I would suggest to him that he alter his colorful charts. My recommendation would be that alongside his picture of stepping-stones leading to the mountaintop, he sketch in a small wooden sign that reads, "Please Watch Out for Vulnerable Children."

8

....

Stepmothers

Tomorrow morning we will take the children out quite early into the thickest part of the forest. We will light a fire and give each of them a piece of bread. Then we will go to our work and leave them alone. They won't be able to find their way back, and so we shall be rid of them.

—The stepmother
in the Brothers Grimm's "Hansel and Gretel"

In this house I have nothing to keep me. I have no roots here. The children are not mine. They don't love me. They have never loved me. . . . I haven't even a key to give up or any instructions to leave behind. I have been outside—outside everything. From the first day I came here.

—The stepmother
in Henrik Ibsen's *Lady from the Sea*

Most little girls dream of becoming mothers. But has any little girl ever dreamed of becoming a stepmother? The folktales of virtually every culture portray the stepmother as a wicked creature, certainly not one to be emulated. In our Western tradition, she is the conniving wife who persuades Hansel and Gretel's father to abandon the children in a dark forest;

she is also the envious queen who, threatened by Snow White's youthful beauty, arranges for her murder; and she is the child-abuser who pits her own spoiled children against poor, neglected Cinderella. And yet, despite the fact that they have not planned for this outcome, millions of little girls do grow up to become stepmothers. And rather than being wicked, most of them are kind-hearted women who do their best to care for their husbands' children.

The role of stepmother, however, is not an easy one to assume. Indeed, TV sitcoms, such as *The Brady Bunch*, which portray the stepfamily as a warm and fun-loving unit where problems can be neatly solved in half-hour segments, have little to do with reality. To my mind, of all the family roles, stepmothering is the one fraught with the most difficulties and the fewest immediate rewards. This perception is confirmed by several research studies, which indicate that stepmothers experience a great deal more stress, anxiety, depression, and anger regarding family life than mothers in other family arrangements.[1] There is some evidence that stepmothers and stepsons get along better than stepmothers and stepdaughters.[2] But there is contrary evidence that stepmothers feel more confident in their role with stepdaughters than they do in their role with stepsons.[3] Researchers John Santrock and Karen Sitterle speculate, "One 'does best' when one 'knows best' and there may be a greater familiarity with the same sex child."[4]

One of my clients describes stepmothering her young stepson as "alternating between feelings of being used, being discounted, being intruded upon, and being unsure of myself." Another client says, "Being a stepmother feels like I'm pulling out my own teeth: self-inflicted and painful." Still another remarks, "As a stepmother, I can't be my natural, spontaneous self. I've become so self-conscious—always worried that I'm slighting my husband's children or not measuring up to his expectations."

In my role as counselor, I have helped clients who are stepmothers most by encouraging them to share their complicated feelings. Talking about the distress that accompanies stepmothering seems to relieve some of it. Often, it also leads to deeper self-understanding and self-compassion, which, in turn, lead to a readiness to understand and feel compassion for the other members in the blended family. In this chapter, I will follow the steps that my clients and I take during the course of therapy. We will first take a long and detailed look at the stepmother-stepchild relationship from the woman's perspective; then we will look at this relationship through the eyes of the stepson, of the father/husband, and, finally, of the stepson's mother.

I have never counseled a stepmother who did not share with me her expectation that she should have loving and motherly feelings for her stepchild. Usually, her husband also expects this of her, especially when his children are young or when their own mother is not available for them. "Surely," he reasons, "this warm woman who loves me so generously will find it a simple matter to love my child as well." And society in general seems to reinforce the notion that loving children—all children—is what normal, good women naturally do.

Hence, when a woman steps into the role of stepmother, she almost always brings to it an assignment that she may not be able to fulfill. Contrary to conventional wisdom, most of us do not unconditionally love a child who is not our own. Indeed, there is a wise old Russian adage that tells us that a mother, who would not give up her child for all the money in the world, would be hard pressed to find anyone willing to take the child forever, free of charge! I remember that when as a young mother I would take care of my friends' toddlers, I was always put off at the thought of changing their dirty diapers; diapering my own babies, however, did not repulse me in the slightest.

Despite the stepmother's intentions to feel only love for her husband's child, especially if this child lost its natural mother through death or abandonment, she may discover that what she mostly feels is antagonism; at times she may wish that her new husband did not come to her encumbered by a child, that this child was not part of their life, that the "intruder" would just magically disappear. One of my clients confided that there was an "uncomfortable fit" between her stepchildren and herself and that she could not help being tense around them. "I get the same visceral feeling around them that I used to get being around my ex-husband's mother, who, though she was a nice lady, got on my nerves; when I'm with the stepkids, my stomach muscles tighten and I have an urge to bite my nails." Another client confided that her stepson's behavior problems made him so unpleasant to be with that she cherished the times he spent away from home. "I know that he's developed problems because his mother's long illness and consequent death traumatized him, but knowing this doesn't seem to make me want to be around him."

Instead of accepting her less-than-loving feelings as fairly normal ones, which may change for the better in the future (among the family therapists I know there is a shared sense that step relationships do improve with time), the stepmother is often appalled by her lack of motherly love; and she is often shocked by the anger that she discovers in its place. "What is wrong with me that I do not have a warm place in my heart for this innocent child?" she asks herself. "What is wrong with you that you do not love my lovable child?" her husband echoes. "What is wrong with me that I feel so angry around him?" she asks herself. "What is wrong with you that you jump all over my son?" her husband echoes. And in response to these accusing questions, the stepmother may begin to doubt her own goodness: "Am I a bad person? Am I becoming like the wicked stepmothers in all those fairy tales?"

For some women, less-than-loving feelings for their stepchildren are so intolerable that they pretend the opposite. For example, a stepmother may become solicitous to her stepchild in a desperate attempt to convince herself, the child, and her husband that she is a nurturing person. Or she may tell the child again and again, "I love you. You know how much I love you," as if these words will make an untruth come true. Or she may project her unacceptable unloving feelings onto the child: "Clearly, my stepson dislikes me. I assure you that it is never, *never* the other way around!" Or she may give up precious and deserved time with her husband so as not to disturb the stepchild. Or she may indulge her stepchild more than her own child. As the following vignette illustrates, she may even displace her negative feelings for her stepchild onto her own child.

Beverly, a sleek professional woman in her middle forties, initiated therapy because she had recurring fantasies of abandoning her own child. After we had spent a few sessions talking about her family life, it became clear to both of us that Beverly's real anger was toward her stepson, not her daughter. The abandonment fantasies were unconscious expressions of her hostility, which she had dared not admit to herself or to her husband. We came to understand that it was psychologically safer for Beverly to fantasize abandoning her daughter, whom she knew she would never leave, than to fantasize abandoning her deeply disturbed stepson, whom she frequently wished would go away. And for good reasons! Not only did he create one crisis after another for the family, but he also demanded so much of his father's attention that Beverly felt she had lost her new husband to the boy. (One could also speculate that Beverly's persistent fantasies were a reversal of her reality, in which she was the one threatened with abandonment.)

Initially, the realization that she harbored hostile feelings for her stepson troubled Beverly. "So, I guess I am like Hansel and Gretel's cruel stepmother," she said bitterly. "Perhaps, in the sense that you are angry at your stepson for burdening the family with his great needs and jealous that he is so central to your husband," I answered; "but the big difference between you and the fairy-tale stepmother is that you will not give up on him without a real battle, and that she gave up on hers without a pang of conscience." Beverly knew this to be true about herself and was relieved. Her husband's son had been abandoned by his natural mother when he was a toddler, and she was determined to do everything in her power not to be the second female caregiver to reject him.

When a stepmother accepts the fact that she is not obliged to love her stepchild, which Beverly was eventually able to accept, she often asks herself, What *is* my obligation to this child? In their book *Living in Step*, Ruth Roosevelt and Jeanette Lofas, both stepmothers, supply what I think is the best answer to this question: "The extent of [the stepmother's] moral imperative is to treat a child kindly as a human being."[5] I should like to add that one can have unkind thoughts about a person but decide not to act these out; feeling and doing are separate human functions.

To be sure, some stepmothers genuinely come to love their stepchildren and their stepchildren come to love them. Bonding is most likely when the children are very young and eager for intimate relationships with adults. Young children are also most likely to accept the stepmother when their own mothers are deceased—when loving and being loved by the second mother is not perceived as a betrayal of the first mother. And, of course, it follows that when the stepmother feels accepted, she will be more accepting. The love between stepmother and stepchild is least likely to flourish when the child shuttles back and forth from his stepmother's home to his mother's home, where he feels the greater allegiance.

Julie, who is in therapy with me, is a soft-spoken woman who radiates kindness and gentleness. Several years ago, having decided not to have children of her own, Julie let herself fall in love with her new husband's two-year-old son, and the little boy was, in turn, affectionate and sweet with her. But as she explained,

> For personal reasons, his mother took Sammy to live out of state when he was four. My husband and I were very upset when this happened. His legal efforts to block this move failed. Before we had been with Sammy a couple of times a week. Now he visits with us only during vacation times, and then he is on his way again, back to his real mother, his real home. I still have the warmest feelings for Sammy. But it would be too painful for me to con-

tinue loving him as fervently as I once did, because
I am continually faced with losing him.

I do not think Julie's reaction is unusual or unhealthy. When
the stepmother knows that, in a couple of days or a week or
a month's time, she will have to return to the "rightful owner"
the little boy or girl with whom she is bonding, she may
protectively hold herself back from becoming too close to
the child.

But even when a stepmother and stepchild have regular
and frequent contacts, a stepmother may become painfully
aware of the limits inherent in their relationship. Ruth Roosevelt and Jeanette Lofas write that the stepchild does not
allow the stepmother to cross over into what they call "the
holy land of mother love" and that if the stepmother gives
too much, "it will be fired back at her, bent and distorted."[6]
Recognizing and respecting the inherent limits of the stepmother-stepchild relationship when the natural mother is in
the picture, the wise and self-protective stepmother holds
herself back; she allows herself to love but not too much;
she allows herself to be attentive to the child but not to make
the child the center of her world. Especially for women who
do not have children of their own, this self-imposed restraint
may bring on feelings of sadness, frustration, and loss; the
gushing maternal feelings have no outlet.

In our fairy tales, the stepmother is cast as the villain; in
real life, however, she is often the one who is neglected and
discounted. During our sessions, Julie often talks about the
hurt of being the "nonmember" of Sammy's family. Although,
for the past six years, Julie has been Sammy's primary caregiver during his biannual visits, her role is hardly recognized.

When Sammy arrived in Colorado for his winter va-
cation, he brought with him, as he always does on
his visits, a long, computer-typed list of instructions
from his mother addressed to his father. Addressed
only to his father, as if I do not exist for her or for
her son.

When Sammy fell on a rusty nail and I took him to the emergency room at the local hospital for a tetanus shot, I was told that we needed his legal guardian's signature; my signature as the step-mother, the nurse tried to tell me tactfully, was not acceptable. When I tell my mother about Sammy—or at least try to—she gets bored and shifts the topic of conversation to anecdotes about her biological grandchildren. When my husband and I talked to Sammy's skiing instructor about his progress, once she discovered that I am the stepmother, not the real mother, she directed her conversation to my husband and didn't even look at me.

But worst of all, Sammy himself seems to discount me these days. It's always "My Mom says . . . my Dad says . . ." It's never, never "Julie says . . ."

Like Julie, many stepmothers are deprived of an honored position in their stepchildren's lives. The feelings of ineffectuality that come from not having a sanctioned role and the concomitant longing to be a "real" mother are poignantly told in Ruth Roosevelt's poem:

I am, and I am not.
I must be, and I may not be.
I have a job to do,
But I must not do it too well.

I am that sound of one hand clapping.
I play tennis without a ball and golf without a club.
In this game, they've changed all the rules.
And they never admit I'm playing.

Can I look at the flowers and never pick one?
Can I listen to the birds and never name one?
Can I raise all his children,
And never have his baby?

Don't tell me to draw the lines
And never cross beyond
To anger, and expectation, and love.
Hell, who do you take me for?[7]

In an intact family, husbands and wives normally give one another feedback about matters of childrearing, and this new information helps them become better parents. In a step-family, the natural parent may not accept the stepparent's advice or criticism. Consequently, the stepparent feels further diminished. Julie confides how frustrating it is to keep her ideas about what might be best for Sammy to herself. She sighs in resignation as she explains that her husband, who is sensitive to her in most ways, dismisses her comments when it comes to his son, especially when they suggest his short-comings as a parent. One mother for his son is all he can seem to take, and that mother is not Julie but his ex-wife. A stepmother I interviewed reflected Julie's perceptions:

> Perhaps for the very reason that I am an outsider in the family, I can observe interactions between my husband and his son with a certain objectivity. I am keenly aware how he ignores the boy's subtle pleas for attention and praise. But when I try to point things out to my husband, he acts very defensively. Because he's not a confrontational sort of guy, he doesn't put this to me in so many words, but I'm sure he has a mind to say, "Don't tell *me* how to raise *my* son. *You* have no expertise in this department; *you're not his mother!*"

Being treated by everyone as the unreal parent—the im-poster mother, the irrelevant one—erodes the stepmother's self-esteem until there is less and less of it. When this happens, her tendency may be to try harder and still harder, to do more and still more for the family, in the hope that these efforts will lead to being valued. What they often lead to, however, is emotional exhaustion rather than validation.

Dr. Katalin Morrison and Airdrie Thompson-Guppy, researchers who practice in Canada, have named the distress that is common to stepmothers the "Cinderella's Stepmother Syndrome." In an article in the *Canadian Journal of Psychiatry*, they describe the symptoms associated with this syndrome:

1. The symptoms fluctuate, depending on the interaction with the stepchildren. Anticipation of the interaction as well as the reaction to the interaction can have significant influence on the symptoms.
2. Several of the following symptoms are present:
   a. Preoccupation with position in family.
   b. Identity confusion regarding the stepmother role.
   c. Feelings of anxiety, which at times may lead to loss of sleep, appetite disturbance and tension symptoms.
   d. Feelings of rejection in the stepfamily situation.
   e. Feelings of ineffectiveness, incompetence, and failure regarding the fulfillment of the maternal function with the stepchildren.
   f. Guilt and hostility toward the stepchildren when the stepmother cannot help them and cannot feel accepted.
   g. Inability to resolve problems regarding the stepmother role with the father of the children, thus creating tension, hostility and fear of rejection in the marital relationship.
   h. Loss of self-esteem.
   i. Overcompensation as a method of dealing with these problems, leading to exhaustion.[8]

"The Cinderella myth of the wicked stepmother should be laid to rest once and for all," the two researchers say. "The problems of modern stepmothers should be seen for what they are: reactions to an inherently difficult and complex situation exacerbated by society's perception of the role of women in general and of stepmothers in particular."[9] It has been my experience that when stepmothers no longer attribute their problems as stepmothers to defects in themselves, they breathe a deep sigh of relief. The family problems may still exist, but the knowledge that they belong to the situation rather than to the stepmother brings comfort. When a woman no longer feels that she is to blame for the discontents in the family and that everything she does will come out wrong, she is much more likely to initiate changes in the family system.

I had the pleasure of hearing about such a positive development from a client I saw recently. Ever since she married her second husband, the custodial parent of a teenage boy, Bee had felt that she was the cause of the boy's unhappiness. Indeed, Charlie was not shy to tell her that life for him was much better before she had come on the scene to disrupt the father-and-son household. Not wanting to make life still worse for the aggrieved boy, Bee had ignored his derogatory remarks about her and had tried to act in a conciliatory manner. One day, however, when Charlie put her down as usual, she was able to say to him without faltering, "I'm sorry that you're not happy about my marrying your father, but from now on, I expect that you will nevertheless treat me with tact and common decency. I want you to know that I have feelings too and that you have no right to hurt them at will." The boy was apparently shocked at her forthrightness but seemed to take what she said seriously. As Bee told me, "Charlie looked contrite. For the first time since I've known him, he said that he was sorry."

Though every person's history is unique, we can say for certain that every boy who becomes a stepchild has suffered a trauma. He has lost the security and sense of wellness that come from being loved and nurtured by one's own parents in one's own home for all the years of one's dependency. Even when Mommy or Daddy has glaring faults, nothing can replace—nothing can be as good as—having Mommydaddy, Daddymommy close by.

When there has been a divorce, the new stepmother is a reminder to the boy of his losses: in his imagination, she is the one who has come between the severed parents and who ensures that they will not be pieced together; she is proof that the fantasy of a reunited nuclear family is no more than that—a fantasy. I remember the sad anecdote that a friend once shared with me. "I am really very happy to meet you," she warmly told the eleven-year-old boy who had just become her stepson. "Well, I sure as hell am not happy to meet you," he shot back. Another friend confided that during her wedding ceremony her nine-year-old stepson ran away. "I am probably the only bride in history to have stood on the receiving line all alone; instead of being at my side, my groom was running all over town looking for his angry, runaway son." These boys' responses are to be expected; as the preponderance of research in the field of stepfamilies suggests, children do not usually take kindly to their stepmothers.[10]

There are several explanations for a boy's negative attitudes toward his stepmother. As the vignette about Bee and Charlie illustrates, a boy may resent the new woman who comes between him and his father and threatens to replace him as father's primary love. If the father does not spend much one-on-one time with the son, the son may become overprotective of the little time that they do have together and resentful of the new wife who cuts into it.

Another compelling explanation is that the stepmother threatens the boy's attachment to his natural mother. Boys, we will do well to remember, are extraordinarily devoted to their mothers. Like young knights in shining armor, they will defend their "lady fair" against anyone who threatens to usurp her esteemed position. Simply by virtue of the fact that the stepmother is a parental presence, the stepson may perceive her as the potential replacement for his mother, which provokes his hostility or withdrawal. Of course, if the stepmother actively competes with the boy's natural mother for his affections or approval, he is even more likely to reject her.

Most stepmothers know that it is a mistake to disparage the stepson's mother in front of him, but in some cases the temptation to do so is great. Beverly, the client I described earlier, often told me how hard it was to go along with her stepson's portrayal of his mother as good and loving, when, in reality, she had neglected him as an infant and ultimately abandoned him altogether at the time that she had taken up with a new boyfriend: "I am left to take care of a very troubled boy because his biological mother failed him so miserably. What I hear from him, however, is that he loves only his real mother and that one day they will be together again, and he will be happy."

Whether the mother is right or wrong, her son will try to defend her integrity. Flesh of her flesh, blood of her blood, he wants desperately to believe that she is inherently good because this belief enables him to trust his own goodness; he wants desperately to know that she loves him because this love assures him that he is lovable; he wants desperately to protect her because if she is not safe in the world, he does not feel altogether safe either.

Beverly was ultimately able to find, if not a perfect solution, a reasonable one. She agreed with her stepson that his mother was inherently good and that she did love him, but she let him know that his mother's leaving him had been wrong and had hurt him very deeply; and she told him what she knew to be true—that, for now, his mother, who was down and out, was not able to take care of him. She also told the boy what every stepson waits to hear: "Even though your mother isn't with you right now, she's still your mother—the only mother you'll ever have. And you never have to worry, not even for a microsecond, that I will try to replace her. I will be your good adult friend and when you are with me I will take care of you, but I will not—cannot— be your mother."

There are, of course, endless variations to the tensions between stepmothers and natural mothers. A close friend, who married a widower with two school-age boys, confided how difficult it has been for her to accept that in the boys' eyes and in her own, she would never measure up to their idealized mother.

In our living room, there is a small oil painting of my husband's first wife, my stepsons' beloved mother, which hangs above the mantelpiece. She—this eternally beautiful, young woman wearing a blue tulle gown—gazes down at us while I—a harried housewife in T-shirt and sweats—am vacuuming and nagging at the boys to pick up after themselves. It is, of course, irrational to resent my predecessor, and in my finer moments I feel great compassion for this young mother who lost her life when a drunk driver rammed into her car. But there is a part of me that wants to scream out, "It's not fair!" when the boys do nothing but idealize her and find plenty that is wrong with me.

The stepson's early antagonisms against his stepmother come as no surprise; in the popular and clinical literature, much has been written about them. What has been discussed far less frequently is the possibility that the stepson will be sexually attracted to his stepmother. Especially when he is a pre-teenager or teenager, a boy can be stirred by his father's attractive new wife, which may cause all manner of conflicts for the boy. For example, his sexual and romantic fantasies may overstimulate him and may also make him feel guilty and anxious. After all, a son depends on his father's trust and comradery and does not want to incur his wrath. Because his yearnings for his father's wife will certainly be disturbing to him, the lovestruck youth may try to keep them a secret. For example, he may withdraw from his stepmother, feigning indifference toward her, or he may even treat her with hostility.

The fortunate stepson has a stepmother who is sensitive to his sexual and romantic vulnerabilities and who never, never mocks or exploits or teases him for these. Aware that he can be easily aroused, she makes efforts not to be seductive with him—although, being human and sexual herself, she may in fact have transient sexual feelings for him. In Euripides' ancient tragedy *Hippolytus*, the stepmother, Phaedra, does pursue her handsome stepson, whom she madly loves and, as a consequence, brings destruction and death to all in the family. Then, as now—in ancient Greece, as well as in contemporary America—erotic love acted out between family members can only be disastrous.

Ruth Roosevelt and Jeanette Lofas tell the story of a boy who wrote his stepmother an impassioned letter while he was at boarding school. Years later, he recalled with gratitude her delicacy in responding to it. The stepmother *and father* wrote the boy how delighted they were that he accepted his stepmother and that she was equally pleased to have a new stepson. They wrote that his acceptance of their marriage was very important to them and that they loved each other very much. With this letter, the boy was able to put aside his romantic fantasies and settle, with relief, into a non-eroticized role as stepson.

In spite of the complications inherent in the stepmother-stepson relationship, there are possibilities for a warm bond between the two. As a rule—an exception might be a very young child who has lost his natural mother through death or abandonment—a stepmother cannot become a second mother to her stepson; however, over time, she can become his adult friend.

For the past five years I have been watching from a distance the relationship that is developing between a dear friend, whom I will call Elizabeth, and the fifteen-year-old boy, whom I will call Adam, who is her love partner's son. During the first years of my friend's romantic involvement, she would from time to time confide that her partner's son rejected her overtures of kindness. The boy returned to her, holiday wrappings perfectly intact, the first Christmas present that she had carefully selected for him. "I'm sorry, but I can't accept a gift from you," his hand-scribbled note said. Respecting Adam's wish to create a distance between them, Elizabeth did not try to force a relationship with him: she simply stepped back. And, unpressured, Adam gradually—very gradually—began to let her in to his life.

Lately, when I see them at social events, I cannot help but notice that Adam looks happy around Elizabeth. He smiles and laughs when they are talking; he listens intently when she shares with him tidbits of her life; he tells her about his girlfriend; he accepts her light hugs and an occasional kiss on the cheek. Having lived through his parents' angry and mutually undermining relationship, Adam has, I suspect, learned from his father's and Elizabeth's positive companionship that the relationship between a man and a woman need not be hurtful but can be enhancing and that perhaps he too can have a wonderful love of his own someday. I also notice that Adam takes precautions that the growing bond with Elizabeth does not compromise his primary loyalty to his own mother. Each time that I have been with my friend and the boy, I observe that he brings up something nice about his mother. It is as if he must remind us, "My mother may not be here in person, but I want you to know that she is here with me in spirit."

Let us now turn our attention from the stepson to the new husband. Recalling the stepmothers I have seen in therapy, I cannot think of one who was not at least mildly disappointed with her husband's role as family man; and most were quite disgruntled. As these women came to understand their husband's conflicts regarding the new family, however, they often developed a greater sympathy for them, which strengthened their married love and also improved family life in general.

It goes without saying that a woman's husband can positively or negatively affect her relationship to his son. In the best of all worlds, the husband intuitively knows how difficult stepmothering is, and he makes every effort to make this task easier. He does not put pressure on his new wife to love his children; rather, he understands that mother love is the province of mothers, not stepmothers, and he is satisfied when his wife is simply kind, attentive, and fair to his child. He also does not allow his children to treat his new wife with disrespect or indifference; rather, he sets and enforces rules with his children for their appropriate behavior in the home. And he does not dismiss his wife's advice about parenting; rather, he honors her observations and, when appropriate, acts on her suggestions. But alas, most worlds are not the best. Husbands with children from previous marriages often stumble into new marriages with heavy psychological baggage, which they tend to unload at the feet of their new wives.

Although most husbands understand at an intellectual level that their new wives cannot love their stepchildren instantaneously and unconditionally, at an emotional level, many may expect precisely this—not just when these children have lost their natural mothers through death or abandonment but when there has been a divorce as well. Children who become part of a stepfamily are always burdened with a legacy of loss. Divorced fathers are usually burdened with a legacy of guilt for having failed to keep the original family intact. Many remarried men want their new wives to mitigate this failure by creating warm, loving, unconditionally accepting, stress-free home lives for their children; commonly, they want their new stepfamilies to fit the mold of the idealized nuclear family. Moreover, if their earlier marriages followed traditional lines and they were not involved in their children's daily care, they may repeat the pattern in their present marriages and expect their new wives to assume with gladness the role of primary parent. When the new wives cannot meet these high expectations—as inevitably happens—the new husbands may feel angry with or disappointed in them.

It is not unusual that at about the time the new wife slips from her pedestal, the husband develops protective and fond feelings for his ex-wife. I have heard many stepmothers say in frustration, "My husband demands so much of me, but he treats his ex-spouse with kid gloves. He makes all sorts of excuses for her most outrageous demands on him. It's so unfair!"

Sometimes, especially when he was the one to end the marriage, a man may have kindly feelings for his "ex" only to compensate for the guilt he harbors for having rejected and hurt her; at other times, however, he may have genuine gratitude and respect for the woman who mothered his child and to whom he is, in a profound way, still connected. He may sometimes, in fact, be swept up by nostalgia for his lost bride, his lost family, and his lost early dreams. As is the case for every member of the reconstituted family, the father/husband has feelings of loyalty that are at times divided between the old relationships and the new ones. A woman must be blessed with confidence in her own worth and with an unpossessive, generous spirit (or learn to cultivate these attributes) in order to accept the fact that her husband, while committed to her, cannot be totally hers—that a small part of him belongs to a former life.

As part of my research for this chapter, I interviewed a recently remarried friend, a writer who is the father of a six-year-old boy. The question I put to him was, "What would you like your wife to know about you in regard to your roles as father and husband?" Here, in essence, is what he said:

> I would want her to know that I love her very much and that I am committed to share the rest of my life with her. I know that the life we make together can't be an easy one, however, and I pray that she can accept me in spite of this.
>
> My first marriage, with all its nastiness, betrayals, and fights, has taken a toll on me. So I come to my present marriage not as the young prince on the white horse with a perfect red rose in hand, but as an old warrior with many scars, some open wounds, and a good deal of defensive armor.
>
> I also come to my new wife with a little boy, whom I love more than words can say and to whom I am devoted. Sometimes my son does pull me away from my wife. Sometimes I take his side against her; when this happens, I feel guilty and torn in two.
>
> Above all else, I want my wife to know that I try to make her life and his life happy, but that I know I don't always succeed. This weakness makes me less than proud of myself and also somewhat grumpy toward her. As a man, I have learned to

believe that I should fix every problem, and it's discouraging to know that I can't always make things work just right in my family.

Although my eloquent friend's experience is uniquely his, I suspect that his sentiments are shared, though perhaps not expressed, by millions of other remarried men.

Of all the relationships in the blended family, the one that is the most complicated, the most ridden with negative feelings, is the relationship between the stepmother and her stepchild's natural mother.

So many forces—jealousy, envy, competition, mistrust—conspire against an amicable relationship between stepmother and mother that it rarely seems to happen. From my clients and friends who are stepmothers, I hear mostly horror stories about the other woman: she is "manipulative" or "undermining" or "narcissistic" or "completely unreasonable" or "neglectful" or "abusive" or "off the wall" or "a space cadet." Some of these depictions are accurate; we all know that many people on this earth are not decent or competent and that sometimes these people become mothers. However, most of these depictions are distortions. It is easy for a stepmother to develop distorted, negative perceptions about her husband's former wife because she rarely gets the chance to know this woman; much of what she "knows" about her is mediated by the husband's perceptions, which may not be favorable. Not surprisingly, there is no English term to describe a *direct* relationship between stepmother and natural mother, who remain "my former husband's present wife" and "my husband's former wife." As human beings, we are programmed to be suspicious of strangers; stepmothers and natural mothers almost always remain estranged from one another.

Like stepmothers, divorced mothers with children tend to be decent women who try their best to cope in difficult family circumstances. These women have experienced great losses: the loss of a spouse, the loss of a family that was meant to stay together, the loss of self-esteem that results from failing in marriage, and, often, the loss of financial well-being. It is natural for them to feel ambivalent toward their ex-husbands' new wives—the women who have replaced them. One of my long-term clients, an insightful, warm-hearted woman, sums it up: "On the one hand, I want my ex-husband's new wife to be successful in her marriage so that my children's second home will be secure. On the other hand, I have mean moments when I want her to be a terrible flop because her failure as a wife would vindicate me as a failed wife; it would be proof that my ex-husband is impossible to live with after all!" My client also expresses what I believe the overwhelming majority of mothers feel. "I suppose that I can accept that my ex-husband has found a wife to replace me. But what I could never accept is that my children would love her more than they love me."

In the course of interviewing for this chapter, I spoke to one woman who had enjoyed a warm relationship with her son's stepmother. I shared with Dana my impression that this was a rare phenomenon indeed and asked if she could explain it. Dana thought for a while and then said, "I suppose it's because Edie and I knew and liked each other before she began dating Vance, my former husband. I had always appreciated Edie's love of children; she is wonderfully maternal and has domestic talents that I don't have. And so when she became my son's stepmother, I was very happy for him. Having liked Edie before she married my ex-husband, it was kind of natural to keep on liking and trusting her afterward. We get together from time to time to review practical matters about my son, her stepson. And we usually end up gossiping and giggling about Vance's relatives, who are the oddest people either of us has ever known."

Dana and Edie's friendship is a reminder that women have a great capacity to bridge unfavorable circumstances in order to make connections with one another. It brings to mind the delightful story by French novelist Guy de Maupassant, "The Double Pins." A bon vivant keeps two mistresses. By alternating the days he is with each woman, he manages to keep each one from finding out about the other. On one of her visits, however, the older mistress notices a particular black-headed pin, obviously belonging to a lady, in her lover's quarters. Without a word to him, she substitutes one of her own pins, which the younger mistress soon discovers. Before long the two women, by cross-hatching one pin with another, devise a communication, which, to the dismay of the bon vivant, eventually leads to an intimate friendship between the two.[11]

After the interview with Dana, I considered how healing it would be for most stepmothers to come to know and develop empathy for "the other woman" so that, instead of being competitors and antagonists, as is so often the case, they can cooperate in the care of the son/stepson. My musings led to an imaginary, healing correspondence between the two women.

Dear Stepmother,

Because you have married my son's father, you will play an important part in my son's life. In advance, I would like to thank you for all the times that you will wipe his runny nose, pick up after him, prepare his meals, take him to the doctor, and lend him a sympathetic ear when he confides his small and big problems. When you decided to marry my son's father, you probably didn't relish the idea that he and his son were a package deal; I respect you for taking on the difficult role of part-time caregiver; I thank you for making my son's needs your concern.

Because I love my son very, very much, I hope that he can make a positive adjustment to his new family and, of course, this means feeling comfortable with you. Be assured that I will do what I can to promote a good relationship between the two of you.

Sincerely yours,
The Mother

To my stepson's Mother,

    Thank you for your recognition and coopera-
tion. For my part, I would like to assure you that I
will take good care of your precious son when he
is in my charge. I imagine that it cannot be easy for
you to turn him over to me—someone you hardly
know. At these times, you must miss him a lot and
worry about him too.

    I would also like to assure you that I will never
presume to be his mother. He has only one mother,
and you are she. However, I gratefully accept your
offer to help your son and me develop a positive
relationship. In every child's heart, there is room for
a kind adult friend, and perhaps I can fill this place.

Sincerely yours,
The Stepmother

    If such correspondences were commonplace, if women
sharing the hard task of bringing up a child reached out to
one another and tried to understand the other's circumstances, I imagine that blended families might become much
nicer environments—for all their members.

    In "Hansel and Gretel," the Brothers Grimm provide one
solution for the beleaguered stepmother: she convinces her
husband to abandon the troublesome kids in the dark woods.
They provide another resolution for the abused stepchildren:
their stepmother conveniently dies, and they return from the
dark woods to live happily in their father's home. Neither
solution, however, will do very well for today's stepmothers
and stepchildren. Hard as it may sometimes seem, they must
try to get along—and then try some more.

9

....

Mothers of Gay Sons

Human nature is not a machine to be built after a model . . . but a tree, which [must] grow and develop on all sides. It is not by wearing down into uniformity all that is individual in themselves, but by cultivating it, and calling it forth . . . that human beings become a noble and beautiful object of contemplation.

—JOHN STUART MILL

While wandering through the stacks at the university library, on the lookout for books about mothers and sons, I happened on a slim volume of letters called *Like Coming Home*. Puzzled by the title, I pulled it from the shelf. The letter that follows, which was written by a twenty-seven-year-old graduate student in chemistry, comes from this book.

Dear Mother,
    In the last few months, I have become aware of a problem that concerns me a great deal. It seems

that lately, we've been talking less and less. We used to call each other every two or three weeks, but now it is every six weeks or so, and it is you who has to call me. I feel a wall forming between us. The problem, however, is my creation. In the last year and a half, a great deal has happened in my life that has changed it tremendously, but I have been afraid to tell you about it. It was about a year and a half ago that I finally admitted something to myself that I have known for years but refused to face, and that is the fact that I am gay.

I know that this is a shock to you. . . . I know that you may be angry or upset, but I'm very afraid. I know how close we have been in the past, and I've seen us drift apart. I am afraid because now I have set something into motion that could completely destroy our relationship. I am afraid of you, that you may cut me off, not just financially, but worst of all, emotionally. Quite honestly, I am afraid that you will not love me anymore. But as frightened as I am by these possibilities, I am frightened more by not being able to be myself, by not being able to share with you the things that are happening in my life. That is why I take this risk now, because I have imagined not only a worst case scenario, but also a happy ending, one in which you are able to accept me completely for what I am. . . .

All my love,
Vince

P.S. I hope that you are still planning to come out and visit this summer. There is someone I want you to meet.[1]

After I read Vince's brave and tender letter, I could not imagine that his mother would stop loving him. Unless a mother suffers from a terrible deformation of character, she will love her children always. But I am not so naive as to believe that the love that Vince's mother gives her son can be light and easy. On the contrary, I expect that hers will be a love weighted down by anxieties and confusions—which is not to say that this love cannot also have its great rewards. My purpose in writing this chapter is to explore the experiences of the gay son and his straight mother as each comes to terms with his homosexuality and with their changing relationship.

According to the preponderance of evidence available, the gay man does not *choose* to be gay; he simply *is* gay. Moreover, one's sexual orientation—whether homosexual, bisexual, or heterosexual—seems to be a given, natural, and, for almost all, unchangeable part of one's makeup. However, accepting his homosexuality in a world that, for the most part, ridicules, despises, and fears it is never an easy matter for a young man; and, all too often, it is a painful crisis of identity for him. Similarly, being proud and supportive of her gay son when, all her life, she has been exposed to caricatures of homosexual men as sinful, strange, silly, perverse, preying, or criminal is never an easy matter for a mother; and the widespread incidence of AIDS and the increasing violence against gays add to her trauma.

A colleague once told me a story I will always remember. Late one night, he got a telephone call from a distraught woman who was in treatment with him. Although she realized that her request was unusual, she nevertheless asked him to please come to her home. When he arrived there, he discovered her teenage son, who had recently "come out" to her, banging his body against a living room wall. Fists tightly clenched, tears streaming down his face, the boy was screaming, "I don't want to be gay. I don't want to be a 'faggot.' Why did God have to make me this way? Why did He make me all wrong?" Confused and frightened herself, the boy's mother was unable to say what the boy needed to hear from her: "You are a fine young man. You are a fine young *gay* man. There is nothing wrong with you. In time you'll become part of the gay community, and you won't feel like such an outcast. But until then you can count on me to support you when you are down or scared. And even when the other kids at school taunt you, you can trust that your mom loves you always." Instead, immobilized by her own considerable emotional pain, this mother (understandably) stood by helplessly.

We should not underestimate the personal suffering that the young homosexual male experiences at the hands of his peers. And we should understand that even the most supportive mother does not have the power to protect her son from his peers' abuse, although her loving understanding can make it hurt less. When she heard that I was writing about gay sons, Claudia Stein, a friend who is a high school teacher, sent me an article from the *Denver Post* that included the following vignette:

> At the door, his heart starts racing and his hands sweat. He feels like running away but he keeps on going. If it were just the words, he could handle it.
>
> He hasn't had a day in high school without them.
>
> Faggot. Queer. Gay.
>
> It goes on and on, all day long. Lez, Dyke, Homo.
>
> He didn't always feel so different from everyone else, but now he does. He listens to the words all day long.
>
> He's been openly gay—"out"—since he was 14 and now he's big, big enough to be a football player, but he's a "queer" instead. He's strong enough to take care of himself, so unless they shoot him or jump him in the alley, he's OK. Maybe. He knows the teachers are talking about him. He feels alone. He's never sure anyone would stand up for him.[2]

Fearing the hate, the violent assaults, the mean jokes, the snide smiles, the rejection, many gay boys and men try to hide their true sexual natures from their peers and their family—and even from themselves. Some boys, tormented by the knowledge that they are homosexual, run away from home or try to kill themselves; in fact, it is estimated that one-third of teen suicides are gay teens.[3]

Dr. Don Johnson, a Boulder psychologist who has counseled many gay men and who is himself gay, points out that the experience of homosexual people is, in one significant way, different from that of other persecuted minority groups: unlike members of ethnic groups, homosexual people do not usually share their minority status with blood relatives and, as a consequence, may feel alienated from their own families.

I remember, as a young girl, tearfully telling my grandmother that on my way home from Hebrew school some neighborhood kids had tried to stick my friends and me with thistles and had called us Christ-killers. She calmly gave me my first lesson about bigotry and told me exactly how to respond to anti-Semitic remarks in the future. The gay youngster who has been born into a straight family does not usually have such empathic support. Because his parents and grandparents have never directly experienced what he is experiencing, they may not know how to give him the understanding and encouragement that he longs for. As loving as they may be, they may not be able to teach him what it means to be gay in a non-gay world. In fact, they may not even know that he is gay and secretly struggling to come to terms with the fact. When this is the case, the parents and child may begin to feel like strangers: they are always slightly out of rhythm; they reach out for one another but cannot make contact.

The father of a gay son, whom I spoke with at a meeting of a P-Flag (Parents and Friends of Lesbians and Gays) support group, confided that, never having suspected that his son was gay, he had often taken him aside for man-to-man talks about women and dating. Later he realized how painful these intimate conversations must have been for the boy and how different and separate from him his son must have felt. Moreover, this father acknowledged that even if he had known that his son was gay, he would not have been able to resonate with the boy's same-sex love relationships. As he said, "I know from my teenage years the thrill of going to the prom with a special girl; but I don't know the thrill of meeting a special boy at a gay bar."

In a similar vein, the single mother of a gay son, whom I also met at P-Flag, shared with me the sadness that she felt in not having been able to help her teenage son deal with the anguish of coming out. "Not having any idea what he was going through—the confusion and fear that he must have felt when he first became aware of his affection for other boys and the rageful rejections when he revealed his affections—I could not be there for him in the way that other mothers are there for their children in pain, and this breaks my heart."

Because the young gay son may feel continually misunderstood by his parents, he may become especially irritable with or even abusive toward them. One woman to whom I spoke at the meeting said that during his early teen years, her son, who had not yet come out, had made her feel absolutely ineffectual as a mother.

> I felt that he hated me—and I didn't understand why. I was really a good mom, but he let me know that whatever I did was wrong. I tried to convince myself that his bad nature was part of his being a teenager, but, in my heart, I knew that this was more than normal teenage acting out. I knew that there was something profoundly wrong between us. Teenagers roll their eyes at their mothers, but my son looked as if he wanted to spit at me.

Most often, it seems to me, the estrangements between parents and their gay sons come about as a result of mutual misunderstandings and missed connections, but sometimes they are the consequence of irreconcilable differences. Certainly, one of the most damaging family conditions for a gay young man is one in which his parents harbor the same prejudices against him as the society at large; in that case, those who are meant to be his comfort-givers are, instead, his oppressors.

A few months ago, after I gave a talk on mothers and sons, a young man in a red sleeveless T-shirt asked if he could speak to me privately. He told me that because he is gay his mother wants nothing more to do with him. Tears running down his cheeks, he went on to say, "I have a recurring dream of going home. From a distance, I see my mom and her arms are outstretched in a welcoming gesture. I run toward her. But as I get closer, I see that in one hand she is holding a gun, and that she is pointing the gun at me."

Hans Christian Andersen, who is reputed to have been gay, described the torment and rejection of the "different" child within his own family in his classic tale "The Ugly Duckling." In rereading the story that Andersen wrote in 1845, I kept thinking how relevant it is for today's gay young men and how little things have changed in 150 years as far as intolerance goes. Although the "ugly" duckling is born with a good character and is able to swim as well as the other ducklings in his mother's brood, the fact that he has an unfamiliar shape makes him the target of unrelenting abuse. The old ducks and the turkey cock who are part of his farm community disparage him; his siblings hiss, peck, and scream at him constantly; one of the "regular" ducks on the farm bites him on the neck because "he's big and he doesn't look like everybody else! . . . And that's reason enough to beat him."[4] Worst of all, the "ugly" duckling's own mother, who first nurtured and protected him but is eventually made to feel ashamed of him by her duck friends, rejects him too. "I wish you were far away," she says.[5] Of course, what she means is, "You bring me nothing but embarrassment and heartache. Because you are odd, I am ashamed of you. I really would be better off without you. In fact, I wish that you had never been born."

Painfully aware that he is an unwanted child, the duckling runs away. He runs and runs, but wherever he finds himself, he cannot escape the meanness of strangers; wherever he is, he does not fit in. All he can do is grieve for his "ugliness." The world has been unkind to the little duckling as it often is to the gay boy. Worst of all, his mother has given up on him. Blinded by her own prejudices, she has not helped him see that he is beautiful. Looking only for proper drake qualities in him, she has not noticed that he is not a drake at all but a young swan.

Eventually the "ugly duckling" discovers on his own that he is a beautiful swan, and he finds loving companionship among other swans. But had he been nurtured by his mother's acceptance all along, I suspect that he would not have suffered so long and so hard before realizing his unique beauty. I also suspect that had his mother gotten approving clucks ("What a fine son you have!") instead of disapproving squawks ("He didn't turn out very well!") from her duck companions, she may have developed into the proud mother of a special child instead of the rejecting mother of a runaway. As human mothers can attest, it is difficult indeed—perhaps impossible—to be accepting when one feels devalued and inadequate oneself. One of the finest contributions of support groups for parents of gay and lesbian children, such as P-Flag, is assuring mothers and fathers that both they and their homosexual children are lovable and valuable people.

Invariably, the gay boys and men I interviewed told me that despite the differences in sexual orientation between themselves and their parents, what they longed for from their mothers and fathers—and expected especially from their mothers—was acceptance. Not tolerance, certainly not pity, but *acceptance:* an unquestioning, loving, laughing, overflowing acceptance. Unconditional acceptance has always been a mother's finest gift to her (young and adult) children. A mother's acceptance of her children's true natures nourishes their self-acceptance as surely as sunshine and raindrops nourish plants and flowers. Conversely, the absence of maternal acceptance leaves all sons and daughters feeling not right with themselves or with the world. Self-esteem is undermined by such thoughts as, "If my own mother rejects me, I must be damaged goods; if *she* does not respect me, how can I expect that anyone else will?"

Because the gay man is disapproved of by the majority culture, his desire for maternal approval may be especially intense and even desperate. This sense of desperation comes through in Arnold's dialogue with his mother from the play *Torch Song Trilogy* by Harvey Fierstein.

MA: You haven't spoken a sentence since I got here without the word "Gay" in it.

ARNOLD: Because that's what I am.

MA: If that were all you could leave it in there [Points to the bedroom] where it belongs; in private. No, you're obsessed with it. You're not happy unless everyone is talking about it. . . .

ARNOLD: [Bordering on hysteria] I don't know what to say to you. I really don't. I'm not trying to throw it in your face, but it is what I am and it's not just a matter of who I sleep with.[6]

What Arnold asks of his mother is not *partial* acceptance of him but acceptance of *all* of him, which includes recognition of him as a human being, as a man, as a gay man, *and* as a sexual gay man. I suspect that Arnold, like every man, wishes that his mother could be happy for him; that instead of holding her nose and telling him to keep his dirty business in the bedroom and out of her face, she could rejoice in the fact that he is emotionally and sexually alive. What seems to be happening with Arnold is that the more he senses his mother's denial of his gay life-style, the more he is pressed to flaunt it, to parade it in front of her. Arnold insists that his mother see him in the full, glaring light of his reality, but his insistence only drives her to shield her eyes from him.

In my conversations with the mothers of gay men who had recently come out to them, a few women implied that they were open to their sons' loving men in a spiritual but not a sexual way. For example, one woman said that although everything else about a gay man's life is acceptable to her, his sexual practices are not. Another woman confided that when her son refers to his roommate as "my lover" she cringes "because then I know we're not talking about a platonic relationship; we're talking about *sex*." The difficulty that these women were having is most understandable when one considers that, historically and traditionally, homosexual practices have been condemned as sinful and unnatural.

The late Howard Brown, known for his leadership in community medicine, recognized both the difficulty for a parent to come to terms with a son's homosexuality and the diminished relationship that necessarily accompanies such denial: "I did not tell my parents that I was homosexual. Nor did most homosexual men of my generation tell their parents. We excused our reticence with the thought that we were sparing them the agony of having to think about us as sexual beings—or, to put it another way, of having to understand us. . . . Instead, we shared with them a version of our lives from which all the essential pages had been expurgated."[7]

Happily, in researching this chapter, I also learned of many women who fully accepted their gay sons—and their sons' love partners. For example, I was told about a mother who, after giving her heterosexual daughter a lovely, traditional church wedding, approached her gay son and his lover and told them that she had put aside an equal amount of money for the lovely, albeit nontraditional wedding that she hoped they would soon have.

Most moving was an anecdote that a woman, the mother of an actor son, shared during a telephone interview.

> I recently confessed to Les that for a long time after he had come out to me I used to wish that he were heterosexual. I also told him that this is no longer true for me. When he asked me why the change of mind, I said, "Because if you weren't gay, you wouldn't be you. And it is you I love."

However, just as accepting that he is a gay person is usually difficult for a young man, accepting that her child is gay does not come easily or all at once for most mothers, even for the most tolerant, generous ones. The following story, told to me by a woman I got to know through P-Flag, is one with which other mothers of gay sons may resonate. Jill, a dark-haired graceful woman who wears long, flowing skirts and colorful scarves, is a married homemaker and a community leader. Open and intelligent, she is the kind of person who invites human contact; for this reason, I found it easy to approach her at the P-Flag meeting and, over a number of subsequent interviews, to ask about her personal experiences as the mother of a gay son.

Two years ago, Jill and her husband learned that their son was gay. The young man, then in his early twenties, had asked his parents to visit with him in San Francisco, where he worked as an architect; during the visit he broke the news to them. Because Rick had never been very interested in girls, Jill had mildly suspected all along that he might be gay; but she had not dwelt on these suspicions or articulated them to anyone, not even to her husband. "At an unconscious level, I must have felt that by neither thinking nor talking about the possibility that Rick was homosexual, it wouldn't come to be," she explained.

When Rick nervously came out to them, both Jill and her husband went numb. But within a few moments, they were flooded with feelings of tenderness for their son and told him that he had their full support and love. "This is not a problem for us," they assured him. Yet, that evening and the following day, alone in their hotel room, Jill and Henry cried; clinging to each other, they cried long and hard.

"I didn't know exactly why I felt such overwhelming sadness," Jill told me. "I had always prided myself on being an open-minded person and, intellectually at least, accepted gay and lesbian people. I knew that I had not lost Rick to a warped or evil force. He was still the same wonderful, bright, caring person that he had always been. And yet I felt horrible. It was as if something very precious had been suddenly taken from me. But I could not name what this something was."

Dr. Don Johnson maintains that upon learning that their

son is gay, parents, all at once, are robbed of the dream that they have cherished since their child was a tiny infant: the dream that they will lead this beloved child into a safe, known, and beneficent world. In truth, this dream is unrealizable for all parents—after all, no such world exists—and all parents must, sooner or later, let go of their illusions. But for the parents of lesbian or gay children, the shards of this shattered dream are especially sharp; the world in which their grown children find themselves is even more dangerous, more unpredictable, more malevolent than the world in which heterosexual people live.

Jill remarked,

> After months of self-examination, I realized that the great, nameless sadness that I had felt after Rick had come out was grief for my own powerlessness. I was helpless to protect Rick from some very real dangers: the hateful acts of homophobic people, the blatant and subtle discrimination aimed at gay men, and the terrifying plague AIDS, which was decimating the gay community.[8]

Jill also indicated that her great sadness had much to do with suddenly being robbed of other sweet dreams: the dreamed-for son who would fall in love with a fine young woman, get married, and raise beautiful children—her future grandchildren; the dreamed-for son who would pattern his life after that of his parents; the dreamed-for son who would do things the "right" way and whose life-style she would never have to *explain* to her own parents and friends.

As Jill told me, the sadness stayed with her for months; sometimes it was a hardly perceptible pain, but other times it was a knife going through her. After returning from San Francisco, she tried to throw herself into her volunteer work, but she found that she did not have the heart for it. And although she had always been a "people person," she also found herself making excuses when friends asked to get together with her. "What I felt was a strong wish to be alone,"

Jill explained. "I needed more time to think and I needed more time to cry. I was really very unhappy."

In the tale of "The Ugly Duckling," Hans Christian Andersen writes that for a long and hard winter the young bird hides himself in a swamp under the cover of snow-laden reeds. Cold and ragged, he is quite convinced that he will simply waste away and die there. But this does not happen. The warm spring sun comes and, with it, new possibility. When the young "duckling" spreads his wings, he discovers, to his great amazement, that they are now strong and powerful. They lift him up, and he flies far away from the swamp, over a flowering garden, toward the clear waters of a winding canal.

Similarly, Jill sought out her own hiding place, where she could give in to her sadness, sort things out for herself, and gradually consolidate her new identity as the mother of a gay person. We normally think of depression, with its disengagement from the everyday world, as an undesirable condition, but sometimes depression is nature's growth tonic. It presses us to be with our troubles *and* to discover our internal sources of understanding, love, and strength, which will allow us to cope with them.

Allow me to digress from Jill's story. After a child comes out, parents will have varying issues to sort through. Although this was not the case for Jill, some parents have difficulty reconciling their child's homosexuality with their religious beliefs. If parents believe that homosexuality is against God's will and that the practicing homosexual person will not go to heaven, they may be overcome with panic: not only are they losing their child on this earth to a life that is unacceptable to them, but they expect to lose the child for all eternity. Torn between impulses to love and support the child and to obey what they are certain is God's word, these parents face a heart-wrenching conflict. Yet I am learning that this conflict is not irreconcilable and that belief in God leads some parents to their gay and lesbian children rather than away from them. The following letter, written by the devout Baptist father of three, appears in Mary Borhek's book, *Coming Out to Parents*.

> For a few minutes [after our son had told the family that he is gay] we just sat in silence. Then I kneeled and began to pray aloud that God would lead us, that He would open our hearts as well as our minds to His will.
>
> The answer did not come at once. Nor did it come easily. . . . The answer came gradually. We observed no outward change in Peter, except that he seemed even happier than usual, if that were possible. He was always a good boy, and we realized that he is still a good boy. He is, in fact, still the same fine person he was before we knew. . . . We continued to pray for God's guidance, and eventually the answer came. We at last knew that God was saying to us, "This is your son. He is the way I made him. Love him the way he is." We know in our hearts that this is the answer God has given us.[9]

This letter brings to mind a story about Bishop Melvin Wheatley, Jr., a well-respected Methodist religious leader in Boulder. When their son told them that he was gay, the bishop and his wife, Lucille Wheatley, responded in words like these:

> Knowing that you are homosexual tells us that we need to learn a whole lot more about what that means. It certainly does not change the way we feel about you. You are a superb human being and we love you. What [do] need to change are the false myths and negative stereotypes about homosexuality both church and society keep holding on to.

And true to their word, Bishop and Mrs. Wheatley have worked tirelessly to open and affirm relations among gay and non-gay individuals both within the church and outside of it.

Another issue with which many parents wrestle is their role in the son's homosexual development. "Am I to blame? Did I do something wrong? Is my son gay because of me?" are questions that torture them. Soul-searching fathers may privately ask themselves, "Was I too weak a role model for my son?" while mothers may guiltily wonder, "Was I so over-powering that I permanently scared him away from other women?" Confused and angry couples may also blame one another: "If only my husband had been more available to him." "If only my wife had not pushed me out of his life." The truth is that no one can say with authority exactly what causes some people to become homosexual and others to become heterosexual. At this time, perhaps the best response to the question of cause is that a complex and mysterious interplay of nature (genetic and biological factors) and nur-ture (parental and/or other environmental influences) seems to define a human being's sexual orientation.

If a parent looks upon the son's homosexuality as warped or sinful, the thought of being in the least bit re-sponsible for its development has to be terrible. So terrible, in fact, that the parent may not be able to bear it and may, quite unconsciously, project the "badness" onto the son, la-beling him as a bad seed, a degenerate, a *mistake*. Or the guilt-ridden parent may withdraw from the gay child, who is a living reminder of the parent's "failure."

All too often, friends, family members, and even ac-quaintances will imply or explicitly tell the parent of a gay or lesbian child that the child is defective. I am reminded of the callous question put to an acquaintance. "If you had known that your son would turn out gay," she was asked by a woman at a cocktail party with whom she had talked about her son's coming out, "would you have had an abortion?" For people who *especially* need others' approval (we all need some, of course), a steady flow of remarks and insinuations that their child is a misfit will feed their own sense of inad-equacy and shame.

However, if parents accept homosexuality as a natural

phenomenon, the idea that they may have played some part in its emergence is less threatening. Not long ago, as I was doing the research in preparation for this chapter, I came across Michael's "Letter to Mama" from *More Tales of the City* by Armistead Maupin.

> I know what you must be thinking now. You're asking yourself: What did we do wrong? How did we let this happen? Which one of us made him that way?
>
> I can't answer that, Mama. In the long run, I guess I really don't care. All I know is this: If you and Papa are responsible for the way I am, then, I thank you with all my heart, for it's the light and joy of my life.[10]

And when Dr. Johnson is asked, as he often is, "What made you gay?" he smiles and answers, "A wonderful stroke of good luck!"

Let us now return to Jill's story. Jill explained to me that her son's coming out and the depression that his announcement precipitated led to some major changes in her life. She gradually accepted the fact that she could not protect Rick from the hardships that his gay life-style promised—the gay-bashing, the job discrimination, and most threatening of all, AIDS—and she made a conscious decision to worry less about him. (Indeed, to accept with grace our limitations—that we do not have the power to save our children, especially as they grow into adulthood, from life's hardness and dangers—is the challenge that faces all of us parents.) She also began to recognize that although there was suffering in the gay community, there was also joy, laughter, comradery, and love; indeed, Jill began to feel a deep satisfaction that her son had found his true self and a sense of belonging in his new community.

Jill was changed in still another way. Ordinarily pleasant and easy-going, she now became angry—angry that her son and millions of other gay, lesbian, and bisexual people suffer abuse and discrimination in our country. Jill's great sadness had transformed itself into a great and powerful indignation, which again transformed itself into a determination to effect social change. Jill, together with her husband, went on to establish the first P-Flag group in her area and to fight vigorously against ordinances and laws that discriminate against the gay population. It has been said that when the gay or lesbian person comes out of the closet, his/her parent goes in and, unable to work through feelings of shame, blame, and guilt, frequently stays in. This is surely not the case for Jill.

Jill expresses a sentiment that I have heard from other mothers of gay and lesbian children: that coming to understand and appreciate her son's world has opened up her own.

> Through my son and my own activism in the gay/lesbian community, I have gotten to know many new, wonderful people—people whom I may have avoided otherwise. These people contribute to our planet in any number of ways. Some are artists; some adopt children whom no one else wants; some are just quiet, ordinary folk working hard to make a living. I have had low-key, young same-sex couples to my home for dinner—and I've opened my home and my heart to a couple of flamboyant drag queens, too. I was always a tolerant person, but I am more than that now. I *enjoy* the way we're all different as human beings. I have a calling to protect what is different in each of us.

I asked Jill to share with me her perceptions of the changes in her relationship with Rick; here, in essence, is what she said.

> From his pre-adolescent years through his early adulthood, Rick was struggling with his emerging

identity as a homosexual man. Because I was not aware of what was going on for him, I couldn't lend him the support and guidance he deserved. I just wasn't there for him. But since Rick has come out, I have the extraordinary opportunity to have a genuine relationship with him. He honors me by being himself around me: by talking candidly about the ideas and the people who are important to him; he has even taken me to gay bars. I have become what Rick tenderly calls his "mother-friend."

The saddest mother-son stories tell about estrangements and rejections. The happiest—such as Jill's—tell about growing empathy, respect, and love.

Part Three

....

MOTHER LOVE

I am the earth, I am the root.
—JUDITH WRIGHT,
"Woman to Child"

10

....

The Language
of Mother Love

Oh what a power is motherhood,
Possessing a potent spell.
                              —EURIPIDES

I once knew a little boy—the son of one of my husband's close friends—whose mother had died in a car accident when he was just a toddler. For months after his mother's death, the child would not speak. Instead, he produced only animal-like noises. Danny's psychiatrist attributed the boy's refusal to speak to the *unspeakable* pain of early mother loss, a loss that he thought left the child with no human words to express its devastation. However, I could not help but believe that Danny's self-imposed mutism also symbolized the sudden absence of his mother's human and humanizing voice: the maternal voice that had soothed, warmed, and affirmed, that had given names to things and feelings, sung lullabies, recited Mother Goose nursery rhymes, and told stories of all kinds.

Danny's sad tale came back to and took hold of me just as I was about to begin a chapter on the mother's caretaking functions—a chapter for which I had accumulated pages of notes. Musing about Danny, however, I felt suddenly compelled to explore instead the influence of the maternal voice; I wanted to understand and to write about the ways mothers shape their sons' self-concepts through the things they say to them.

From the moment of birth (and often for the months preceding birth), a mother talks to her child. And according to studies on infant behavior, it is the mother's voice that both newborn daughters and sons prefer more than any other.[1] There is even scientific evidence that the fetus attends to and will, after birth, have some memory of the stories mother tells it. In an intriguing series of studies, Dr. Anthony DeCasper and his colleagues at the University of North Carolina directed women during the last six and a half weeks of their pregnancies to read aloud to their fetuses twice a day either Dr. Seuss's *The Cat in the Hat* or a poem called "The King, the Mice and the Cheese." At three days of age, the newborns were outfitted with padded earphones. By sucking rapidly or slowly, they could control whether the recording of the Dr. Seuss story or of the poem was piped through their earphones. Amazingly, fifteen of the sixteen infants sucked at the right rate to hear what their mothers had read to them when they were fetuses. In utero, mothers' words had already made an impression on them.[2]

Mother's soothing words, her warnings, assessments, prophecies, and stories accompany her children throughout their growing years and, to a great extent, define their self-concepts. Young children believe that their mothers know everything and that they always tell the truth; for these reasons the maternal voice wields great power. My friend and colleague Dr. Wayne Phillips calls the mother "the most trusted interpreter"; she is the one to define her children's inner and outer worlds. She tells them what they can safely approach in the world, what they must avoid; whom to like, whom to dislike. She gives them words to name the things around them and the feelings within them. She lets them know which of their behaviors and feelings are acceptable and will elicit her smile, which are unacceptable and will bring her frown.

Although from an early age a boy normally pulls away from his mother and seems to tune her out, he does to stop taking to heart the things that she tells him; on the contrary, he clings to her words and draws on them even when he is grown. It is not at all difficult to come up with examples of the powerful effects that mother's words create. A young man I counseled told me that when he was little his first-grade teacher frequently shamed him for doing things in odd and "unacceptable" ways; when he shared with his mother how humiliated he often felt in school, she explained that the behaviors his teacher had labeled as odd were really original and that he could be very proud of being endowed with an original way of thinking and of doing things. She also explained that only people with original minds would recognize this special quality in him, which is why his conventional teacher failed to do so. With her kind and clever tongue, this mother was able to give new meaning to her son's behavior, which he has put to good use. Taking full advantage of his gift to see the world from unusual perspectives, he is becoming a successful stand-up comedian.

In her book *Mothers and Sons*, Carol Klein includes a lovely vignette about poet Robert Graves that also illustrates the constructive and enduring effect that the maternal voice can have. When Graves was a young boy, his mother gave him the following advice: "Robert," she said, "this is a great secret, never forget it! Work is far more interesting than play!" Robert went on to become a prolific writer—even during hard times, his literary output was prodigious. And giving praise where praise is due, he fully attributed his achievements to the "secret" that his mother had revealed to him.[3]

Edward Kennedy "Duke" Ellington also listened carefully to his mother's voice. "As though I were some very, very special child," he recalled, "my mother would say, 'Edward, you are blessed. You don't have anything to worry about. Edward, you are blessed!' "[4] And for the very reason that his mother believed that he was a very, very special child and blessed, Ellington, according to his biographer Geoffrey C. Ward, became convinced of it too. For him, nothing seemed impossible. An African-American performer living in the Jim Crow era, Ellington earned the recognition of presidents of the United States as well as the Queen of England; and he was responsible for so many pieces of music that music scholars have not yet agreed on a final tally, although it is believed to be somewhere near 2,000.[5]

Stories told by Sigmund Freud about his mother, Amalie, also exemplify the power of the maternal voice. Intuitive and sentimental, she had always believed in signs and omens. In part because her firstborn had been born with a caul, a traditional omen of fame and happiness, Amalie was convinced that he was destined for greatness. Hence, she named him Sigmund, which derives from the German word meaning "victorious." Although Amalie's life was centered on the conviction that Sigmund was fated to become a great man and she regaled the boy (as well as her seven other children) with stories and portents of her "golden Sigi's" glorious birth and brilliant destiny, Sigmund's father, Jakob, did not indulge in such "fantasies." When, on one occasion, Jakob, in a fit of anger, commented that Sigmund would "never amount to anything," the young boy promised himself to prove his father wrong and to vindicate his mother.[6]

In truth, Sigmund Freud grew up to be much more like his father—inquiring, skeptical, dryly funny—than like his fanciful and intuitive mother. (Similarly, Duke Ellington is said to have taken more after his father than after his mother, although it was always her approval that he sought.) Nevertheless, Freud was convinced that his mother's adoring trust in him was the reason for his self-confidence, his intellectual courage, his inner sustenance, and his drive. He also speculated that it may have accounted for his "thirst for grandeur,"[7] from which we can infer that it may not be wise for a mother to make her son feel *too* special.

A mother's words can also undermine the son's self-confidence, as the story of my friend Charles, a confirmed bachelor, illustrates. Charles was brought up by his mother and his mother's sister, both of whom had been deserted by their husbands. As a child, Charles often heard his two "mothers" remark that "anything in pants can't be trusted." "My mother's and my aunt's words have never stopped reverberating in my head," Charles confided. "After years of therapy, it became clear to me that one of the reasons that I am afraid to commit to a life-long relationship is that I still believe my mother's and aunt's assessment of men. Since I am one of those unfortunate creatures who wears pants, I fear I cannot be trusted."

The enduring power of the mother's words—for good and for bad—is reflected in the old adage: "What the mother sings to the cradle goes all the way down to the coffin." It is also illustrated by the archetype called the Great Spinner, who is said to determine man's future by spinning stories and prophecies. The Great Spinner—almost always a female figure—makes frequent appearances in our civilization's most famous tales. For instance, she appears as the three Weird Sisters who use their cunning words to deceive Macbeth. She is also represented by the bad fairy who prophesies that Sleeping Beauty will prick her finger on a poisoned spindle and die and by the good fairy whose life-affirming prophecy saves the girl from this fate. And she is the benevolent Clotho, the first of the three Fates, who, in ancient Greek myths, spins the cloth of human destiny with golden threads.

We can say that the mother who tells her young son, "You will grow up to be a handsome, good, and courageous man!" is a modern-day version of the good fairy or of a Clotho: her positive assessments, which her son trusts absolutely, help instill a positive self-concept in him. On the other hand, the mother who tells her son, "You will grow up to be a bum!" is like the bad fairy who poisons the child's future.

The power of the maternal voice finds support not only in story but in scientific research. After testing one hundred children and their parents, Dr. Martin Seligman, who is widely respected for his research on depression, concluded that the way mothers talk about the world strongly influences their sons' and daughters' perceptions. Indeed, the mother's level of optimism and the children's levels are very similar. According to Seligman's research, the father's level of optimism does not affect that of his sons or daughters. "If the child has an optimistic mother, this is great," Seligman remarks; "but it can be a disaster for the child if the child has a pessimistic mother."[8] As Seligman's research also demonstrates, an optimistic outlook is a powerful antidote for depression, and, conversely, a pessimistic outlook is one of the major causes of depression.[9]

Of course, all of us mothers, when we are tired or grumpy or frustrated or emotionally depleted, are bound to slip and to say hurtful things to our children. Still, we can usually make a conscious effort to speak to our children with sensitivity—to enhance them rather than to cut them down, to offer them positive rather than negative prophecies, and after having said something unkind, to make our apologies. Knowing that what we say does matter is reason enough for trying as best we can to choose our words with care.

To be sure, what we mothers choose to tell our children has much to do with our own basically optimistic or basically pessimistic outlook, whether it reflects our half-full glass or our half-empty one. This is one reason depressed mothers are well advised to get treatment rather than to endure their melancholia, which, inevitably, casts a long shadow over their children's developing selfhoods.

In a passage from *Maternal Thinking*, Sara Ruddick, drawing on Spinoza's ideas, describes the positive influences of a mother's optimism, or *cheerfulness*. "To be cheerful," she writes, "is to see a child hopefully and to welcome her hopes; for children, hope is as important as breathing, certainly more important than sleep. According to Spinoza, 'cheerfulness is always a good thing and never excessive.' "[10]

As Ruddick notes, cheerfulness as a virtue does not include cheery denial of reality, whether reality is a troubled family situation or a child's anger, fear, or disappointment. It is rather an attitude that suggests that life—despite all its uncertainties and injustices, its ups and downs—is worth living fully and joyfully; it is an attitude that promotes respect and compassion for the human race and the human condition; and it is an attitude that encourages one to cope in the face of adversity. Drawing from Bruce Springsteen, my son notes that "cheerfulness means recognizing the realities without forgetting the possibilities."

When a mother is blessed with (or consciously cultivates) cheerfulness, she will naturally pass on stories—anecdotes, proverbs, prophecies—to her children that teach them courage instead of despair. In my childhood family, whenever I felt overwhelmed, I could count on being assured by my maternal grandmother's German words "*Nicht so gefahrlich,*" which to me meant "Don't fret—it's not so terrible; you can handle whatever happens" or her directive "*Mach spass,*" which I interpreted as "Try to find something funny about the trouble that visits you; make a joke out of it." I remember too that after I was bitten by a squirrel that I was feeding, my grandmother explained that the squirrel had certainly not meant to bite me but was suffering from weak eyes and so mistook my finger for a peanut—and that although I should probably not hand-feed wild animals, I need not become afraid of them. Not surprisingly, my cheerful grandmother had an uncanny talent for finding four-leaf clovers. Indeed, one of my precious mementos is a four-leaf clover that she carefully pressed for me when I was a little girl.

In my present family, whenever Bruce, Jonathan, Leah, or I experience a minor misfortune—getting a rejection notice or missing a plane connection, for example—we can count on my cheerful mother-in-law's response, "Well, *everything* is an experience! You'll learn from this too." When, some months ago, I told Leah that I had sliced off part of the car door by hitting a pole in a parking garage, I was not surprised when she smiled mischievously and said, "Don't feel so bad, Mom. Remember, everything is an experience."

Even in the grimmest situations, mothers can infuse their children with courage. From the testimonies of survivors of Hitler's death camps, we know that mothers (and mother surrogates) soothed their children with words of cheer even as they accompanied them to the gas chambers. And through my practice and experience, I know mothers of sons who are HIV positive whose cheerful words help the young men face life with hope and optimism.

I do not think it is surprising that the folk stories and fairy tales children love most and that have endured the test of time have at their root an attitude of cheerfulness. Through them, boys and girls learn that like the heroes and heroines who outsmart witches, escape from giants, and slay dragons, they can face and handle life's fearful situations and inner pressures. As renowned child psychiatrist and author Bruno Bettelheim said so well, the message that fairy tales get across to the child is "that a struggle against severe difficulties in life is unavoidable, is an intrinsic part of human existence—but that if one does not shy away, but steadfastly meets unexpected and often unjust hardships, one masters all obstacles and at the end emerges victorious."[11] I have come to believe that this is exactly the message we mothers need to communicate to our children, again and again, through our own sayings, anecdotes, prophecies, and stories.

The harming effect of the *absence* of cheerfulness in the home became clear to me a few years ago when Jonathan told my husband and me that as a little boy he had often been alarmed by our casual remarks about the "dismal state of the planet." Hearing us say that no one, not even the president of the United States, could control the threats to the environment or the worldwide problems of war, disease, overpopulation, crime, and famine, Jonathan had become convinced that we were all doomed. Despite Jonathan's anxiety, my husband and I knew that we could not be hypocrites and pretend to him that the world was in good shape. However, we decided to talk about the problems of the world in a different way: to convey to him (and to our daughter) that situations are never hopeless, that we are not helpless, and that problems have at least partial solutions, which we are obligated to seek. I have learned that by saying things in a more cheerful manner for the sake of Jonathan and Leah, I have come to feel more hopeful about the future myself.

In the introduction to her novel *Ceremony*, Leslie Marmon Silko writes:

> I will tell you something about stories . . .
> They are all we have, you see,
>   all we have to fight off
>   illness and death.
> You don't have anything
> If you don't have stories.[12]

Certainly, fathers tell their sons stories, stories that connect the growing boys to the male experience and, as Robert Bly would say, give them a face, a history, an identity. At their best, the father's stories lead the son out into the world, away from the familiar, the home, the mother; telling of heroic deeds, they whet the boy's appetite for life's adventures. However, the stories that we mothers tell have their own life-giving power. At their best, they draw our sons inward, into the world of feelings and relatedness; they enlarge our sons' understanding of the human experience—loving, caring, compromising, enduring, suffering, overcoming, triumphing —and the human cycle—being born, growing up, nurturing new life, and dying.

In Chinua Achebe's classic novel *Things Fall Apart*, which is about Ibo tribal life in Nigeria, a marvelous passage points to the boy's need for both the father stories and the mother stories.

> So Okonkwo [the father] encouraged the boys to sit with him in his *obi*, and he told them the stories of the land—masculine stories of violence and bloodshed. Nwoye [the son] knew that it was right to be

masculine and to be violent,[13] but somehow he still preferred the stories that his mother used to tell, and which she no doubt still told to her younger children—stories of the tortoise and his wily ways, and of the bird *eneke-ntioba*. . . . He remembered the story she often told of the quarrel between Earth and Sky long ago, and how Sky withheld rain for seven years, until crops withered and the dead could not be buried because the hoes broke on the stony Earth. At last Vulture was sent to plead with Sky, and to soften his heart with a song of the suffering of the sons of men. . . . That was the kind of story that Nwoye loved.[14]

Reading Achebe's description, I thought of our own maternal traditions of story-telling. I flashed on images of mothers checking out armloads of picture books at my local library; I remembered my own story-telling grandmother, whose made-up tales of benign forest animals, talking flowers, and good fairies cast a magic spell over my childhood. But with sadness, I also thought about the mothers who, depressed or chronically exhausted from overwork and stress, plop their young children in front of the TV rather than tell them stories. How much these children miss! And how dangerously powerful the TV becomes when it, rather than mother, is the storyteller.

After my son left home for college, I dared to step into his storage closet, which had, throughout his growing-up years, been a dumping ground for everything from his Superman comic books to his Star Wars figures to his school papers. The closet was now in reasonable order—I had, in fact, threatened Jonathan that I would not let him go off to college until he had cleaned it out—and, neatly stacked in one corner, were the story books from his childhood. As I began turning the pages of some of our favorite books, *Where the Wild Things Are*, *The Rats of NIMH*, and *The Giving Tree*, it occurred to me that Jonathan and I had spent his early years in story—stories that I had read to him, stories that I had made up for him, stories that he had invented and told to me.

Even after Jonathan was too old for "make-believe," the story-telling did not stop. There were stories about the grandfather, my father, who had died before my children were born but who, I am sure, Jonathan would have loved and admired; stories about Jonathan himself—the clever, funny, sweet, and mischievous things that he had done when he was very little; stories about the sixties and the civil rights movement and the peace marches and the Beatles.

Now that Jonathan is a young adult, I have begun to tell him stories that I would never have thought of sharing earlier: stories about myself. I am quite sure that when Jonathan was in his early teens and distancing himself from me, he would not have been interested in these stories. These days, however, he seems eager to hear them. Moreover, because he is no longer the little boy who deserved to be shielded from life's grim realities, I can be open with him.

I am telling him about the insecurities and fears that wove through my own growing-up years as the only child of immigrant parents who lived through the Holocaust; about my determination to make something of myself, in part because my parents and relatives—a number of whom perished at Hitler's hands—were robbed of the chances to realize their ambitions; about my early friendships and romances and my enduring love for his father; about my hopes and dreams for the future. I also feel free to talk about such "women's issues" as freedom of choice, gender discrimination, date rape, and the struggles of combining motherhood and career.

Although I derive great pleasure from sharing these intimacies and from discussing women's issues with my son, I do not think that I am deluding myself when I say that my primary motivation in revealing myself and my concerns is not to make me feel good or to turn my son into a confidant, which would be inappropriate indeed. My primary motivation is to enlarge Jonathan's perspective. My hope is that in helping him know me not only as the caregiving mother of his childhood but also as a woman and a person in my own right, I am indirectly helping him to see the other women who will touch his life in their fullness and complexity. The fact that he is drawn to young women who have strong opinions and lofty ambitions leads me to believe that I am on the right track.

All too frequently, sons have come to believe that their mothers (and the caretaking wives who eventually take the place of their mothers) exist only for them and live only in the role of mother. By failing to know their mothers as real people, sons commonly project onto them (and onto their wives) distorted images: the image of the all-providing, all-available Good Mother; or her opposite, the image of the castrating, withholding Bad Mother. Speaking for the many, novelist Alfred Kazin writes, "I could never really take it in that there had been a time, even in *der heym* [the home], when [my mother] had been simply a woman alone, with a life in which I had no part."[15]

If, however, the many conversations that I have had with adult sons during the course of writing this book reflect a general sentiment, men want to know their mothers as people and are hungry for their mothers' autobiographical stories. When we mothers are willing to share these stories, we give our sons priceless gifts.

As I write this, I recall an interview with the husband of a colleague. Jeffrey unwrapped from wads of tissue paper a small leather-bound book: a journal in which his mother, once an accomplished sportswoman but now incapacitated by Alzheimer's disease, had kept detailed notes of her hikes into the wilderness with the young Jeffrey. For an hour, Jeffrey and I pored over his mother's journal. And Jeffrey's face lit up whenever, reading between the lines, we could infer from her descriptions of their outdoor adventures a new aspect of his mother's life and outlook.

In her analysis of over a hundred oral histories of mothers of sons, Linda Rennie Forcey, a professor at the State University of New York in Binghamton, concluded that mothers generally do not share their personal lives with their sons. They assume that their own experiences are of little interest to their sons, and that by speaking to them at a personal level they may alienate them from male culture. One mother told Forcey, "I've never thought of asking them what they think of my being in school. I've just assumed they find it sort of embarrassing." Another confided, "I am so excited about the things that I am studying, but I don't share it with my son. It seems like sort of an egotistical thing to do." And still another shared, "When I had my first two cancer operations it blew my mind. . . . I couldn't say a word to the boys. I think my husband talked to them but I'm not sure."[16] It is sadly ironic that women generally encourage close relationships—certainly with their daughters—but they avoid them with their own sons.

Surely, both mothers and sons lose out when mothers withhold their personal stories. As a result of finally getting to know his mother during his middle years, writer John Updike understood how much he had missed as a younger man by not knowing her, by not hearing her stories. "How festive and limpid her wit is, and with what graceful irony she illuminates every corner of her brave life. . . . All this for decades was muffled . . . behind the giant mask of motherhood," he wrote in an article for *Vogue* magazine.[17]

Certainly, we mothers must be careful not to confide to our sons details (especially sexual ones) of our lives for which they are not prepared to cope or which would promote an inappropriate intimacy between us. However, in our efforts to protect our sons from knowing too much—because we think that our personal stories would bore or burden them or alienate them from the male world—have we fallen into the habit of telling them too little? Isn't it time for many of us to remove "the giant mask of motherhood" that muffles the words of the woman hidden behind it and to tell our sons stories that represent us?

In Tillie Olsen's heart-rending "Tell Me a Riddle," we gradually learn that the dying old mother—the central character of this short story—has had a difficult life. She and her husband had come to America to escape the poverty of Russia but were forced to struggle through equal hardships in their new country. The mother in particular was constricted by the poverty in which she raised seven children. Though the husband allowed himself to go out and to attend reading circles, she stayed home, encumbered by the obligations of childcare and embittered by the grievances against her husband's selfishness. Despite the humiliations and terrors of poverty that weighed her down, however, she never gave up her youthful ideals, although she kept these hidden. And as she is dying, her children become aware that they have never really seen the vital, intelligent, idealistic woman who is their mother; they have seen only her flattened, downtrodden shadow. Now that she is dying, the grown children feel a sudden need to see her in all her fullness, all her aliveness, all her strength, all her *possibility:* "Where did we lose each other, first mother, singing mother?" one asks. Another, her son, says that he has never known her; and yet another son suffers, he says, for "that in her which never lived (for that which in him might never live)."[18]

We mothers have much to learn from the grieving adult children in Olsen's masterpiece: By hiding who we are from our sons and daughters, we deprive them; however, by telling our stories—by singing our songs—we ensure that the most vital and loving parts of ourselves will live on in them.

11

....

The Transformation
of Mother Love

I do not want to die. . . . I do not want to go until I have faithfully made the most of my talent and cultivated the seed that was placed in me, until the last small twig has grown.

—KÄTHE KOLLWITZ,
Diaries and Letters

When my son, Jonathan, was very little, we spent a lot of time snuggling on the couch reading picture books. One of my favorites was Shel Silverstein's *The Giving Tree*.[1] It is about an apple tree and a little boy. Each day the little boy comes to be with the apple tree: he gathers her leaves and weaves them into a kingly crown; he eats her juicy apples; he scrambles up her trunk and swings from her branches. And when he is exhausted from all his play, he sleeps peacefully in her shade. The apple tree and the little boy are very, very happy together. However, as the years go by and the boy grows older, he stops coming to the tree to play, to eat her apples, and to be comforted.

At the time, I did not fully understand why reading this book to the little boy curled up on my lap made me teary-eyed. I realize now that I became sad in anticipation of the day when Jonathan, like the boy in the story, would grow older and turn away from my sheltering arms—when the tender intimacy between us would be lost and we would have to let each other go.

The irony of motherhood is that it comprises two seemingly opposite tasks: the loving mother first creates a unity with her child, and then, piece by piece, over years and years of parenting, disassembles it. For most mothers, the second task is harder than the first—so hard, in fact, that some mothers find all kinds of reasons not to let go. But by holding on too tightly or too long, they impair not only their sons' development but their own. Conversely, as we will see throughout this chapter, by encouraging the necessary separations from them, they foster their sons' vitality and their own.

During pregnancy, the mother experiences her infant as part of herself; indeed, in the beginning, maternal love is akin to self-love. Although the birth process ruptures the condition of perfect oneness, it is partially restored as the mother assumes her caregiving and soothing functions. Holding and nursing her infant, whose smile is meant only for her, she can easily lose herself in their merging oneness. Andrea Boroff Eagan, who has extensively researched the development of mothers, writes that although the term symbiosis has been used only to describe the baby's view of the world, it is an accurate metaphor for the mother's as well. "The infant feels that she and her mother constitute a single entity, and her mother feels much the same. This is not a hallucination; the ties that bind the two are real and complicated."[2]

As poet Adrienne Rich writes,

> I recall the time when, suckling each of my children,
> I saw his eyes full open to mine, and realized each

of us was fastened to the other, not only through mouth and breast, but through our mutual gaze: the depth, calm, passion of that dark blue, maturely focused look."[3]

My editor, Alexia Dorszynski, calls the period of mother-infant oneness—so shimmering and pure—"the golden age." Of course, like all golden ages, it necessarily comes to an end. Just as the child must "hatch" from the symbiotic bond to achieve selfhood, so must the mother "struggle," as Rich says, "from that one-to-one intensity into a new realization, or reaffirmation, of her being-unto-herself."[4]

Relinquishing the early unity with the infant is hardest for women who do not have loving partners. For these women, the sweet pleasures of the symbiotic love-bond with the baby may fill a deep and hungry hole. If this hole has no bottom, as is often true for the woman who has never herself received tender care, the new mother may prolong the intimacy with her baby long after it is appropriate to do so. For instance, she may find nursing so gratifying that she resists weaning her baby; or in order for her to feel safe and warm, she may sleep in the same bed with her growing child. I have observed that unwed teenage mothers, who commonly have babies in order to feel loved and special, are often responsive, caring parents during the symbiotic phase of mothering, when their own needs for closeness and warmth are being met. However, as soon as their children begin to assert their autonomy and opposition, they want little to do with them. Their tragic solution may then be to have a second baby while they neglect or abuse the first one, who no longer meets their needs for nurturance.

It is also common for the woman who was not adequately mothered when she was a child to expect her baby to mother her—to affirm and adore her, to be a source of endless comfort, and to never, never abandon her for other relationships. Similarly, a woman who has been or who is undervalued as a person may also have special difficulty dissolving the symbiotic bond and letting others into her baby's life. The baby's absolute dependence may endow a new mother with a feeling of worthiness, power, and purpose that she has never known. No one—not Daddy, not Grandma, not Nanny—can comfort the way Mommy can; and there is no one with whom baby would rather be. For a woman who has felt like a "nothing" in her daily existence, the recognition that she is *everything* to her baby can be exhilarating.

And if the baby is a son, the new mother may experience in their relationship what Carol Klein describes as "a special soaring exultation."[5] If only in mother's fantasy, the male infant nestled in her arms is the key to her own longed-for prestige. Addressing the displaced dreams and ambitions of powerless women, existential philosopher Simone de Beauvoir writes, "A son will be a leader of men, a soldier, a creator; he will bend the world to his will, and his mother will share his immortal fame; he will give her the houses she has not constructed, the lands she has not explored, the books she has not read."[6] As de Beauvoir further notes, the women who expect to transcend their own limited lives by engendering hero sons whom they will live through are inevitably disappointed; psychologically healthy sons invariably leave their mothers to create lives separate from them. And as we discussed in Chapter 3, the movement away from the mother begins very early in the son's life.

Although dissolving the unity with her baby is especially wrenching for a woman who depends on the child to fill her up, the transition from oneness to twoness is difficult for most new mothers. Even after her children are grown, a woman may still long, from time to time, for the lost golden age. When she was forty-nine, German sculptor and graphic artist Käthe Kollwitz wrote in her diary, "Last night I dreamed once more that I had a baby. There was much in the dream that was painful, but I recall one sensation distinctly. I was holding the tiny infant in my arms and I had a feeling of great bliss as I thought that I could go on always holding it in my arms. It would be one year old and then only two, and I would not have to give it away."[7] Like Kollwitz, I too have sometimes dreamed that my grown children are still my babies. For the first minute or two after I awaken from these dreams, I feel utterly bereft. It is as if I have suddenly lost a pure and lovely part of myself.

Some mysterious inner force urges the child to separate itself from the mother. However, no such comparable force compels the mother to separate from the child. Mothers, it seems, must learn when and how to let go. Some cultures ritualize the maternal act of separation. For example, for centuries pregnant Thai women purchased clay figurines of a mother with babe in arms. After the birth of their babies, the new mothers would throw these figurines into the river, thereby shattering the image of prenatal oneness and psychologically readying themselves for their postnatal twoness. Among the Aztec, it was customary for new mothers to sever the umbilical cord with a flint stone while saying, "I cut from your middle the navel string. . . . Here you sprout, here you flower. Here you are severed from your mother as the chip is struck from the stone."[8]

Unfortunately, modern American mothers are usually not given any instruction in the art of letting go (and of being let go). Unlike the ancient Aztec and the Thai people, we have no rituals to mark the leave-takings between mother and child, no models to guide the separating pair. Quite the opposite. In our culture, the mothers who remain always available to their children, always the "essential" ones, are deified as the "good mother," while the mothers who discourage their children's dependence may be labeled "cold" or "unmotherly."

The maternal task of separation is further complicated by the fact that "letting go" is not a single event. Indeed, how much easier it would all be if, let us say, after a mother weaned her baby (or left her toddler with the daycare worker or helped her eight-year-old pack a duffel bag for his first "overnight" at camp or put her ten-year-old on a plane all by himself or handed her teenager the car keys), she could confidently say, "Okay, now I've mastered the separation part of being a mother once and for all, and that's that!" The reality is that throughout the course of raising children, mothers must keep on learning to let go—to practice saying their goodbyes cheerfully; to push back the tears and accept ever-greater distances between their children and themselves.

With a son attending an out-of-state college and a daughter who recently graduated from college and is making her way in the "real" world, I know that I am still learning how to let go with grace; each time Jonathan and Leah take another step toward emancipation I must silence the anxious inner voice that warns of the dangers and uncertainties out there and tell myself (and them) that they will manage just fine.

As the following vignettes illustrate, when women do not understand that their children's separation is a normal and necessary development, they may view it as a sign of their maternal inadequacy or as a rejection of them. However, when they are given instruction in the art of letting go (and of being let go), they have a much better chance of fostering their children's well-being and growth—as well as their own.

My client Linda, the mother of two-and-a-half-year-old fraternal twins, told me that her daughter tries mostly to please her, but her son often provokes and frustrates her.

> He argues and argues, makes mean faces at me, and tries to push me out of his way. And then I lose my temper and, not knowing what else to do, send him to his room. Oh, it seems like I'm always sending him to his room. And when I isolate him like this I wind up feeling like such a bad mother.

I suggested to Linda that without being aware, she was being a very good mother; by sending her little son to his room when he was angry with her, she was doing exactly what he needed her to do for him—provide some space between them and free him temporarily from her maternal protection and control. Indeed, Linda herself pointed out that after her son spent a few minutes alone in his room, he always seemed happier and more at peace with the world—and with her.

Moreover, by sending her little son to his room, Linda was doing exactly what she needed to do for herself—enjoy a few moments of solitude and separation from her son. After all, unrelieved, round-the-clock ministrations to one's young children exhaust a mother's mental and physical resources; being ever-available, a mother can end up feeling spent. I find it quite interesting that the middle- and upper-class Victorian women who were expected to devote themselves exclusively to motherhood and the management of the household would nevertheless retire to their bedrooms each afternoon for an hour of solitude. The nineteenth-century mother seemed to know what the twentieth-century mother often fails to recognize: that every human being needs some time to be alone, to be unaccountable, to be quiet, to turn inward.

Mara, the mother of a six-year-old son who no longer welcomed her hugs and kisses, told me, "When Zak rejects my tenderness, I feel diminished and slapped down. It seems that my very essence—this generous maternal nature of mine—is being devalued." What helped my client was hearing from me that Zak's refusals were not intended to hurt her. Rather, they signified that he was growing out of little boyhood. It also helped Mara when I explained that although she meant no harm, her hugs and kisses threatened her son, perhaps because they aroused him or perhaps because they made him feel like a little baby again or perhaps because he thought "kissy-facey" stuff was only for girls. Once Mara could better understand what was going on for Zak, she felt less resentful and was more willing to honor the physical distance comfortable for him.

My hope and expectation is that Mara will also discover there are advantages to being the mother of a "big boy"—that instead of finding connections with her son only through their physical closeness, which he necessarily outgrows, she will find them by talking with him, by listening to him, by teaching him, by learning from him, and by exploring the world with him. I also hope and expect that Mara will discover new outlets for her generous maternal nature, that she will find ways of giving care and affection to a neglected child or a homeless woman or a lonely old person.

Mara's feelings of rejection as a mother remind me of the reactions of another client. Cynthia, who tends to be reserved and decorous, burst into my office one afternoon, obviously distraught. She told me that a counselor from her son's prestigious college, where he was a senior, had just telephoned to inform her that the young man had been hospitalized for depression. Although she had wanted to take the next plane from Denver to be with him, the psychiatrist assigned to the case had sternly advised against this, explaining that maternal solicitude would have the effect of weakening her son even more. "I feel like such a bad person," Cynthia sobbed. "She is telling me that my motherly love is not a cure but a poison, and that Carl needs me to be absent, not present, in order to get well." Nevertheless, Cynthia decided to take the psychiatrist's advice and did not visit her depressed son in the hospital. She realized that if she saw him while he was so ill, she would not be able to hold back her tears or to keep the "Oh, you poor, poor baby" look from her face.

In our therapy, Cynthia came to understand that her maternal nurture needed to take a new form. Having always felt sorry for her son, who, like Cynthia, was hypersensitive and easily knocked down by life's vicissitudes, Cynthia was used to commiserating with his troubles. In fact, as she came to recognize, this response was one way of remaining close with him. But in order to encourage his confidence and competence as he stepped out into the world, which is what she really wanted to do, Cynthia needed to nurture him differently; she needed to assert her faith in his personal power rather than to join him in his weakness. Nurture, after all, is not equivalent to indulgence; to nurture means to foster growth—to promote what is most alive and resilient in the other.

Shortly before her son's discharge from the hospital, Cynthia wrote to him.

Dear Carl,

Just a brief note to say that I do not doubt for a moment that learning to manage your depression is making you a stronger and wiser man. Now that we live apart, I am so glad that when you were in trouble you found kind and qualified people to help you. I love you with all my heart and have every confidence that you will face the world with courage and integrity. Drop me a line or give me a call when it's convenient!

Mom

Not surprisingly, as Cynthia has separated from Carl, she is able to focus more on the relationship with her husband, who is delighted by her attentions. Rather than talk about Carl in our sessions, we are now talking about the trip to London that Cynthia and her husband are happily planning or about the pleasure they find in reading books aloud to one another or about the new confidences that they are sharing. Once, as I was walking home from work, I passed one of Boulder's outdoor cafés and could not help but smile when I caught sight of the two, oblivious to me and all the other passersby, sipping their iced teas and gazing lovingly at one another.

For some women, feelings of being rejected peak when their sons marry. The developmental task of the young man is to transfer his feelings of primary loyalty and love from his mother to his wife, and in order to accomplish this, he will, in fact, seek greater physical and emotional distances from his mother, which may hurt and confuse her. As my long-time friend Charlotte put it, "I can't understand the reason for it, but now that Mel is married, he treats me more like a mother-in-law than like a mother." And a colleague, Marianne, confided, "When Robert was single we would have wonderful telephone conversations that went on a long time, but now that he's married, our calls are short and almost businesslike; rather than *talk* to me, Robert *checks in* with me." Saddest of all was the confidence shared by my client Mimi, a pediatric nurse and the mother of five:

> When my son and daughter-in-law gave birth to my first grandchild, I was bursting with good advice for them. I had so much to give them—babycare, after all, was my area of expertise. Not only did I bring up my own brood, but I have ministered to the needs of hundreds of new mothers and their babies over the years as a career nurse. My son, however, made it clear to me that I was not to impose my views on them. He strongly implied that my advice-giving made his wife feel dominated, and that he needed to protect her from my domination. I felt like a Santa Claus, laden with gifts, who is barred from coming down the chimney and sent back out into the cold.

Although the famous proverb "A daughter's a daughter the rest of her life, a son's a son 'til he takes a wife" is an exaggeration, it points to the long-held tradition that the roles of son and of husband are in conflict with one another; although the continuous and close bond between mother and married daughter has generally been encouraged, the one between mother and married son, which is perceived as a threat to the young man's developing independence, has been discouraged.

As we have discussed in earlier chapters, the male child, beginning at a very young age, disidentifies from his mother. Nevertheless, throughout boyhood, adolescence, and early adulthood, he remains emotionally dependent on her to one extent or another. Normally, he ends this dependency at the time of his marriage: he understands that it is no longer appropriate for him to whisper his tender, vulnerable feelings into his mother's ear, that he must learn to share these with his wife instead. He understands that he should no longer turn to his mother for her expert opinions, that he must learn to trust his wife's counsel above all others. And the new wife typically reinforces her young husband's attempts to free himself from the powerful attachment to his mother; like him, she may perceive this attachment as a threat to his manhood; and just as no man wants to be pulled back into childishness, no woman wants to be married to a boy.

However, as the young married man normally pulls away from his mother voluntarily, the mother typically feels abandoned as her son shifts his allegiance from her and his original family to his chosen life partner. In order to soften this loss, some mothers compete with their daughters-in-law for the son/husband's loyalty; they may pamper the married son or demand his time and attention. The mother who indulges her married son or makes excessive demands on him is sure to incur her daughter-in-law's ire. In her book *Worlds of Pain: Life in the Working Class Family,* Lillian Rubin writes that young working-class husbands, who are often still in their teens, tend to drop by their mothers' homes and sometimes continue to have regular meals there. Not surprisingly, their wives are furious. The young women want their young men to relinquish their roles as pampered sons and to establish themselves as self-sufficient husbands: to move out of their mothers' homes into their own.

The response of more secure mothers to their newly married sons is to accept a less glorified, a less central role in their lives. Maternal love transforms as it matures. The wisest and loveliest older mothers I know tell me that the pleasures of being a parent continue across the life cycle. As my mother-in-law, Sylvia Bassoff, told me, when her son married me and as the two of us raised a family, she was filled with pleasure and pride. There was for her—and, when she beholds her grandchildren, continues to be—great joy in watching the lives of the younger generations unfold. In Sylvia's words, "I savor every moment."

In Germany, my friend Charlotte explained to me, the advice offered to parents of grown children is summed up in three words: *staunen, schweigen,* and *schenken. Staunen* is to marvel at from a respectful distance. Wise parents take delight in and praise the goodness and power of their grown children while they honor the boundaries that separate them. *Schweigen* refers to a disciplined silence. Wise parents give up the right to advise, criticize, lecture, and impose ideas upon their grown children; they offer a listening ear rather than an instructive word. *Schenken* refers to giving gifts. Wise parents give gifts that empower their grown children—material gifts, when appropriate, but also emotional gifts such as compassion, affirmation, support, encouragement, and praise.

Allow me a short digression. When I planned this book, I expected that its concluding chapter would be about friendships between mothers and adult sons. If mothers mothered intelligently and lovingly during their sons' growing-up years, I was convinced they had every reason to expect close friendships with their adult sons. However, my interviews with many well-adjusted men led me to change my mind. Although I met several men who loved and liked and cared about their mothers and who gladly shared *parts* of their lives with them, I did not meet one who called his mother his "friend," i.e., his confidante and companion. (In contrast, I have known many women who say that their mothers are not only their friends but their *best* friends.) Having struggled so hard and so long to become separate from their mothers —that is, to become adult men—they are not about to break down the protective fences between them and risk falling back into infantile intimacies with them. Similarly, the women who enjoy positive relationships with their sons do not try to take these fences down but learn instead to love within their bounds. Hence, my concluding chapter is not about mothers becoming friends with their sons but about mothers separating from them and taking new pleasure in their own selfhood.

The universal task of mothers is to respect their sons' needs to create a certain distance from them. Unfortunately, mistaking normal separation for cruel rejection, some mothers "retaliate" by abandoning their sons physically or emotionally. For example, at one point, after my client Cynthia was advised by her son's psychiatrist not to visit him, she told me, "Maybe the best thing for Carl and me is just not to have anything to do with each other from here on in. If he doesn't need me in his life, I certainly don't need him in mine." Cynthia's hostile proclamation was a temporary re-action to feeling discounted. In time, she came to understand that she was indeed important to her son—although, as we have seen, her presence in his life would need to take a new form.

Although some mothers, in response to their sons' sep-arating from them, may withdraw their love, care, or interest in them, others may become excessively accommodating. I observed this tendency in myself. As Jonathan approached adolescence—a period typically marked by the teenager's opposing wishes to assert adult independence and to regress to infantile dependence—I responded with exquisite atten-tion to his childish needs. I recall, for example, that when he told me that he was going for days without eating anything because "you never have any *good* food in the house," I did not smile at his wild exaggerations or send him to the neigh-borhood grocery store with a shopping list or teach him how to make an omelet. Rather, overwhelmed with guilt, I traipsed to the supermarket and overstocked the refrigerator with his favorite ready-to-eat foods—yogurt in every flavor, jars and jars of pickles, olives, and salsa. And when he wanted to toast a bagel, I was always there to slice it in two for him. My husband's gentle admonishments put a stop to my oversolicitude: "Evi, it's not healthy for Jonathan or for you to pamper him this way; you're keeping him stuck in 'little boyhood'—and you're knocking yourself out un-necessarily."

However, looking back, I perfectly understand the sub-conscious reasons for my oversolicitude. Because Jonathan at twelve was so obviously pulling away—acting surly and sharing so little of himself with me—I became unsure that we would have any connection in the years to come. Unlike my husband, who shared with Jonathan a passion for sports and enjoyed a natural comradery, I sensed that my son and

I might not have common interests to bind us in the future. Only by meticulously catering to Jonathan's wishes would I remain important to him—or so I mistakenly assumed. It is interesting that I was not similarly insecure when my daughter, with whom I strongly identified and who strongly identified with me, pulled away during her adolescence. Although Leah's efforts to differentiate herself from me sometimes stung—"I'm not you, *I'm me*," she would often say—I did not believe that we would ever become strangers to one another.

It is my impression that many other mothers overindulge their sons in an effort to remain important to and needed by them. A colleague recently told me that when as a college student, he had hitchhiked home for the holidays, his mother was forlorn that he had not brought along his dirty laundry for her to wash. This colleague also confided his sadness that his mother could relate to him only as caretaker and that they never developed a more engaging relationship. As he said, "Without my laundry to wash, there was nothing between my mother and me." Indeed, for all too many women it is the failure to get beyond their impulses to caretake and to develop more mature forms of maternal love—such as being empathic, encouraging, and affirming—that undermines their relationships with grown children.

I began this chapter with a reference to *The Giving Tree*. Let us return to this story, which, with great simplicity and heart, tells about the mother who, wanting only to please her son and ensure a close relationship with him, indulges him and, in so doing, stunts his growth and her own.

The boy, whom the mother-tree loves very much, goes off into the world, leaving her behind, sad and lonely. Then one day he returns. To her disappointment, however, he no longer wants to gather her leaves, scramble up her trunk, swing from her branches, eat her apples, or sleep in her shade. Instead, he wants money to buy the toys and gadgets that he believes will bring him happiness. Apologetic, the mother-tree explains that she has no money to give but encourages the boy to take all her apples and sell them to city folk. The boy does just that.

Years pass, and the boy disappears from the mother-tree's life once again. Then one day he returns. Now he asks her for a house to keep him warm. Admitting that she has no house other than the forest, the mother-tree tells the boy to cut off her branches and use these to build a house for himself. He is satisfied for the time being and, after stripping the mother-tree of her limbs and branches, departs from her.

Once again, he stays away for years, and once again, on his return, he wants something more. This time it is a boat that can carry him to faraway places. Sad that she does not have a ready-made boat to give, the mother-tree tells the boy to cut down her trunk and to make a boat from it.

Having sailed the seas, the boy, now an old man, returns. The old mother-tree, anticipating that he will want still more from her, confesses that she has nothing left to give. Now that her apples, her branches and leaves, and her trunk are gone, she is nothing but an old stump.

That Shel Silverstein uses a tree to represent the mother is quite fitting. Throughout the ages and across many cultures, the tree is identified with the mother. In their positive forms, both are life-giving and life-affirming; both bear, transform, nourish, anchor, and shelter. In Greek legend, the mother tree splits open her trunk to birth the beautiful god Adonis; in ancient Egyptian myth, the tree goddesses, Hathor and Nut, give birth to the sun.[9] But in her negative form, like the human mother who will not let her children go and grow, the mother tree is life-denying: she is the hanging tree, the gallow tree, the cross, the stake. As the giant baobab tree of eastern Africa, she entombs the dead in her belly; as the Egyptian tree goddess Nut, she not only births the sun but is the keeper of its coffin.

I find it interesting that the tree is also associated with a woman's personal development and inner growth. Just as a tree reconciles the opposites of above and below, of heaven and earth, by both reaching toward the sky and penetrating deep into the earth, a woman must learn to reconcile her spiritual needs—to create, to develop the intellect, to define moral or religious beliefs, to dream, to aspire—and her down-to-earth (grounding) functions—to protect, nourish, and shelter her dependent children. By allowing her limbs and branches to be cut, Silverstein's Giving Tree, unable to reach for the stars, is deprived of dreams and aspirations.

Like the Giving Tree, many mothers sacrifice what is most alive and potentially fruitful in themselves for their children; by staying overinvolved in their children's lives, they do not get on with their own lives. But a woman with a truncated life cannot really be happy; neither can she be a good-enough mother to her sons and daughters. Ironically, the woman who gives up her personal interests and talents in order to be ever-available to children who have outgrown their need for her physical care is likely to discover that they come to resent her for her indulgence of them, which perpetuates their dependency on her and saps their vitality, and for her unending self-sacrifice, which instills guilt in them.

The soothing, caring "mother of oneness" is essential to the present and future well-being of her babies and very young children. By virtue of her attunement to their needs, they come to trust the world and the people in it as basically good. A mother's doting love will enable them to love others as well as to value themselves. But once her children are no longer babies, it is the wise "mother of separation" who encourages them to take care of themselves. And just as the wise "mother of separation" fosters her children's growth, she makes sure that she herself continues to grow—to take an active part in the world around her, to realize her talents and ambitions, to stimulate her intellect, to nourish her senses.

I sometimes used to worry that by pursuing a career in psychology and by writing books—by not being all-available to my children when they were growing up—they would resent me when they were adults. But now I know the opposite to be true. Leah, who has graduated from Carleton College and works in New York City, recently told me, "Mom, if you hadn't created a rich life of your own I would have been scared that you'd have wanted to take mine away—or, maybe, I'd have felt obligated to let you live through me. Your interest in your work made it easier, not harder, for me to feel comfortable with you." And a few months ago, during his winter break from college, Jonathan gave me a gift that I never expected. After reading the chapter that I had written about boys and their male role models, he took me aside and said, "I like your chapter a lot, and it's true that when I was a kid you couldn't be my role model. But you are now, just as much as Dad is. You know, Mom, how you always tell me that you're proud of me. Well, I've never told you this, but I'm proud of you too."

I do not believe that Jonathan's sentiment is unique. In my interviews with adult sons, I am reminded again and again that sons are most likely to respect their mothers when they see them as vital people—people who are engaged in their own enterprises, whatever these might be, and who maintain a lively interest in the world around them. In the earliest years of motherhood, a mother's role is to mirror and echo, coddle and dote. When a little boy explains why he loves his mother, he tells only about the nurturing things that she does for him. However, when a grown man reflects on his feelings for his mother, he tends to talk about her as a person in her own right.

Several examples of men who have high regard for their mothers come to mind. My client Ian recently spent a session talking about his mother's love of learning, which has inspired his own passion for books, and the way, undaunted, she is putting her life back together after the death of her husband of fifty years. My husband's eyes shine as he describes his mother's political activities—conducted by telephone from her apartment, where she is confined—on behalf of other frail and handicapped elderly. And when I asked my dear friend Rich if there were times when he was filled with love for his mother, he did not tell me about her acts of caretaking; choking back the sudden tears of emotion that took him by surprise, he simply said, "Yes, when I see that she is engaged in life and happy—when her face is beaming—I love her very much."

Sadly, many women are discouraged—by spouses, lovers, grown children, parents, and general opinion—from engaging in creative, social, political, and intellectual work because they might be accused of neglecting their family obligations. Several of my clients tell me that they even feel guilty for reading a book! For example, although her sons are in their late teens and quite capable, one of my clients explains that she still believes she should be always available to them: "When I snuggle up with a book and suddenly notice that one, two, or God forbid, three hours have gone by, I feel like I'm doing something that I shouldn't—that I'm acting selfishly. It seems so foolish, but there's a part of me that says I should be doing for the boys but not for myself."

In addition to guilt, fear can also hold women back from their development. Adam Phillips, a British psychotherapist, describes a consultation with a frantic mother of a toddler. The mother explained that her son prevented her from doing anything by hanging on to her and always being wound round her legs. The woman's repeated complaint that the child was always in the way prompted Phillips to ask her where she would be going if her son were not in the way, to which she replied, "Oh, I wouldn't know where I was!" Phillips suggests that this mother, afraid of realizing her ambitions, unconsciously encouraged her son's clinginess. As long as the little boy was the obstacle in her way, she had an excuse for going nowhere in her life.[10]

There are a number of reasons that mothers hold on to their sons too tightly or too long. The eminent Jungian analyst M. Esther Harding suggests that a mother may be unwilling to release her son from his dependency on her for fear of diminishing her power, which derives from doing and, sometimes, overdoing for him. Of course, the mother's protracted caretaking makes it hard, if not impossible, for the boy to develop his own competencies.

Harding describes the necessary maternal transformation as relinquishing her position of superiority as *giver* in order that the son can be released from his demeaning position of *taker*. This transformation is illustrated in some ancient Egyptian myths, whose themes are the ritualistic sacrifices of the adolescent sons (Attis, Horus, and Osiris), which are carried out by the mother, not in spite of her love but because of it.

The archetypal mother is depicted as two-sided: on the one side, she is soft and all-providing; on the other side, she is hard and withholding, intolerant of the son's inappropriately childish dependence. The "hard" mother refuses to clean her seven-year-old's room, which has become a disaster area, and insists that he put it in order himself. The "hard" mother does not rescue her crying son from his father, who is furious at him for having left his new mountain bike, unlocked, on the soccer field. The "hard" mother refrains from making excuses for her son when the high school attendance officer calls to tell her that the boy has cut chemistry class five times and may fail the class. The "hard" mother reminds her college-age son to pay back the $50 that he borrowed from her for tickets to a rock concert.

Again and again, over the course of parenting, the mother's "hardness" allows her to turn her back on her child—or symbolically sacrifice him—in order that he will become a strong and capable man. Too much of a mother's soft side, which is her maternal solicitude and caretaking, undermines the son's passage into independence and adulthood; it cripples his confidence to cope without her—or without the motherly wife he eventually marries to take the place of his doting mother. Harding further points out that too much maternal softness not only affects the son but also undermines the woman's own passage into greater autonomy. Only as the mother releases her son from his dependent ties on her does she release herself from the constricting role of caretaker.

For a mother, the art of letting go involves balancing her soft and hard sides—becoming increasingly aware when she is leaning too heavily on one side so that she can make adjustments. One of the many benefits of the intact family is that husbands and wives shape each other as parents; married women can and should turn to their husbands to help them recognize when they are tilting out of balance. In my experience, without another's viewpoint, it is often difficult to accurately judge when one is being too hard or too soft as a parent. Single mothers, who do not have the advantage of ongoing feedback from their sons' fathers, are wise to turn to trusted friends and relatives or to a family therapist for feedback and guidance in this area.

The transformation of mother love is wonderfully described in a tale told by the Bella Coola people, who live along the coastal areas of British Columbia. I happily discovered this tale in Merlin Stone's book *Ancient Mirrors of Womanhood;* of all the mother-son stories that I have read, this one is my favorite."[11]

Mother Somagalags came down from the heavens that stretch across the lands of the North Pacific waters. There she found a man to love and with his seed brought forth three children in the form of three great mountains. When the mountains were fully grown, Somagalags left them and journeyed long and far to a beach made of the finest grains of sand. Once having reached her destination, Somagalags did not stop to rest. Instead, she went back and forth, time and again, from the beach to a nearby forest from which she collected and carried away many dry fallen cedars. From these cedars, whose branches and bark she painstakingly cleaned and smoothed, Somagalags built herself a sturdy wooden cabin in which to live.

Having settled into her cedar-wood cabin, which stood at the edge of the great ocean waters, Somagalags once again gave birth, this time to four young wolves, who howled for food and warmth. Placing the infant cubs in the warmest corner of the cabin, she did not stop to rest from the great labor of childbirth but went off to dig for clams. When, weighted down with her basket of clams, she returned to the cabin, she was surprised to hear the laughter of human children coming from inside. But upon entering the cabin, all she saw were four tender cubs sleeping peacefully. Trying to forget the puzzle of the human voices, Somagalags made a fire in the hearth and over it cooked the clams for her hungry cubs.

The days passed, the seasons turned, the years went by. One evening as Somagalags, digging stick in one hand, basket filled with clams in the other, stood by the water's edge she was filled with weariness. "How many times has it been that I have fetched for clams, made the fire, fed my young?" she sighed to herself as she trudged across the white sands to her cabin. Then as she reached the Great Cedar Tree, which had grown alongside her house, something in her made her stop momentarily in her tracks, and a sudden sound of human laughter brought her thoughts to a halt.

In silence, Somagalags drew close to the window of the cedar cabin and, peering inside, saw, to her astonishment, four nearly grown young men in place of her four wolf cubs. Now a great anger rose in her heart and fatigue filled her body. She thought of the many long, unrelieved days that she had spent doing and doing still more to take care of her young. Furious, clutching her digging stick, Somagalags climbed through the window. Madly waving the stick, she chastised the four young men for tricking her into believing that they were helpless cubs, that they could not fetch their own wood or make their own evening fire. Though quick to make excuses, the young men finally admitted that they had taken advantage of their mother. Each agreed that if she taught them how to care for themselves, they would make her proud of them.

The very next day Somagalags took her sons to the beach to teach them the secrets of finding the clam beds. She took them to the edge of the forest, where she pointed out the straightest cedars and told them how they could be felled and used to build new shelters that would protect them from the cold sea winds. Finally, she took them to a sunlit grove deep in the forest where, patiently and lovingly, she taught them how to use the wood of life to carve the sacred totem, so that they and their children and their children's children would never forget the proud clan to which they belonged.

Let us compare the meanings of the tree imagery in Shel Silverstein's *The Giving Tree* and in the story of Mother So-magalags. The Giving Tree is self-sacrificing and also passive. Out of love for her son, she allows her son to use her for his purposes, even though this use entails having her leafy branches, limbs, and trunk cut down so that she is reduced to an old stump. And the boy is not better but worse off for having been indulged by the mother tree who cannot say no to him. Over the years, he grows increasingly selfish and materialistic; having been given too much, he knows only how to take.

In the tale of Mother Somagalags, the tree is a symbol of the mother's agency rather than passivity, her self-respect rather than self-abnegation. With her own strong hands, Somagalags builds her house from the wood of the tree—not any tree, but the cedar tree, which, like Somagalags herself, is hard and durable, capable of protecting her family from the harsh winds that would knock down flimsier material. For several years Somagalags carries on her mother work without complaint. But when the role as caretaker begins to feel like a lifelong bondage, it is the Great Cedar Tree, which has taken root in the sandy soil on which her house stands, that signals to her that she must change—and this is exactly what Somagalags proceeds to do.

Empowered by her own sense of indignation, Somagalags no longer bends to her sons' infantile appeals for the mother care that they have outgrown and that, if continued, would doom them to eternal boyhood. Instead, she passes on to them the secrets of her experience so that they can take care of themselves by building their own sturdy houses and carving their own magnificent totem—so that they can become competent men.

Thus, having honorably and lovingly fulfilled her maternal obligations, the mythical Mother Somagalags—who, we would do well to remember, represents all ordinary mothers—will return, alone, to the fine wooden house, built with her own hands, that sits by the edge of the sea in the shade of the Great Cedar Tree that never stops growing.

And, surely, we have every reason to speculate that when Mother Somagalags is in her fine wooden house she is not twiddling her thumbs. Perhaps she is learning how to play the piano or perhaps she is writing a poem or, perhaps, like my mother-in-law, she is making phone calls to the mayor's office on behalf of those who are in need.

AFTERWORD

A Letter to Jonathan

September 12, 1993

Dear Jonathan,

I was strolling on the mall yesterday when from a distance I caught sight of a bunch of eight- or nine-year-old boys in baseball uniforms. They were knocking each other around, falling all over themselves, laughing hard. Among this group of husky towheads was a slender dark-haired boy, and I said to myself, "Why, there's Jonathan. His game must be over. He looks so happy. I bet his team won." I rushed toward "you." And then I remembered. *You* are all grown up; you live 700 miles away from me; you have a beard and drive a sixteen-foot truck and cook your own meals. Were you now standing among these boys in baseball uniforms, you would tower over them, especially the slender dark-haired one.

I miss you, little Jonathan. I miss my wild, my sweet, my innocent boy.

Of course, there are advantages to your having grown

up. Being little Jonathan's mother was not always a breeze. Did I ever tell you that when you were a toddler—a toddler who discovered the wonders of his new world by trying to *eat* everything in it—I developed, on your behalf, an intimate, ongoing relationship with the Poison Control Center? (Funny now, not funny then.) And your sloppiness—the trail of dirty dishes, smelly socks, balls and bats, bottle caps and empty yogurt containers with sticky spoons that followed you around the house—well, it drove me crazy. Then there was your argumentativeness, the relentless questioning and contradicting. By the time you turned twelve, you had honed the skills of an Alan Dershowitz; living with a trial lawyer was not something I had bargained for.

More than anyone else, Jonathan, you could wear me down, frustrate me, make me want to scream. And more than anyone else, Jonathan, you could break my heart. When you brought me your sorrows, your worries, your fears, when you bared your tender soul and your good heart to me, my anger melted away like snow on a warm winter day. I wanted to make it all right for you, to remove every stone from your path. But most of the time all I could do was listen; all I could offer was a sympathetic ear and an optimistic word. Some of my happiest moments were when I felt that my listening to you and affirming you had helped; some of my worst times were when I believed that my offerings were inadequate, when your tear-filled eyes revealed your disappointment in me.

And yet, for all the difficulties of being a mother, I know that without you my life would be infinitely inferior. In Hebrew Jonathan means "gift of God," and you are that to me.

Perhaps in part because you are a male and I am a female, we look at the world differently. No doubt because you and I have strong personalities and strong opinions, we do not smooth over our differences but draw each other's attention to them. Sometimes I feel as if I must stand on my head to see your perspective, but I do just that. You convince me to stretch and to see anew. You prevent me from becoming smug, absolute, stuck in one position.

Without your being aware, you bring out the best in me. Because you are determined to overcome your insecurities by facing life bravely and cheerfully, I would feel embarrassed wimping out on my life, taking the easy path, backing down; so I try to do the right thing. Just like you want me to be proud of you, I want you to be proud of me. Do you remember that, years ago, when I was battling to overcome stage fright, you gave me your treasured baseball card of Dave Winfield? "When you're on that TV program and feeling scared, just touch this card and it will give you all the power you need," you assured me. As you promised, the magic—the magic of your love and confidence in me—worked.

Life is full of paradoxes. In the process of helping you grow, I grow too; in making you strong, I become strong; by observing your tolerance of people and ideas, I become more tolerant. As I am a role model for you, you are one for me; as I am your teacher, you are mine. For all this, thank you, Jonathan.

With love and respect,

Mom

NOTES

Introduction

1. I have adopted the term "overfunctioning" from HARRIET GOLDHOR LERNER, *The Dance of Anger: A Woman's Guide to Changing the Patterns of Intimate Relationships* (New York: Harper & Row, 1985).

2. SARA RUDDICK, *Maternal Thinking: Towards a Politics of Peace* (New York: Ballantine, 1989), p. 120.

3. SIBYLLE BIRKHÄUSER-OERI, *The Mother: Archetypal Image in Fairy Tales* (Toronto: Inner City Books, 1988), p. 116.

Chapter I

1. ELEANOR MACCOBY and CAROL JACKLIN have conducted the most definitive research of male-female differences; their analyses, which are based on studies done in the United

States, cross-cultural data, animal studies, and hormonal research, show that boys on the whole hit and insult each other more, respond faster and more strongly when they are hit or insulted, and engage in more rough-and-tumble play than girls on the whole. However, not all boys are more aggressive than girls and some are less (*The Psychology of Sex Differences*, vol. 1 [Stanford: Stanford University Press, 1974]; "Sex Differences in Aggression: A Rejoinder and Reprise," *Child Development*, vol. 51 [1980], pp. 964–980).

2. See CHRISTINE GORMAN ("Sizing Up the Sexes," *Time*, January 20, 1992, pp. 42–51) for an interesting commentary on parents' observations that girls and boys are different in nature.

3. DEBORAH TANNEN provides a well-researched account of gender differences in speaking patterns (*You Just Don't Understand: Women and Men in Conversation* [New York: Ballantine Books, 1990]).

4. Giving credit where credit is due, DIANE GREEN points out that Linda Lowenstein, a columnist for the *Daily Camera* (Boulder, Colorado), was the first to note that boys have an internal "vroom."

5. ROBERT BLY, *Iron John: A Book About Men* (Reading, Mass.: Addison-Wesley, 1990), p. 6.

6. JOHN WELWOOD, *Journey of the Heart: Intimate Relationship and the Path of Love* (New York: Harper Perennial, 1991), p. 146.

7. RICK FIELDS, *The Code of the Warrior in History, Myth, and Everyday Life* (New York: Harper Perennial, 1991), p. 30.

8. ROBERT MOORE and DOUGLAS GILLETTE, *King, Warrior, Magician, Lover: Rediscovering the Archetypes of the Mature Masculine* (San Francisco: Harper, 1990), p. 79.

9. See "Children's Conduct Disorders," *Harvard Mental Health Letter*, vol. 5 (9) (March 1989), for a description of antisocial behavior in youngsters.

10. See MYRIAM MIEDZIAN (*Boys Will Be Boys: Breaking the Link Between Masculinity and Violence* [New York: Doubleday, 1991], pp. 63–69) for a comprehensive review of the

situational and psychological conditions associated with violence in boys.

11. See MICHAEL E. LAMB ("Fathers and Child Development: An Integrative Review," in *The Role of the Father in Child Development*, edited by Michael E. Lamb [New York: Wiley, 1981], pp. 1–70) for a review of studies on the influence of the father in the boy's development.

12. SCOTT COLTRANE, "Father-Child Relationships and the Status of Women: A Cross-Cultural Study," *American Journal of Sociology*, vol. 93 (5) (1988), pp. 1060–1095.

13. MUNRO LEAF, *The Story of Ferdinand* (1936; reprint, New York: Puffin Books, 1977).

14. A version of this story appears in BERNIE ZILBERGELD, *Male Sexuality* (Toronto: Bantam Books, 1978), p. 91.

15. See GORMAN, pp. 42–51, for a discussion of children's resistance to play with toys associated with the opposite sex.

16. WELWOOD, p. 156.

17. CAROL KLEIN, *Mothers and Sons* (Boston: G. K. Hall, 1985), p. 14.

18. Ibid., p. 15.

19. MIEDZIAN, p. 98.

20. KLEIN, p. 15.

21. Cited in ALEXANDRA TOWLE, ed., *Mothers* (New York: Simon and Schuster, 1988), p. 64.

22. Cited in ibid., p. 42.

23. BLY, pp. 2–3.

24. MIEDZIAN, p. 197.

25. BLY, p. 29.

26. JOSÉ ORTEGA Y GASSET, *Meditations on Hunting* (New York: McGraw-Hill, 1986), p. 100.

27. SARA RUDDICK, *Maternal Thinking: Towards a Politics of Peace* (New York: Ballantine, 1989), p. 19.

28. Ibid., p. 72.

Chapter 2

1. FELIX SALTEN, *Bambi*, translated by Whittaker Chambers (New York: Grosset & Dunlap, 1929), p. 88.

2. Ibid., p. 112.

3. Ibid., p. 104.

4. J. LANG, "Brooding Behind the Steel Wall," *Inroads*, January 1991, pp. 27–28.

5. SALTEN, p. 103.

6. As quoted in ROSS FIRESTONE (ed.), *A Book of Men: Visions of the Male Experience* (New York: Stonehill, 1978), pp. 30–31.

7. RONALD CLARK, *Freud: The Man and the Case* (New York: Random House, 1980), p. 12.

8. SALTEN, p. 62.

9. GUY CORNEAU, *Absent Fathers, Lost Sons: The Search for Masculine Identity*, translated by Larry Shouldice (Boston: Shambala, 1991), p. 22.

10. Cited in WILLIAM RASPBERRY, *Denver Post*, January 26, 1992.

11. Ibid.

12. CORNEAU, p. 17.

Chapter 3

1. Psychoanalyst RALPH GREENSON seems to have been the first to describe the boy's developmental processes of "dis-identification" from the mother and "counter-identification" with the father. According to Greenson, the first step establishes the boy's separateness, and the second his maleness ("Dis-identification from Mother: Its Special Importance for the Boy," *International Journal of Psycho-Analysis*, vol. 49 [1968], pp. 370–375).

2. For a fascinating interpretation of gender development and its implications for creativity, readers are encouraged to refer to LIAM HUDSON and BERNADINE JACOT, *The Way Men*

Think: Intellect, Intimacy, and the Erotic Imagination (New Haven: Yale University Press, 1991).

3. DORIS BERNSTEIN, *Female Identity Conflict in Clinical Practice*, edited by Norbert Freedman and Betsy Distler (Northvale, N.J.: Jason Aronson, 1993), p. 25.

4. Ibid., p. 26.

5. LINDA RENNIE FORCEY, *Mothers of Sons: Toward an Understanding of Responsibility* (New York: Praeger, 1987), p. 52.

6. HUDSON and JACOT, p. 41.

7. The traditional fatherly function of separating mother and son is clearly illustrated in FELIX SALTEN's *Bambi*. For example, in one scene from the book, Bambi's mother leaves the young deer alone so that she can be relieved of caretaking and enjoy some moments of solitude. But Bambi is utterly miserable without her and calls for her. Suddenly, he observes his father standing beside him. The old stag reprimands Bambi for crying for his mother and suggests that he is certainly capable of staying by himself for a little while. Although Bambi trembles at his father's words, he also wants to win his approval. As Salten writes, "When his mother came back he did not tell her anything of the encounter. He did not call her any more either the next time she disappeared. He thought of the old stag while he wandered around. He wanted very much to meet him. He wanted to say to him, 'See I don't call my mother any more,' so the old stag would praise him." (pp. 81–82)

8. See, for example, SAMUEL OSHERSON, *Finding Our Fathers: How a Man's Life Is Shaped by His Relationship with His Father* (New York: Fawcett Columbine, 1986), p. 6; J. LEVER, "Sex Differences in the Games Children Play," *Social Problems*, vol. 23 (1976), pp. 478–487; E. PRITCHER and L. S. SCHULTZ, *Boys and Girls at Play: The Development of Sex Roles* (New York: Praeger, 1983); CHRISTINE GORMAN, "Sizing Up the Sexes," *Time*, January 20, 1992, pp. 42–51.

9. ERICH NEUMANN, "Fear of the Feminine," *Quadrant: Journal of the C. G. Jung Foundation for Analytic Psychology*, Spring 1986, p. 11.

10. OSHERSON, p. 10.

11. Ibid., p. 98.

12. LOREN E. PEDERSEN, *Dark Hearts: The Unconscious Forces that Shape Men's Lives* (Boston: Shambala, 1991), p. 7.

13. I would like to point out that the mother who, rather than holding the son back, pushes him out of her nest too abruptly may also become the "terrible mother" of his fantasy world. For example, in fairy tales, she is sometimes depicted as the wicked mother (stepmother) who sends her young deep into the cold, dark woods where they must fend for themselves or die. And in one version of the Greek myth, she takes the form of the goddess Hera, who flings her newborn son, Hephaestus, from the peak of Mount Olympus into the void, permanently crippling him.

14. ROBERT A. JOHNSON, *He: Understanding Masculine Psychology*, rev. ed. (New York: Harper & Row, 1989), p. 49.

15. CAROL KLEIN, *Mothers and Sons* (Boston: G. K. Hall, 1985), p. 50.

16. BRUNO BETTELHEIM, *The Uses of Enchantment: The Meaning and Importance of Fairy Tales* (New York: Vintage Books, 1977), p. 145.

17. KLEIN, pp. 46–47.

18. ROBERT J. STOLLER, "Symbiosis Anxiety and the Development of Masculinity," *Archives of General Psychiatry*, vol. 30 (1974), p. 170.

19. ERNEST JONES, *The Life and Work of Sigmund Freud*, vol. 1 (New York: Basic Books, 1953), p. 8.

20. D. H. LAWRENCE, "New Heaven and Earth," *The Complete Poems of D. H. Lawrence* (New York: Viking Press, 1964), p. 259.

Chapter 4

1. Cited in ANTONIA FRASER, *The Warrior Queens* (New York: Alfred A. Knopf, 1989), p. 330.

2. In this chapter, we deal with heterosexuality rather

than with homosexuality. Mothers' responses to the sexuality of gay sons are addressed in Chapter 9.

3. JUDITH ARCANA, *Every Mother's Son: The Role of Mothers in the Making of Men* (Garden City, N.Y.: Doubleday, 1983), p. 16.

4. Ibid., p. 14.

5. JOHN MUNDER ROSS, "Beyond the Phallic Illusion: Notes on Man's Heterosexuality," *The Psychology of Men: New Psychoanalytic Perspectives*, edited by Gerald Fogel, Frederick Lane, and Robert Liebert (New York: Basic Books, 1986), p. 65.

6. CHRISTIANE OLIVIER, *Jocasta's Children: The Imprint of the Mother*, translated by George Craig (London: Routledge, 1989), p. 36.

7. DAVID M. TERMAN, "Affect and Parenthood: The Impact of the Past Upon the Present," *Parenthood: A Psychodynamic Perspective*, edited by Rebecca Cohen, Bertram Cohler, and Sidney Weissman (New York: Guilford Press, 1984), p. 330.

8. OLIVIER, p. 82.

9. Cited in ANGELA BARRON MCBRIDE, *The Growth and Development of Mothers* (New York: Harper Colophon, 1973), p. 85.

10. OLIVIER, p. 83.

11. CAROL KLEIN, *Mothers and Sons* (Boston: G. K. Hall, 1985), p. 114.

12. ANNE BANNING, "Mother-Son Incest: Confronting a Prejudice," *Child Abuse and Neglect*, vol. 13 (1989), p. 567.

13. Interestingly, in SOPHOCLES' ancient tragedy, Jocasta does not appear so innocent. Unlike her son who says, "I had to face a thing most terrible/Not willed by me, I swear," Jocasta appears to have some premonition of the incest and an interest in minimizing it: "As to your mother's bed, don't fear it/Before this, in dreams too as well as oracles/Many a man has lain with his own mother" (*Sophocles: Oedipus at Colonus*, in David Grene and Richard Lattimore, eds., *Greek Tragedies*, vol. 3 [Chicago: University of Chicago Press, 1961], pp. 107–187).

14. OLIVIER, p. 2.

15. KLEIN, p. 106.

16. ROBERT BLY, *Iron John: A Book About Men* (Reading, Mass.: Addison-Wesley, 1990), p. 185.

17. BANNING, p. 565.

18. ESTELA V. WELLDON, *Mother, Madonna, Whore: The Idealization and Denigration of Motherhood* (London: Free Association Books, 1988), pp. 88–89.

19. PENNY BILOFSKY and FREDDA SACHAROW, *In-laws/Outlaws; How to Make Peace with His Family and Yours.* (New York: Fawcett Crest, 1991), p. xi.

Chapter 5

1. KARL ZINSMEISTER, "The Nature of Fatherhood," An Institute for American Values Working Paper for the Symposium on Fatherhood in America Publication No. 11 (1991), p. 25.

2. EVELYN BASSOFF, "Q & A: Marriage," *Parents* Magazine, June 1993, p. 54.

3. BASSOFF, "Q & A: Marriage," *Parents* Magazine, May 1992, p. 45.

4. BASSOFF, "Q & A: Marriage," *Parents* Magazine, June 1992, p. 41.

5. NOR HALL and WARREN DAWSON, *Broodmales* (Dallas: Spring Publications, 1989), p. 28.

6. MARTIN GREENBERG and NORMAN MORRIS, "Engrossment: The Newborn's Impact upon the Father," *American Journal of Orthopsychiatry*, vol. 44 (1974), pp. 520–531.

7. HOMER, *The Odyssey*, translated by Robert Fitzgerald (New York: Anchor, 1963), pp. 295–296.

8. LINDA RENNIE FORCEY, *Mothers of Sons: Toward an Understanding of Responsibility* (New York: Praeger, 1987), p. 60.

9. ROBERT A. JOHNSON, *We: Understanding the Psychology of Romantic Love* (New York: Harper & Row, 1983), p. 164.

10. There is accumulating evidence of the nurturing father's impact on the child's development. For example,

a twenty-six-year longitudinal study shows that paternal involvement is the single strongest parent-related factor in the development of empathy in sons and daughters; fathers who spent time alone with their children—giving baths, meals, and basic care—reared the most compassionate adults (RICHARD KOESTNER, CAROL FRANZ, and JOEL WEINBERGER, "The Family Origins of Empathic Concern: A 26-Year Longitudinal Study," *Journal of Personality and Social Psychology*, vol. 58 [1990], pp. 709–717).

11. *Zohar III*, 77b–78a, quoted from Raphael Patai, *The Hebrew Goddess* (New York: Avon Books, 1978), p. 137.

Chapter 6

1. TAMAR LEWIN (*New York Times*), "Single, a Parent and Proud," reported in *Denver Post*, October 11, 1992, p. 31A.

2. See, for example, NEIL KALTER, *Growing Up with Divorce: Helping Your Child Avoid Immediate and Later Emotional Problems* (New York: Fawcett Columbine, 1990), pp. 2–3; JOHN GUIDUBALDI and JOSEPH PERRY, "Divorce and Mental Health Sequelae for Children: A Two-Year Follow-up of a Nationwide Sample," *Journal of the American Academy of Child Psychiatry*, vol. 24 (1985), pp. 531–537; JUDITH WALLERSTEIN and JOAN BERLIN KELLY, *Surviving the Break-up: How Children and Parents Cope with Divorce* (New York: Basic Books, 1980).

3. Findings are from RICHARD A. WARSHAK, "The Texas Custody Research Project" described in Richard A. Warshak, *The Custody Revolution: The Father Factor and the Motherhood Mystique* (New York: Poseidon Press, 1992), pp. 136–151. For further corroboration, see KATHLEEN A. CAMARA and GARY RESNICK, "Interparental Conflict and Cooperation: Factors Modifying Children's Post-Divorce Adjustment," in E. MAVIS HETHERINGTON and JOSEPHINE D. ARASTEH, eds., *Impact of Divorce, Single Parenting, and Stepparenting on Children* (Hillsdale, N.J.: Lawrence Erlbaum Associates, 1988), pp. 169–195.

4. ROBERT BLY, *Iron John: A Book About Men* (Reading, Mass.: Addison-Wesley, 1990), p. 17.

5. Ibid., p. 17.

6. KALTER, p. 249.

7. The moving story of the Jews who lived in the internment camp in Oswego, New York, is reported in RUTH KRUBER, *Haven: The Unknown Story of 1,000 World War II Refugees* (New York: Coward McCann, 1983).

8. ROMAIN GARY, *Promises at Dawn* (New York: Harper & Bros., 1961), p. 26.

9. MARTIN HOFFMAN, "Father Absence and Conscience Development," *Developmental Psychology*, vol. 4 (1971), pp. 400–406.

10. MARGUERITE KELLY wrote, "It is in the history of a family . . . that a child finds his place best and no one explains it better than a grandparent." Cited in BETH MENDE CONNY, "The Quotable Family," manuscript, p. 18.

11. KALTER, p. 394.

12. WALLERSTEIN and KELLY, p. 167.

Chapter 7

1. HOMER, *The Odyssey of Homer*, translated by Allen Mandelbaum (Berkeley: University of California Press, 1990), p. 19.

2. Ibid., p. 442.

3. Ibid., p. 455.

4. JOHN BALZAR (*Los Angeles Times*), "America's Phobia of Gays Brewed from Potent Mix," reported in *Denver Post*, February 18, 1993, p. 2A.

5. SARALIE BISNOVICH PENNINGTON, "Children of Lesbian Mothers," in *Gay and Lesbian Parents*, edited by Frederick W. Bozett (New York: Praeger, 1987).

6. See, for example, DAVID CRAMER, "Gay Parents and Their Children: A Review of Research and Practical Implications," *Journal of Counseling and Development*, vol. 64 (1986), pp. 504–507.

7. E. MAVIS HETHERINGTON, "Family Relations Six Years After Divorce," *Remarriage and Stepparenting: Current Research and Theory*, edited by Kay Pasley and Marilyn Ihinger-Tallman (New York: Guilford Press, 1987), pp. 185–205.

Chapter 8

1. See, for example, WILLIAM A. BARRY, "Marriage Research and Conflict: An Integrative Review," *Psychological Bulletin*, vol. 73 (1979), pp. 41–45; JANICE HOROWITZ NADLER, "The Psychological Stress of the Stepmother" (Ph.D. diss., abstract in *Dissertation Abstracts International*, vol. 37B [1976], p. 5367).

2. W. GLENN CLINGEMPEEL, EULALEE BRAND, and R. LEVOLI, "Stepparent-Stepchild Relationships in Stepmother and Stepfather Families: A Multi-method Study," *Family Relationships*, vol. 33 (1984), pp. 465–473.

3. JOHN SANTROCK and KAREN SITTERLE, "Parent-Child Relationships in Stepmother Families," *Remarriage and Stepparenting: Current Research and Theory*, edited by Kay Pasley and Marilyn Ihinger-Tallman (New York: Guilford Press, 1987), pp. 283–299.

4. Ibid., p. 292.

5. RUTH ROOSEVELT and JEANETTE LOFAS, *Living in Step: A Remarriage Manual for Parents and Children* (Chelsea, Mich.: Scarborough House, originally published by Stein & Day, 1976), p. 47.

6. Ibid., p. 49.

7. Ibid., p. 44.

8. KATALIN MORRISON and AIRDRIE THOMPSON-GUPPY, "The Cinderella's Stepmother Syndrome," *Canadian Journal of Psychiatry*, vol. 30 (1985), p. 526.

9. Ibid., p. 527.

10. See, for example, JESSE BERNARD, *Remarriage: A Study of Marriage* (New York: Russell & Russell, 1956); LUCILLE DUBERMAN, "Step-Kin Relationships," *Journal of Marriage and the Family*, vol. 35 (1973), pp. 283–292.

11. GUY DE MAUPASSANT, *Short Stories of the Tragedy and Comedy of Life*, vol. 17 (New York: Dunne, 1903).

Chapter 9

1. MEG UMANS (ed.), *Like Coming Home* (Austin: Banned Books, 1988), unpaged.

2. MAUREEN HARRINGTON, "Support Groups Offer Teens Solace in a Difficult Time," *Denver Post*, June 4, 1992, pp. 1E, 2E.

3. Ibid., p. 1E.

4. HANS CHRISTIAN ANDERSEN, *The Complete Fairy Tales and Stories*, translated by Erik Christian Haugaard (New York: Doubleday, 1974), p. 218.

5. Ibid., p. 219.

6. HARVEY FIERSTEIN, *Torch Song Trilogy: Three Plays* (New York: Villard Books, 1983).

7. HOWARD BROWN, *Familiar Faces, Hidden Lives: The Story of Homosexual Men in America Today* (New York: Harcourt Brace Jovanovich, 1976), p. 68.

8. I would like to point out that because AIDS now threatens heterosexuals—sexually active teenagers being especially vulnerable—the way it used to threaten only homosexuals, Jill's remark to me: "I worry as much about my single, heterosexual daughter as I do about my gay son" seems especially apt. The fear of having one's child struck down by this terrible disease no longer belongs only to parents of gay men.

9. MARY V. BORHEK, *Coming Out to Parents: A Two-Way Survival Guide for Lesbians and Gay Men and Their Parents* (Cleveland: Pilgrim Press, 1983), p. 181.

10. ARMISTEAD MAUPIN, *More Tales of the City* (New York: Harper & Row, 1980), p. 160.

Chapter 10

1. ANTHONY DECASPER and W. P. FIFER, "Of Human Bonding: Newborns Prefer Their Mothers' Voices," *Science*, vol. 208 (1980), pp. 1174–1176.

2. Cited in MARSHALL KLAUS and PHYLLIS KLAUS, *The Amazing Newborn* (Reading, Mass.: Addison-Wesley, 1985), p. 52.

3. CAROL KLEIN, *Mothers and Sons* (Boston: G. K. Hall, 1985), p. 232.

4. GEOFFREY C. WARD, "Elegant Duke Ellington: A Feast for Eye and Ear," *Smithsonian*, vol. 24 (1993), p. 64.

5. Ibid., p. 63.

6. MERCEDES LYNCH MALONEY and ANNE MALONEY, *The Hand that Rocks the Cradle: Mothers, Sons, and Leadership* (Englewood Cliffs, N.J.: Prentice-Hall, 1985), p. 19.

7. RONALD CLARK, *Freud: The Man and the Case* (New York: Random House, 1980), p. 9.

8. MARTIN SELIGMAN, *Learned Optimism* (New York: Alfred A. Knopf, 1991), p. 128.

9. Ibid., pp. 76–82.

10. SARA RUDDICK, *Maternal Thinking: Towards a Politics of Peace* (New York: Ballantine, 1989), pp. 74–75.

11. BRUNO BETTELHEIM, *The Uses of Enchantment: The Meaning and Importance of Fairy Tales* (New York: Vintage, 1977), p. 8.

12. LESLIE MARMON SILKO, *Ceremony* (New York: Penguin, 1977), p. 2.

13. "Violent," in this case, connotes the warrior spirit, which was necessary for survival in Nigeria during a time of tribal warfare. It does not connote the crazy, destructive acting out that violence means to us in America today.

14. CHINUA ACHEBE, *Things Fall Apart* (New York: Fawcett Crest, 1959), pp. 52–53.

15. ALFRED KAZIN, *A Walker in the City* (New York: Harcourt Brace, 1951), p. 122.

16. LINDA RENNIE FORCEY, *Mothers of Sons: Toward an Understanding of Responsibility* (New York: Praeger, 1987), pp. 95–97.

Notes

17. JOHN UPDIKE, "The Most Unforgettable Character I've Ever Met," *Vogue*, November 1984, p. 441.

18. TILLIE OLSEN, *Tell Me a Riddle* (New York: Delta Books, 1961), p. 107.

Chapter 11

1. SHEL SILVERSTEIN, *The Giving Tree* (New York: Harper & Row, 1964), unpaged.

2. ANDREA BOROFF EAGAN, *The Newborn Mother: Stages of Her Growth* (New York: Henry Holt, 1985), p. 77.

3. ADRIENNE RICH, *Of Woman Born: Motherhood as Experience and Institution* (New York: W. W. Norton, 1986), p. 31.

4. Ibid., p. 36.

5. CAROL KLEIN, *Mothers and Sons* (Boston: G. K. Hall, 1985), p. 20.

6. SIMONE DE BEAUVOIR, *The Second Sex* (New York: Random House, 1974), p. 576.

7. Quoted in MARY JANE MOFFAT and CHARLOTTE PAINTER (eds.), *Revelations: Diaries of Women* (New York: Vintage Books, 1975), p. 239.

8. NOR HALL and WARREN DAWSON, *Broodmales* (Dallas: Spring Publications, 1989), p. 15.

9. See ERICH NEUMANN, *The Great Mother: An Analysis of the Archetype*, translated by Ralph Mannheim (Princeton: Princeton University Press, 1963), p. 242.

10. ADAM PHILLIPS, "Obstacles and Desires," *Harper's Magazine*, January 1992, p. 33.

11. MERLIN STONE, *Ancient Mirrors of Womanhood: A Treasury of Goddess and Heroine Lore from Around the World* (Boston: Beacon Press, 1984), pp. 297–299.

BIBLIOGRAPHY

ACHEBE, CHINUA. *Things Fall Apart*. New York: Fawcett Crest, 1959.

ANDERSEN, HANS CHRISTIAN. *The Complete Fairy Tales and Stories*. Translated by Erik Christian Haugaard. New York: Doubleday, 1974.

ARCANA, JUDITH. *Every Mother's Son: The Role of Mothers in the Making of Men*. Garden City, N.Y.: Doubleday, 1983.

ARKIN, A. M. "A Hypothesis Concerning the Incest Taboo." *Psychoanalytic Review*, vol. 71 (1984), pp. 375–381.

BALZAR, JOHN. "America's Phobia of Gays Brewed from Potent Mix." Reported in *Denver Post*, February 18, 1993, p. 2A.

BANNING, ANNE. "Mother-Son Incest: Confronting a Prejudice." *Child Abuse and Neglect*, vol. 13 (1989), pp. 563–570.

BARRY, WILLIAM A. "Marriage Research and Conflict: An Integrative Review." *Psychological Bulletin*, vol. 73 (1979), pp. 41–45.

BASSOFF, EVELYN. *Mothering Ourselves: Help and Healing for Adult Daughters.* New York: Dutton, 1991.

———. *Mothers and Daughters: Loving and Letting Go.* New York: New American Library, 1988.

BASSOFF, EVELYN, and GENE GLASS. "The Relationship Between Sex Roles and Mental Health: A Meta-Analysis of Twenty-Six Studies." *Counseling Psychologist,* vol. 10 (1982), pp. 105–112.

BEAUVOIR, SIMONE DE. *The Second Sex.* New York: Random House, 1974.

BEDOUIN, CHARLES M., and SCOTT W. HENGGELER. "Post-Divorce Mother-Son Relations of Delinquent and Well-Adjusted Adolescents." *Journal of Applied Developmental Psychology,* vol. 8 (1987), pp. 273–288.

BERNARD, JESSE. *Remarriage: A Study of Marriage.* New York: Russell & Russell, 1956.

BERNSTEIN, DORIS. *Female Identity Conflict in Clinical Practice.* Edited by N. Freedman and B. Distler (Northvale, N.J.: Jason Aronson, 1993).

BERRY, PATRICIA (ed.), *Fathers and Mothers.* Dallas: Spring Publications, 1990.

BETTELHEIM, BRUNO. *The Uses of Enchantment: The Meaning and Importance of Fairy Tales.* New York: Vintage, 1977.

BILOFSKY, PENNY, and FREDDA SACHAROW. *In-Laws/Outlaws: How to Make Peace with His Family and Yours.* New York: Fawcett Crest, 1991.

BIRKHÄUSER-OERI, SIBYLLE. *The Mother: Archetypal Image in Fairy Tales.* Edited by Marie-Louise Von Franz. Translated by Michael Mitchell. Toronto: Inner City Books, 1988.

BLANKENHORN, DAVID. "The Good Family Man: Fatherhood and the Pursuit of Happiness in America." An Institute for American Values Working Paper for the Symposium on Fatherhood in America, Publication No. WP12 (1991), 32 pp.

BLY, ROBERT. *Iron John: A Book About Men.* Reading, Mass.: Addison-Wesley, 1990.

BORHEK, MARY V. *Coming Out to Parents: A Two-Way Survival*

Guide for Lesbians and Gay Men and Their Parents. Cleveland: Pilgrim Press, 1983.

BRETHERTON, INGE. *Symbolic Play.* New York: Academic Press, 1984.

BRONSTEIN, PHYLLIS. "Differences in Mothers' and Fathers' Behaviors Toward Children: A Cross-cultural Comparison." *Developmental Psychology,* vol. 20 (1984), pp. 995–1003.

BROWN, HOWARD. *Familiar Faces, Hidden Lives: The Story of Homosexual Men in America Today.* New York: Harcourt Brace Jovanovich, 1976.

CAMARA, KATHLEEN A., and GARY RESNICK. "Interparental Conflict and Cooperation: Factors Modifying Children's Post-Divorce Adjustment." In E. Mavis Hetherington and Josephine D. Arasteh (eds.), *Impact of Divorce, Single Parenting, and Stepparenting on Children.* Hillsdale, N.J.: Lawrence Erlbaum Assoc., 1988.

CLARK, RONALD. *Freud: The Man and the Case.* New York: Random House, 1980.

CLINGEMPEEL, W. GLENN, EULALEE BRAND, and R. LEVOLI. "Stepparent-Stepchild Relationships in Stepmother and Stepfather Families: A Multi-method Study." *Family Relationships,* vol. 33 (1984), pp. 465–473.

COLMAN, ARTHUR, and LIBBY COLMAN. *The Father: Mythology and Changing Roles.* Wilmette, Ill.: Chiron Publications, 1988.

COLTRANE, SCOTT. "Father-Child Relationships and the Status of Women: A Cross-cultural Study." *American Journal of Sociology,* vol. 93 (5) (1988), pp. 1060–1095.

CONNY, BETH MENDE. "The Quotable Family." Manuscript.

CORNEAU, GUY. *Absent Fathers, Lost Sons: The Search for Masculine Identity.* Translated by Larry Shouldice. Boston: Shambala, 1991.

CRAMER, DAVID. "Gay Parents and Their Children: A Review of Research and Practical Implications." *Journal of Counseling and Development,* vol. 64 (1986), pp. 504–507.

DECASPER, ANTHONY, and W. P. FIFER. "Of Human Bonding:

Newborns Prefer Their Mothers' Voices." *Science*, vol. 208 (1980), pp. 1174–1176.

DINNERSTEIN, DOROTHY. *The Mermaid and the Minotaur: Sexual Arrangements and Human Malaise*. New York: Harper Colophon Books, 1977.

DRAPER, THOMAS W. "Sons, Mothers, and Externality: Is There a Father Effect?" *Child Study Journal*, vol. 12 (1982), pp. 271–280.

DUBERMAN, LUCILLE. "Step-Kin Relationships." *Journal of Marriage and the Family*, vol. 35 (1973), pp. 283–292.

EAGAN, ANDREA BOROFF. *The Newborn Mother: Stages of Her Growth*. New York: Henry Holt, 1985.

ELLMAN, RICHARD. *Oscar Wilde*. New York: Alfred A. Knopf, 1988.

FIELDS, RICK. *The Code of the Warrior in History, Myth, and Everyday Life*. Harper Perennial, 1991.

FIERSTEIN, HARVEY. *Torch Song Trilogy: Three Plays*. New York: Villard Books, 1983.

FIRESTONE, ROSS. (ed.), *A Book of Men: Visions of the Male Experience*. New York: Stonehill, 1978.

FISCHER, LUCY ROSE. "Married Men and Their Mothers." *Journal of Comparative Family Studies*, vol. 14 (1983), pp. 393–401.

FOGEL, GERALD I., FREDERICK M. LANE, and ROBERT S. LIEBERT. *The Psychology of Men: New Psychoanalytic Perspectives*. New York: Basic Books, 1986.

FORCEY, LINDA RENNIE. *Mothers of Sons: Toward an Understanding of Responsibility*. New York: Praeger, 1987.

FRASER, ANTONIA. *The Warrior Queens*. New York: Alfred A. Knopf, 1989.

GORMAN, CHRISTINE. "Sizing Up the Sexes." *Time*, January 20, 1992, pp. 42–51.

GREENBERG, MARTIN, and NORMAN MORRIS. "Engrossment: The Newborn's Impact upon the Father." *American Journal of Orthopsychiatry*, vol. 44 (1974), pp. 520–531.

GREENSON, RALPH. "Dis-identification from Mother: Its Special Importance for the Boy." *International Journal of Psycho-Analysis*, vol. 49 (1968), pp. 370–375.

GREGORY, IAN. "Anterospective Data Following Loss of a Parent: Delinquency and High School Dropout." *Archives of General Psychiatry,* vol. 13 (1965), pp. 99–109.

GRENE, DAVID, and RICHARD LATTIMORE, eds. *Greek Tragedies,* vol. 3. Chicago: University of Chicago Press, 1961.

GUIDUBALDI, JOHN, and JOSEPH PERRY. "Divorce and Mental Health Sequelae for Children: A Two-Year Follow-up of a Nationwide Sample." *Journal of the American Academy of Child Psychiatry,* vol. 24 (1985), pp. 531–537.

GUTMANN, DAVID. "The Father and the Masculine Life Cycle." An Institute for American Values Working Paper, for the Symposium on Fatherhood in America, Publication No. WP13, November 1991, 23 pp.

HAMILTON, EDITH. *Mythology: Timeless Tales of Gods and Heroes.* New York: New American Library, 1940.

HARDING, M. ESTHER. *Woman's Mysteries: Ancient and Modern.* New York: Harper Colophon Books, 1971.

HARRINGTON, MAUREEN. "Support Groups Offer Teens Solace in a Difficult Time." *Denver Post,* June 4, 1992, pp. 1E, 2E.

HETHERINGTON, E. MAVIS. "Family Relations Six Years After Divorce." In Kay Pasley and Marilyn Ihinger-Tallman (eds.), *Remarriage and Stepparenting: Current Research and Theory.* New York: Guilford Press, 1987.

HOFFMAN, MARTIN. "Father Absence and Conscience Development." *Developmental Psychology,* vol. 4 (1971), pp. 400–406.

HOMER. *The Odyssey.* Translated by Robert Fitzgerald. New York: Anchor, 1963.

HOMER. *The Odyssey of Homer.* Translated by Allen Mandelbaum. Berkeley: University of California Press, 1990.

HORNEY, KAREN. *Feminine Psychology.* New York: W. W. Norton, 1967.

HUDSON, LIAM, and BERNADINE JACOT. *The Way Men Think: Intellect, Intimacy and the Erotic Imagination.* New Haven: Yale University Press, 1991.

HUGGINS, SHARON L. "A Comparative Study of Self-Esteem of Adolescent Children of Divorced Lesbian Mothers and

Divorced Heterosexual Mothers." *Journal of Homosexuality*, vol. 18 (1989), pp. 123–135.

JOHNSON, MIRIAM M. *Strong Mothers, Weak Wives: The Search for Gender Equality.* Berkeley: University of California Press, 1988.

JOHNSON, ROBERT A. *He: Understanding Masculine Psychology* (rev. ed.). New York: Harper & Row, 1989.

———. *We: Understanding the Psychology of Romantic Love.* New York: Harper & Row, 1983.

JONES, ERNEST. *The Life and Work of Sigmund Freud*, vol. 1. New York: Basic Books, 1953.

KALTER, NEIL. *Growing Up with Divorce: Helping Your Child Avoid Immediate and Later Emotional Problems.* New York: Fawcett Columbine, 1990.

KAZIN, ALFRED. *A Walker in the City.* New York: Harcourt Brace, 1951.

KEEN, SAM. *Fire in the Belly: On Being a Man.* New York: Bantam Books, 1991.

KENEMORE, THOMAS, and LORETTA WINEBERG. "The Tie that Binds: A Clinical Perspective on Divorced Mothers and Adolescent Sons." *Clinical Social Work Journal*, vol. 12 (1984), pp. 332–346.

KERÉNYI, KARL, and JAMES HILLMAN. *Oedipus Variations: Studies in Literature and Psychoanalysis.* Dallas: Spring Publications, 1991.

KLAUS, MARSHALL, and PHYLLIS KLAUS. *The Amazing Newborn.* Reading, Mass.: Addison-Wesley, 1985.

KLEIN, CAROL. *Mothers and Sons.* Boston: G. K. Hall, 1985.

KOESTNER, RICHARD, CAROL FRANZ, and JOEL WEINBERGER. "The Family Origins of Empathic Concern: A 26-Year Longitudinal Study." *Journal of Personality and Social Psychology*, vol. 58 (1990), pp. 709–717.

KRAMER, SAMUEL N. (ed.). *Mythologies of the Ancient World.* New York: Doubleday, 1961.

KRUBER, RUTH. *Haven: The Unknown Story of 1,000 World War II Refugees.* New York: Coward McCann, 1983.

KRUG, RONALD. "Adult Male Report of Childhood Sexual Abuse by Mothers: Case Descriptions, Motivations and Long-

Term Consequences." *Child Abuse and Neglect*, vol. 13 (1989), pp. 111–119.

LAMB, MICHAEL E. "Fathers and Child Development: An Integrative Review." In Michael E. Lamb (ed.), *The Role of the Father in Child Development*. New York: Wiley, 1981.

LANG, J. "Brooding Behind the Steel Wall." *Inroads*, January 1991, pp. 27–28.

LAWRENCE, D. H. *The Complete Poems of D. H. Lawrence*. New York: Viking Press, 1964.

LEAF, MUNRO. *The Story of Ferdinand*. New York: Puffin Books, reprint, 1977.

LEE, JOHN. *The Flying Boy: Healing the Wounded Man*. Deerfield Beach, Fla.: Health Communications, 1987.

LERNER, HARRIET GOLDHOR. *The Dance of Anger: A Woman's Guide to Changing the Patterns of Intimate Relationships*. New York: Harper & Row, 1985.

LEVER, J. "Sex Differences in the Games Children Play." *Social Problems*, vol. 23 (1976), pp. 478–487.

LEWIN, TAMAR. "Single, a Parent and Proud." From *New York Times*, reported in *Denver Post*, October 11, 1992, p. 31A.

LIPSON, CHANNING. "A Case Report of Matricide." *American Journal of Psychiatry*, vol. 143 (1986), pp. 112–113.

MALONEY, MERCEDES LYNCH, and ANNE MALONEY. *The Hand that Rocks the Cradle: Mothers, Sons, and Leadership*. Englewood Cliffs, N.J.: Prentice-Hall, 1985.

MATTIS, MARY. *Sex and the Single Parent*. New York: Henry Holt, 1986.

MAUPIN, ARMISTEAD. *More Tales of the City*. New York: Harper & Row, 1980.

MCBRIDE, ANGELA BARRON. *The Growth and Development of Mothers*. New York: Harper Colophon, 1973.

MIEDZIAN, MYRIAM. *Boys Will Be Boys: Breaking the Link Between Masculinity and Violence*. New York: Doubleday, 1991.

MILES, ROSALIND. *Love, Sex, Death and the Making of the Male*. New York: Summit Books, 1991.

MOFFAT, MARY JANE, and CHARLOTTE PAINTER (eds.). *Revelations: Diaries of Women.* New York: Vintage Books, 1975.

MOORE, ROBERT, and DOUGLAS GILLETTE. *King, Warrior, Magician, Lover: Rediscovering the Archetypes of the Mature Masculine.* San Francisco: Harper, 1990.

MORRISON, KATALIN, and AIRDRIE THOMPSON-GUPPY. "The Cinderella's Stepmother Syndrome." *Canadian Journal of Psychiatry,* vol. 30 (1985), pp. 521–529.

NADLER, JANICE HOROWITZ. "The Psychological Stress of the Stepmother." Ph.D. diss., abstract in *Dissertation Abstracts International,* vol. 37B (1976), p. 5367.

NEUMANN, ERICH. *The Child.* Translated by Ralph Mannheim. Boston: Shambala, 1990.

———. "Fear of the Feminine." *Quadrant: Journal of the C. G. Jung Foundation for Analytic Psychology,* Spring 1986, pp. 1–11.

———. *The Great Mother: An Analysis of the Archetype.* Translated by Ralph Mannheim. Princeton: Princeton University Press, 1963.

OLIVIER, CHRISTIANE. *Jocasta's Children: The Imprint of the Mother.* Translated by G. Craig. London: Routledge, 1989.

OLSEN, TILLIE. *Tell Me a Riddle.* New York: Delta Book, 1961.

ORTEGA Y GASSET, JOSÉ. *Meditations on Hunting.* New York: McGraw-Hill, 1986.

OSHERSON, SAMUEL. *Finding Our Fathers: How a Man's Life Is Shaped by His Relationship with His Father.* New York: Fawcett Columbine, 1986.

PATAI, RAPHAEL. *The Hebrew Goddess.* New York: Avon Books, 1978.

PEDERSEN, ANNE, and PEGGY O'MARA (eds.). *Being a Father: Family, Work, and Self.* Santa Fe: John Muir, 1990.

PEDERSEN, LOREN E. *Dark Hearts: The Unconscious Forces that Shape Men's Lives.* Boston: Shambala, 1991.

PENNINGTON, SARALIE BISNOVICH. "Children of Lesbian Mothers." In Frederick W. Bozett (ed.), *Gay and Lesbian Parents.* New York: Praeger, 1987.

PETERSON, J. L., and NICHOLAS ZILL. "Marital Disruption, Parent-

Child Relationships, and Behavior Problems in Children." *Journal of Marriage and the Family*, vol. 48 (1986), pp. 295–307.

PHILLIPS, ADAM. "Obstacles and Desires," *Harper's* Magazine, January 1992, pp. 33–36.

PRITCHER, E., and L. S. SCHULTZ. *Boys and Girls at Play: The Development of Sex Roles.* New York: Praeger, 1983.

REBELSKY, FREDA, and CHERYL HANKS. "Fathers' Verbal Interactions with Infants in the First Three Months of Life." *Child Development*, vol 42 (1971), pp. 63–68.

RICH, ADRIENNE. *Of Woman Born: Motherhood as Experience and Institution.* New York: W. W. Norton, 1986.

ROOSEVELT, RUTH, and JEANETTE LOFAS. *Living in Step: A Remarriage Manual for Parents and Children.* Chelsea, Mich.: Scarborough House, originally published by Stein & Day, 1976.

ROSS, JOHN MUNDER. "Beyond the Phallic Illusion: Notes on Man's Heterosexuality." In Gerald Fogel, Frederick Lane, and Robert Liebert (eds.), *The Psychology of Men: New Psychoanalytic Perspectives.* New York: Basic Books, 1986.

ROWAN, JOHN. *The Horned God: Feminism and Men as Wounding and Healing.* London: Routledge & Kegan Paul, 1987.

RUBIN, LILLIAN. *World of Pain: Life in the Working Class Family.* New York: Basic Books, 1976.

RUDDICK, SARA. *Maternal Thinking: Towards a Politics of Peace.* New York: Ballantine, 1989.

SALTEN, FELIX. *Bambi.* Translated by Whittaker Chambers. New York: Grosset & Dunlap, 1929.

SANTROCK, JOHN, and KAREN SITTERLE. "Parent-Child Relationships in Stepmother Families." In Kay Pasley and Marilyn Ihinger-Tallman (eds.), *Remarriage and Stepparenting: Current Research and Theory.* New York: Guilford Press, 1987.

SELIGMAN, MARTIN. *Learned Optimism.* New York: Alfred A. Knopf, 1991.

SILKO, LESLIE MARMON. *Ceremony.* New York: Penguin, 1977.

SILVERSTEIN, SHEL. *The Giving Tree.* New York: Harper & Row, 1964.

STOLLER, ROBERT J. *Presentations of Gender.* New Haven: Yale University Press, 1985.

———. "Symbiosis Anxiety and the Development of Masculinity." *Archives of General Psychiatry,* vol. 30 (1974), pp. 164–172.

STONE, MERLIN. *Ancient Mirrors of Womanhood: A Treasury of Goddess and Heroine Lore from Around the World.* Boston: Beacon Press, 1984.

TANNEN, DEBORAH. *You Just Don't Understand: Women and Men in Conversation.* New York: Ballantine Books, 1990.

TERMAN, DAVID. "Affect and Parenthood: The Impact of the Past Upon the Present." In Rebecca Cohen, Bertram Cohler, and Sidney Weissman (eds.), *Parenthood: A Psychodynamic Perspective.* New York: Guilford Press, 1984.

TOWLE, ALEXANDRA (ed.). *Mothers.* New York: Simon and Schuster, 1988.

UMANS, MEG (ed.). *Like Coming Home.* Austin: Banned Books, 1988.

UPDIKE, JOHN. "The Most Unforgettable Character I've Ever Met." *Vogue,* November 1984, p. 441.

WALLERSTEIN, JUDITH S., and JOAN BERLIN KELLY. *Surviving the Break-up: How Children and Parents Cope with Divorce.* New York: Basic Books, 1980.

WARD, GEOFFREY C. "Elegant Duke Ellington: A Feast for Eye and Ear." *Smithsonian,* vol. 24 (1993), pp. 63–67.

WARSHAK, RICHARD A. *The Custody Revolution: The Father Factor and the Motherhood Mystique.* New York: Poseidon Press, 1992.

WELLDON, ESTELA V. *Mother, Madonna, Whore: The Idealization and Denigration of Motherhood.* London: Free Association Books, 1988.

WELWOOD, JOHN. *Journey of the Heart: Intimate Relationship and the Path of Love.* New York: Harper Perennial, 1991.

WHITEHEAD, BARBARA DAFOE. "Perspectives on The New Familism." An Institute for American Values Working Paper for the Symposium on Fatherhood in America, Publication No. WP8, June 1991, 27 pp.

YABLONSKY, LEWIS. *Fathers and Sons: The Most Challenging of All Family Relationships.* New York: Gardner Press, 1990.

ZILBERGELD, BERNIE. *Male Sexuality.* Toronto: Bantam Books, 1978.

ZINSMEISTER, KARL. "The Nature of Fatherhood." An Institute for American Values Working Paper for the Symposium on Fatherhood in America, Publication No. WP11, 1991, 33 pp.

INDEX